Un/Covering the North

Valerie Alia

Un/Covering the North:
News, Media, and Aboriginal People

UBCPress / Vancouver

Printed in Canada on acid-free paper ∞

ISBN 0-7748-0706-7

Canadian Cataloguing in Publication Data

Alia, Valerie, 1942-
  Un/covering the north

  Includes bibliographical references and index.
  ISBN 0-7748-0706-7

  1. Native mass media – Canada, Northern.* 2. Mass media – Canada, Northern.
3. Native peoples in mass media.* I. Title. II. Title: Uncovering the north.

E98.C73A44 1999   302.23′09719   C99-910110-2

This work was published with the assistance of a grant from the Publishing Fund of the International Council of Canadian Studies.

UBC Press also gratefully acknowledges the ongoing support to its publishing program from the Canada Council for the Arts, the British Columbia Arts Council, and the Department of Canadian Heritage of the Government of Canada. We also wish to acknowledge the financial support of the Government of Canada through the Book Publishing Industry Development Program (BPIDP) for our publishing activities.

UBC Press
University of British Columbia
6344 Memorial Road
Vancouver, BC V6T 1Z2
(604) 822-5959
Fax: 1-800-668-0821
E-mail: info@ubcpress.ubc.ca
www.ubcpress.ubc.ca

For the brave and brilliant pioneers of northern journalism. Long may they thrive!

And, of course, for Pete.

Contents

Illustrations and Maps

Illustrations

Maps

Tables

Preface

The focus in this book is on Aboriginal media in the Canadian North, examined in the context of the development of Canadian, North American, and international Aboriginal communications and northern communications in general. Canada has long been a world leader in both northern and Aboriginal communications and especially in the development of Aboriginal communications in the North. Today, Canada maintains this leadership position despite the many setbacks and cutbacks that have followed each increment of progress, the increasing number of new initiatives and improvements to existing services in other countries, and the notable challenges from Australian indigenous radio and television.[1]

Although many of the developments in northern communications have been small-scale and ad hoc, others have been ambitious and far-reaching. The federally funded Project Inukshuk sponsored by Inuit Tapirisat Canada (ITC), for example, helped to establish Inuit broadcasting. Its offspring, the Inuit Broadcasting Corporation, continues to thrive and to expand its radio and television programming. Inuit communications are among the most highly developed and consistently productive of the northern services, reflecting parallels in the political sphere – notably the emergence of the Inuit homeland of Nunavut, which became an official territorial government in April 1999.

In the early 1990s the Anik satellites made it possible to develop Television Northern Canada (TVNC), the unprecedented television programming system produced under the leadership of representatives from thirteen federally funded regional Aboriginal communications societies (discussed in detail in Chapter 3). Its founders hope that it will some day span the circumpolar North to include Alaska, Greenland, Finno-Scandia, and Siberia. Although Ottawa persists in cutting funds, the broadcast explosion continues both in Canada and worldwide, facilitating the expansion of satellite availability and program development everywhere.

With even less consistent funding than broadcasting, and a resultant scarcity of personnel, northern print media have had a more chequered history. Yet despite the greater difficulty in initiating print projects and keeping print media alive, northern publications have made important inroads. Challenge after challenge, cutback after cutback, newspapers and magazines survive and, indeed, thrive. Some disappear, some undergo transformations in format or frequency, others are begun, or (as in the case of *Dännzhà'* in Yukon and *Native Press* in the Northwest Territories) are begun anew.

Despite the international importance of Canada's northern media, no book has examined the representation of the North in northern and southern Canadian news media – or indeed in media generally – or the nature and extent of northern publications, radio and television stations, programs and policies. This is the task at hand. Most of the studies by individual scholars and research groups have focused on northern broadcasting (primarily Inuit broadcasting) and have omitted much of the North, many of the northern peoples, and all of northern print media.

Donald R. Browne's recent comparative study of international indigenous electronic media, for example, takes on too much and – for all its honourable intentions – ends up saying very little. In Browne's study, Canada's indigenous broadcast media are represented solely by a handful of Mohawk radio outlets in Quebec. The Aboriginal communications societies are absent, as is the North, except for fleeting references to the Inuit Broadcasting Corporation and Television Northern Canada (Browne 1996). Yet the northern media services, especially those involving Inuit, have long been the backbone of Canada's indigenous electronic programming.[2]

The present study provides an overview of the history, scope, and nature of northern Aboriginal communications. It is intended not only for North American readers but for those who study the communications of remote communities and first peoples in other countries and regions. Scholars in other countries have already paid considerable attention to Canadian media and media policy (e.g., Browne 1996; Meadows 1993, 1996; Meadows and Brown 1995). Especially through the Inuit Circumpolar Conference – the international Inuit organization – those in other northern nations (Greenland, Denmark, Norway, Russia) have engaged in communications networking with Aboriginal peoples in the Canadian North. It is therefore hoped that this book will interest an international readership and will encourage future scholarship on northern and Aboriginal communications.

The research was conducted in various northern communities and in northern and southern libraries and archives between 1984 and 1997. The material on government, campaigns, elections, and communications was gathered in 1990-3, when I resided in Yukon for several months of each year. Part of the research conducted in 1990-1 was funded by the Royal Commission on Electoral Reform and Party Financing and was reported in presentations before the commission and in a chapter in one of the research volumes published by the commission (Alia 1991a). That portion of the research was supervised by Chairman Pierre Lortie and commissioners Pierre Fortier, Robert Gabor, William Knight, and Lucie Pépin, and guided by Frederick Fletcher, who headed the commission's communications research team, and Robert A. Milen, who edited the volume on Aboriginal peoples, in which the results of the research were published.

Pierre Lortie was responsible for changing the scope of the project. I had originally proposed a study of the northern territories, and he asked that I extend it to include the provincial North. I confess that, at first, I thought this an annoying piece of unnecessary extra work, which I undertook primarily to please the commission. It meant expanding the time frame, staff, and budget. However, I soon saw the wisdom of Lortie's request. First, there are historical reasons to include the provincial North, given the decades of fluctuation of Canada's northern borders. Second, the material on the northern regions of the provinces greatly enriches the portrait of conditions and patterns in the North. Land and weather do not observe borders, nor do many policies and people. The northern areas of the provinces have much more in common with the territories than with the provinces' southern regions. In Canada, "territory" connotes more northernness than does "province," but, for understanding the nature and extent of northern communications, such semantic separations are less useful than the trans-boundary linkages.

Other portions of the research were supported by grants from the Social Sciences and Humanities Research Council, York University, and the University of Western Ontario. Those portions of the research included interviews by the author in spring and summer 1990 with northern and southern journalists who cover the North, and other research conducted by the author or by research teams under her supervision in the eastern Arctic (now Nunavut), the western Northwest Territories, Yukon Territory, and the northern regions of the provinces. A deliberate effort was made to hire researchers from different locations, cultures, and backgrounds. They included members of several First Nations in Yukon, western Arctic, and northern provinces; Inuit from Nunavut; and non-Aboriginal people from several provinces. In addition, a two-year study of coverage of the North by northern and southern print media was conducted by the author and student research assistants from the University of Western Ontario Graduate School of Journalism. This provided much of the data analysed in Chapter 6.

Notes on Terminology
Given the number of people quoted in this book, a wide range of terminology is used, and clarification of some terms is in order. Preferred usage varies among peoples and regions. Current usage at the Council for Yukon First

Nations (CYFN) indicates a preference for "First Nations" or "Aboriginal." "Indian" is used widely in Yukon (until recently, the name of CYFN was the Council for Yukon Indians) and in parts of the United States. In other parts of Canada and the United States, that term is used infrequently or is considered objectionable. Although CYFN and other First Nations organizations have veered away from "Native," and many Aboriginal people in the United States and other countries consider it objectionable, it is still used widely in Canada (for example, Northern Native Broadcasting Yukon is the name of one broadcasting organization).

The term "indigenous" is used internationally as well as within Canada and, less often, in the United States. In my own usage, I have given preference to the terms "indigenous," "first peoples," and "Aboriginal," which are more inclusive than the terms discussed above. It should be noted, however, that many people outside Canada find the term "Aboriginal" objectionable or prefer other terms. Although First Nations is widely preferred by many indigenous Canadians, it is generally thought to exclude Inuit and therefore omits a major portion of indigenous northerners.

In Canada, the word "Inuit" (singular Inuk, language Inuktitut) is preferred by Inuit themselves and has replaced "Eskimo" in current usage. "Inuit" is used generically to refer to all of the members of the Inuit Circumpolar Conference (ICC). They are Aboriginal people from several countries and related subcultures. An Inuk is one Inuit person; two people are Inuuk; and more than two are Inuit. Various Inuit groups use individual terms as well. Inuvialuit are Inuit from the western Arctic; their predominant language is Inuvialuktun. Inuktitut is the predominant language of Nunavut Inuit. Alaskans sometimes refer to themselves as Eskimo, but increasingly prefer the more specific names of their separate cultures. Although indigenous Greenlandic people also have separately named cultures, and use the generic Inuit in relation to their participation in ICC, they usually call themselves Kalaallit to indicate their common allegiance to Kalaallit Nunaat (Greenland under home rule, made official two decades ago).

No one has come up with a wholly successful way to refer to people who are not indigenous. "Non-Aboriginal" is admittedly a dodge. In my earlier work on Inuit culture (Alia 1994, 1995), I have usually used "Qallunaaq" (singular) or "Qallunaat" (plural), the Inuktitut term for non-Inuit – not just white – people. In the broader context of the present book, this is not possible.

The Athapaskan language Gwich'in is also called Gwitch'in, Kuchin, or Loucheux. Gwich'in, the spelling preferred by the Yukon Native Language Centre, is adopted here, except in official titles (e.g., Vuntut Gwitch'in First Nation).

Dene is used to refer to Athapaskan- or Dene-speaking Aboriginal people. Métis are people of mixed Aboriginal and non-Aboriginal (originally French) ancestry. Nunavut means "our land" in Inuktitut and is the name of the Inuit homeland which in 1999 became Nunavut Territory.

A Note about the Cover

The attractive rendering of the North on the cover of this book is a northern-looking landscape, but it represents only a fraction of what is meant by "North." The image resembles some of the northern provincial regions and southern parts of Yukon and the Northwest Territories. In the Arctic, there are no tall trees, and the line between earth and sky is often drawn by rocks. To convey the scope and nature of "North" and "northern media" would take several images.

Acknowledgments

Frederick Fletcher encouraged this project in the first place and, having seen an early research study and book chapter (Alia 1991a), said, "You really should do a book." Rob Milen, David Bell, Gail Valaskakis, Lorna Roth, Carol Geddes, Pamela Freeman, and Pete Steffens read earlier versions or portions of the manuscript.

The researchers often worked under challenging conditions. Those in the North dealt with challenges of winter transportation and weather. The interpreter in the Baffin region had to work by phone. During my long months of residence in the North, the London, Ontario, researchers had to rely on phone-fax-courier lifelines, which in bad weather sometimes failed. Brian Higgins collated several years of data and wrote the first draft of Chapter 6. His research colleagues were Adrienne Arsenault, Stephen Chase, Susan Clairmont, Garth Hardie, Kelley Korbin, Leslie McLaren, Christine Prystay, and Daniel Smythe. Kjersti Strömmen worked in London and in Iqaluit, where she also conducted interviews for the radio documentary *Nunavut: Where Names Never Die* (Alia 1995). Clare Thorbes worked in London and in Whitehorse, where she braved a challenging Yukon winter and, in addition to fulfilling duties for an internship with the *Whitehorse Star* and conducting research for this project, translated some of the writings of the Siberian Aboriginal poet, Vladimir Sangi, from the original Russian.

For the richly rewarding time at Inuit Tapirisat of Canada, I am indebted to Rhoda Inukshuk, Nancy Weeks Doubleday, Sadie Hill, Robert Higgins, and John Bennett. For the ongoing, stimulating dialogue on northern communications, Inuit culture, and just about everything else, I thank Alexina Kublu, Mick Mallon, Keith Crowe, and Jack Hicks.

Warm thanks to Mimi Bahl, Jim Bell, Jim Butler, Patricia Charlie (researcher for Old Crow), Allan Chrisjohn, Greg Coleman, Helen Fallding, Amanda Graham, Catherine Honyust, Peter Hum, Ken Kane, Lenore Keeshig-Tobias, Chitee Kilabuk (researcher for Pangnirtung), SharonAnne LaDue (researcher for Ross River), Anita McCallum (librarian, *London Free Press*), G. Campbell

McDonald, Malcolm Mayes, Michael Meadows, Patrick Nagle (CBC Iqaluit), Lee Selleck, Dan Smoke-Asayenes, and Bud White Eye, and to Don Alper, Robert Monahan, Marty Hitchcock, and Kristen Clapper at Western Washington University's Center for Canadian-American Studies. Brenda G. Nores helped update the data on media outlets and the material on northern Aboriginal communications on the Internet (Appendix E). A special thank you to Robin Angeley for coming to the rescue (and phoning every electrician in town) to facilitate the computer hookup. At UBC Press, Laura Macleod shepherded the project through the first phase and Barbara Tessman and Camilla Jenkins saw it through to the end, thankfully with the requisite humour for dealing with authors and deadlines.

The Social Sciences and Humanities Research Council of Canada provided funding for consultation in spring and summer 1990 with northern and southern journalists covering the North, and for a two-year, three-workshop project in journalistic ethics, 1994-6.

I am as always indebted to Dan Restivo and David Restivo, my wonderful and talented sons, and to Pete Steffens – husband, colleague, soul-mate, and friend – who provided Russian translation, editorial expertise, food, stories, and humour during the final weeks of writing.

A Tribute

Among those to whom thanks are owed, I want to make special mention of Lou Jacquot, whose spirit permeates these pages – especially those which describe Yukon. As I sought to understand the intricacies of Yukon communications, politics, and culture, Lou provided guidance, comfort, a willing ear, and a delightfully irreverent and politically acute sense of humour. When I met him, Lou was Yukon's only Aboriginal PhD and was advisor to the Yukon Native Teacher Education program based at Yukon College.

I wish I could report that his sense of humour sustained him as well as it sustained so many others. He told me that having a PhD was a mixed blessing and a constant struggle. In memory of Lou and his indomitable spirit, the cartoon he gave me just before I left Whitehorse after my first winter there in 1990 is reproduced at the beginning of the Introduction. It was included in the information kit given to participants in the First Nations Intensive Seminar described in Chapter 2, and I invariably hand it to anyone who expresses an interest in Canadian First Nations.

Acronyms

AFN	Assembly of First Nations
AINA	Arctic Institute of North America
AIROS	American Indian Radio on Satellite network distribution system
AMMSA	Aboriginal Multi-Media Society of Alberta
ANCS	Alberta Native Communications Society
BCTV	British Columbia Television
BRACS	Broadcasting for Remote Aboriginal Communities Scheme (Australia)
CAJ	Canadian Association of Journalists
CANCOM	Canadian Satellite Communications Incorporated
CARC	Canadian Arctic Resources Committee
CASNP	Canadian Alliance in Solidarity with Native Peoples
CBC	Canadian Broadcasting Corporation
CP	Canadian Press (wire service)
CRTC	Canadian Radio-Television and Telecommunications Commission
CYFN	Council for Yukon First Nations (formerly the Council for Yukon Indians)
CYI	Council for Yukon Indians (see also CYFN)
FNC	First Nations Communications
HBC	Hudson's Bay Company
ICC	Inuit Circumpolar Conference
IBC	Inuit Broadcasting Corporation
ICS	Inuvialuit Communications Society
INAC	Indian and Northern Affairs Canada
INCA	Indian Communications Arts department at SIFC
ITC	Inuit Tapirisat of Canada

KNA	Kalaallit-Nunaata-Radioa
MAB	Man and the Biosphere
MBC	Missinipi Broadcasting Corporation
MLA	Member of the Legislative Assembly
MP	Member of Parliament
NACS	National Aboriginal Communications Society
NAJA	Native American Journalists' Association (American, also has Canadian members)
NBP	Northern Broadcasting Policy
NCI	Native Communications Incorporated
NCP	Native Communications Programme
NCS	Native Communications Society of the NWT
NDP	New Democratic Party
NFB	National Film Board of Canada
NIC	Nunavut Implementation Commission
NIMAA	National Indigenous Media Association of Australia
NIRS	National Indigenous Radio Service (Australia)
NJA	Native Journalists Association (of Canada)
NNBAP	Northern Native Broadcast Access Program
NNBT	Northern Native Broadcasting Terrace
NNBY	Northern Native Broadcasting Yukon
NNNC	Native News Network of Canada
NSN	Northern Sciences Network
NTI	Nunavut Tunngavik Incorporated
NWT	Northwest Territories
PC	Progressive Conservative Party
PJNP	Program in Journalism for Native People (University of Western Ontario)
RCAP	Royal Commission on Aboriginal People
RCERPF	Royal Commission on Electoral Reform and Party Financing
RCMP	Royal Canadian Mounted Police
SRDU	Satellite relay distribution undertaking
SIFC	Saskatchewan Indian Federated College (University of Regina)
TFN	Tungavik Federation of Nunavut (now NTI)
TNI	Taqramiut Nipingat Incorporated
TVNC	Television Northern Canada
YANSI	Yukon Association of Non-Status Indians
YNB	Yukon Native Brotherhood

Chronology of Northern Events and Developments

c. 985   Norse voyage to Vinland (Greenland) finds Aboriginal people the Norse call "skraelings," who run them out of the country (Nuttall 1994, 3-4)

1576   Martin Frobisher, looking for Northwest Passage to the Orient, sails into Frobisher Bay

1771   Moravian Brethren, first missionaries to Inuit, arrive in Nain, Labrador

1700s   Missionaries introduce the syllabic writing system to the North, adapting the system used for Cree to Inuktitut

1800s   European whaling period

1877   Northwest Territories Council is formed

1894   First permanent mission in Baffin Island established by Anglican Reverend E.J. Peck at Blacklead Island

1896   Klondike Gold Rush

        Yukon Territory is created

1898   *Yukon Midnight Sun* begins publishing in Whitehorse

1901   Thomas Edison's film of Inuit games is shown at the Pan-American Exposition in Buffalo, New York

1909   Start of parliamentary government in Yukon

1912   Captain Frank E. Kleinschmidt's documentary feature on Alaska Eskimo village life has its first public screenings

1917   October Revolution brings technology and social services to the indigenous minorities of the Russian (Soviet) North

1920s   Radio broadcasting begins in Canada

1922   Robert Flaherty's film, *Nanook of the North*, is released

1929   Scheduled air service begins along the Mackenzie Valley

1932	First version of *Micmac News* begins publication (Carriere and Downes 1992, 2)
1941	First Canadian Census to include the North
1944	The Arctic Institute of North America (AINA) is founded jointly by Canadians and Americans
1946-56	Canada and the United States collaborate to build weather stations, signal stations, and air-defence posts across the North
1946	*Native Voice* begins publication, founded and published by the Native Brotherhood of British Columbia
1950s	Communities are established throughout the Canadian North; Aboriginal people are encouraged to come in from the land and make the communities their primary homes
1950	James Houston introduces soapstone to sculptors at Port Harrison, northern Quebec (now Nunavik)
	Inuit first vote in a Canadian election; other Aboriginal people will not be able to vote for more than a decade
1951	The Northwest Territories Council begins to include elected as well as appointed members and starts alternating meetings between Ottawa and the North
1953	Department of Northern Affairs and Natural Resources is formed
1955	Work begins on Distant Early Warning Line (DEW Line), one of a series of American-Canadian northern defence projects
	Inuit families are moved from Port Harrison (now Kuujjuaq), northern Quebec, and Pond Inlet, Baffin Island, to new communities in the High Arctic, at Resolute Bay and Grise Fiord
1958	CBC Northern Service is created
1959	Federal government starts cooperatives for Native people
	James Houston introduces printmaking at Cape Dorset
1960	The first Aboriginal-language radio program is broadcast in Inuktitut, by CBC Northern Service via shortwave from studios in Montreal
1961	Inuit in the eastern Arctic begin radio broadcasts
1962	Inuit in Districts of Keewatin and Franklin vote in a federal election for the first time
1965	Abraham Okpik is appointed the first Native member of the Northwest Territories Council
1967	Elected regional councils are formed throughout the Northwest Territories

Frontier Package is established, bringing radio to seventeen communities in the western Arctic

Kenomadiwin Radio is launched from a travelling van in northern Ontario

1969 Jean Chrétien's White Paper on Indian Policy promotes "assimilationist policies" but, ironically, stimulates Aboriginal communications projects

Michael Mitchell, trained and sponsored by the NFB Challenge for Change program, directs *These Are My People,* the first film by an Aboriginal filmmaker

Anik satellite system is launched

1970 Northwest Territories centennial

Native Communications Society of Nova Scotia is founded and begins publishing *Micmac News*

1971 Northern Pilot Project, Aboriginal radio experimental projects in Keewatin (NWT) and northern Ontario receive funding from the federal Department of Communications

1972 Thay Lun Lin Communications Society is founded in Yukon (changed to Ye Sa To Communications Society in 1975)

1973 Federal government creates the Native Communications Programme (NCP)

CBC Northern Television Service is launched

Landmark Arctic Peoples' Conference is held in Denmark (precursor to ICC)

1974 Wawatay Native Communications Society is founded in northern Ontario

1975 Legislative Assembly of the Northwest Territories becomes fully elected; it has an Aboriginal majority membership and is run by consensus with no political parties

Nunatsiakmiut Community Television Society at Frobisher Bay (now Iqaluit) is launched

1977 Inuit Circumpolar Conference (ICC), the international Inuit organization, is founded

1978 Federally funded Project Inukshuk is launched, marking the start of Inuit television broadcasts over the Anik B satellite

Kalaallit-Nunaata Radioa (national Greenland radio) becomes an associate member of the European Broadcasting Union

First Aboriginal members elected to Yukon Legislative Assembly

1979	Greenland Home Rule becomes official on 1 May, with Denmark relinquishing its powers in a gradual process
1980	Thérrien Report, produced for the CRTC, links communications to the preservation of Aboriginal languages and cultures, setting the stage for a new era in Aboriginal broadcasting
1980s	Northern Native Broadcasting Yukon (NNBY) is developed
1981	Inuit Broadcasting Corporation (IBC), the first Aboriginal television network, is founded
	Satellite radio service for the NWT and Yukon is begun
1982	Inuit Broadcasting Corporation (IBC) is officially launched on 12 January
1983	Northern Broadcasting Policy (NBP) and Northern Native Broadcast Access Program (NNBAP) are launched, supported by a commitment from the federal government to fund thirteen northern Aboriginal communications societies with $40.3 million over four years
1984	CBC Native Access Policy bolsters support for the NBP and NNBAP
1985	CHON-FM Radio launched by NNBY in Whitehorse
	Federal funding cutbacks to NNBAP cause a major upheaval in northern communications
1986	National Aboriginal Communications Society (NACS) is founded
	Second wave of federal funding cutbacks to NNBAP
	Task Force on Broadcasting Policy (Caplan-Sauvageau Report) strongly supports Aboriginal broadcasting
1987	Siberian (then Soviet) delegates attend ICC General Assembly for the first time and are designated "associate members"
	Richard Nerysoo becomes the first Aboriginal speaker of the House for the Northwest Territories Legislative Assembly
1988	The first Aboriginal national television documentary, *Sharing a Dream,* is produced by the Native Communications Society
1990	First Congress of Northern Minorities takes place in Moscow
	Siberian (Soviet/Russian) associate members are made full members of ICC
	More federal funding cuts to NNBAP
	The federal government ends the NCP, cutting all funding to Aboriginal newspapers and magazines

1992	Television Northern Canada (TVNC) begins broadcasting in January
1993	Another wave of federal funding cuts to NNBAP
	Funding cuts to Aboriginal language programs
	The Nunavut Land Claim is signed on 25 May; receives Royal Assent on 9 July; celebrations are held in Coppermine
1994	Yup'ik in Siberia hold the Second Eskimo Assembly and elect a council of elders headed by journalist Svetlana Taliok
1999	The Canadian Territory of Nunavut becomes official on 1 April, completing the separation of the Inuit-majority eastern Arctic from the NWT

Un/Covering the North

Canadians will recognize the heading as a play on the first line of the national anthem, "O Canada, our home and native land." The cartoon appeared during the Oka crisis, involving the federal and Quebec governments, Quebec police, the town of Oka, and the Kanehsatake Mohawk First Nation.

Introduction

> The phone lines are down to the Yukon's most remote
> community. The people of Old Crow won't have any way of
> letting the Chief Returning Officer know who won in their
> riding, short of renting a plane and flying the results in.
> Those results could be crucial.
>
> CBC Radio, Whitehorse

The results were indeed crucial, and they arrived in a most unusual way. A ham radio operator picked up the information from a message radioed from an airplane flying over Old Crow and relayed the results to Whitehorse (Alia 1991a). That convoluted, but effective, mode of transporting information may seem unnecessary and peculiar to someone from Outside.[3] In the North, such occurrences are part of daily life. When it comes to sending or receiving news, northerners are used to improvising.

In the North, people know they need each other. This is especially true in the interrelated areas of communication and transportation. In the northern winter, a breakdown in transportation can be a matter of life or death. A northerner doesn't think twice about whether to stop and help a traveller in trouble. Breakdowns in transportation are not the only crises. A communications breakdown can also be critical in a land where radio or telephone lines link people with survival, as well as with each other.

I often call the North a huge small town. Despite the enormous distances, people know each other. On a six-seater Piper Navajo headed from Whitehorse to Juneau, I ran into an acquaintance from Pangnirtung. In a few minutes, flying between Yukon and Alaska, I was able to catch up on a couple of years of gossip from the Baffin region thousands of miles away. Whenever I land at the airport in Iqaluit, Whitehorse, or Yellowknife, I run into several people I know, and I'm not even a full-time northern resident. I'm from Outside. In most years, I spend several months each year "up here," usually in winter, which keeps me from being classified as a fair-weather tourist. Like a small town, the North features friendliness and hostility in nearly equal parts, reflecting that "family" quality so often seen in small communities, which includes both sibling rivalry and unconditional love.

I continue to be amazed at the speed with which northern news travels through the North – and the slowness with which it reaches (non-northern) people in the South.

Map I.1

The circumpolar North

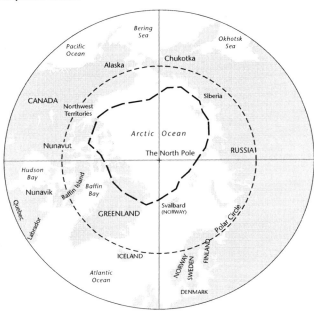

Source: Map adapted from Dorit Olsen, Statistics Greenland, P.S. Box 1025, DK-3900 Nuuk, Greenland. Homepage: www.statgreen.gl. E-mail: stat@greennet.gl. Used with permission

Although the growth of air travel and computers has contributed greatly to the development of the information network, I suspect that the North's small-town atmosphere has as much to do with widely shared conditions and a mythos of northernness. Canadian northerners live in communities of fifty to three thousand or in cities such as Yellowknife or Whitehorse (at 23,474, the latter is the major northern metropolis) that are tiny by southern standards. In this setting communications, politics, and policy making are at once personal, casual, small-scale, and – because of the very nature of circumpolarity – uniquely global.

In this book, "North" refers to those regions that are designated "Middle North," "Far North," and "Extreme North" on Map I.2, which is based on Hamelin's cartographic visualization of Canadian "nordicity." The three regions include portions of the provinces and all of Yukon and the Northwest Territories. As of April 1999 the Canadian North includes a third territory, Nunavut.

Information about how long first peoples have lived in the North varies. Figures range from 7,000 to more than 35,000 years (Alia 1991a, 107) and

Map I.2

The Canadian North: Nordicity zones

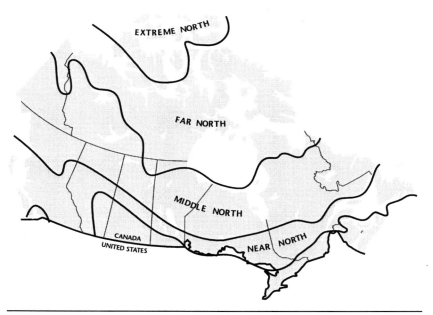

Source: Adapted from Ontario Royal Commission on the Northern Environment; appeared in Alia (1991a, 107).

some recent research suggests an even wider range. In 1997 the British journal *Science* reported that stone tools found at Siring Yuriakh near the Lena River in Siberia dated back to between 240,000 and 366,000 years ago (Bowman 1997, A15). Before Outsiders intervened, community members were related by language, clan, and family; there were no elected chiefs, councils, or administrative centres. Decision making was consensus-based – a political foundation still important to northern governments today. Indigenous people emphasize that their governments long preceded any idea of Canada or the United States.

The following pages introduce some of the key themes and subjects developed in the book. The northern climate is considered in both its journalistic sense – the social, political, and communications climate – and its more literal sense of weather. I survey indigenous broadcasting around the globe as a context for examining indigenous broadcasting in the North. This is followed by a discussion of communications and power relations, an overview of northern political culture, and a discussion of the relationship between indigenous leadership and journalism.

Transportation and Climate in the Canadian North

> Foul weather isolates Yukon. Snow storms ... and ice fog have
> disrupted ... flights for nearly two weeks.
>
> Andrea Buckley, *Yukon News,* 1991

In many places, weather is a subject for small talk. In the North, it is the stuff of hard news and serious concern. In northern Canada, weather, transportation, and communications are tightly intertwined and fraught with challenges unimaginable in the South. Despite such challenges, virtually everyone interviewed in the course of this study said that northern weather and travel conditions are inadequately addressed in government policy. Northerners tend to view government funding initiatives for northern conditions as drop-in-the-bucket remedies for ocean-sized problems. Even in good weather, travel is a challenge. It is difficult for southerners to imagine having to charter a helicopter or an airplane merely to exercise the privilege of voting or running for office, but this is done routinely in the North.

Through the long winter, the weather has a tremendous impact on both transportation and communications. In many parts of the North there is twenty-four-hour darkness, or only a brief period of light. Almost everywhere there is wind and extreme cold. "If it's minus 45 or 50 you don't drive at all. If you get stuck somewhere, you die" (Alia 1991a, 113-4).

I spent the winter of 1991 in Yukon. January began with record-breaking cold. There were days that were in the minus 40s and 50s Celsius, when Whitehorse was socked in by ice fog so thick it was hard to see across a well-lit street. Taxis and trucks gave out. Airplanes were grounded for days. People were stranded in town or out. The mail went nowhere. In an unguarded moment, I slipped into Outside mentality. Thinking only of research deadlines in Ottawa, I dashed across town (forty-eight below, zero visibility) to the post office to use Priority Post. I was not the only creature of habit. In the bookstore/office supply store/post office, others were queued up. I suddenly realized how silly we looked clutching our precious packages. It was several days before the mail went out. There is a mini-van "mail bus" from Whitehorse to Atlin, British Columbia, just over the Yukon border. I was told of a couple of dogsled mail runs between small communities, but these will not get mail from Whitehorse to Ottawa.

Familiarity with conditions in Nunavut, where the only access to communities is slow travel by snowmobile, dogsled, or all-terrain vehicle, or (usually faster) travel by air, led me to wrongly assume that the roads in Yukon would mean easier access among communities. Until I wintered in Yukon, I was unaware that road access meant little in winter. I had no understanding of what happens to a vehicle at minus 45 degrees until I spent part of New Year's Eve in a deceased Whitehorse taxi. In the city, breakdowns and delays are a nuisance. In remote locations, they are deadly.

Although such conditions are particular to northern climates, Aboriginal communications in other parts of the world are affected by comparable conditions. Many people experience isolation, whether poor or nonexistent roads, to use an example, are a result of Arctic, desert, or other terrain, or of a lack of funding. The remoteness of many indigenous communities is one of the main reasons that new technologies are so widely appealing. Internet and satellite broadcast access is increasing at a rapid rate, and indigenous people are energetically working to integrate the new media into their daily lives. Because it travels easily and inexpensively by air without need of vehicles or roads, radio has long been the primary medium for Aboriginal communications internationally.

Aboriginal Broadcasting in the International Context
The first Aboriginal broadcasts in North America were heard on Alaskan radio in the 1930s. The Canadian Broadcasting Corporation (CBC) did not get involved until the late 1950s. Despite Alaska's nearly thirty-year head start, the United States has moved all too slowly to support Aboriginal media. Progress has been more rapid in Canada: once Native people began to broadcast in Canada, indigenous media – particularly the oral-culture-friendly medium of radio – were soon spread across the land. Canada remains the world leader in Aboriginal broadcasting. It now has several hundred local Aboriginal radio stations, eleven regional radio networks, "the beginnings of a national Aboriginal radio network," six television production outlets, and Television Northern Canada (TVNC), the satellite-transmitted service that spans the Canadian North (Royal Commission on Aboriginal Peoples 1997).

Considering its far greater population and collection of diverse indigenous communities, the corresponding figures for the United States are particularly disappointing. According to Gordon Regguinti of the Native American Journalists' Association, there are about thirty Native American radio stations nationwide, of which twenty-two to twenty-four are in the "lower states," with a handful in Alaska (personal communication, 1998). The Native Media Resource Center figures concur. The centre lists twenty-one stations in the "lower 48 states" and ten in Alaska. The Alaska stations are run by Yup'ik, Aleut, Iñupiat, Athabaskan, and "urban Alaska Natives" in Anchorage (Native Media Resource Center 1998; 1996). A fairly recent development is a twenty-four-hour-a-day distribution service via AIROS, the American Indian Radio on Satellite network distribution system, which sends programming over the Internet and public radio to tribal communities throughout the United States. One of the stations that send programming through AIROS is a Native American music program, *Different Drums*, which originates at KBBI in Homer, Alaska.

There is a scattering of stations that provide Sámi programming in Finland, Norway, and Sweden, and Sámi Radio has its own channel based in Finland. It broadcasts in three Sámi languages – North Sámi, Inari Sámi, and Skolt Sámi – and works closely with Sámi Radio in Sweden and Norway. The goal is to have a joint digital channel of multiple services by the year 2000.

New Zealand has twenty-one Maori radio stations linked by Ruia Mai, the national Maori radio service. Founded in 1990, the service began broadcasting in stereo in 1996. The Maori and the New Zealand government are currently discussing ways to improve the promotion of Maori language through broadcasting (Maori Radio Network 1996; New Zealand 1998).

The first exclusively Aboriginal station in Australia did not begin broadcasting until 1985 at Alice Springs. Australia's Northern Territory is akin to Canada's North – vast spaces, small communities, several languages. As of 1998 there are three exclusively indigenous radio stations, at Alice Springs, Brisbane, and Townsville, and one indigenous community television station at Alice Springs. The National Indigenous Media Association of Australia (NIMAA) has a membership of 136 community broadcasting groups, suggesting a growing commitment to indigenous broadcasting.

Despite frequent and extensive funding cuts, Canada still has the lead in Aboriginal communications. One reason the media survive is the extensive network of volunteers who either supplement paid staff or run the media by themselves. For example, in Fort McPherson, NWT, the community radio station is run by a group of volunteers guided by a volunteer committee. Founded in 1983, the station is linked to the Native Communications Society of the NWT. Its annual budget of approximately $6,000 is raised through bingo games, with regular Monday evening radio bingo helping to fill the pot. In addition to regularly scheduled programming, "there are other times the station is on the air for other organizations and just to provide music and messages to those people who are out on the land" (Curt Svendsen in Alia 1991e). The station broadcasts in Gwich'in and English. The radio station in Tuktoyaktuk, NWT, was founded in 1970 and is also run entirely by volunteers. They are supervised by elected officers of the Tuk-Tuk Communications Society and broadcast in English and Inuvialuktun.

Marginalization: Communications and the Hierarchies of Power

There is a frustrating contradiction in northern communications: At the same time that northern leaders and community members have benefited from extensive access to technological breakthroughs in mass media, those outside the North appear to have received little benefit from information generated in the North through these technologies. Jim Butler, editor of the *Whitehorse Star,* has often lamented the lack of coverage of northern issues and perspectives in the southern media. "The southern media's coverage ... [is] largely limited to occasions when northern politicians thrust themselves into major southern spotlights habitually patrolled by the media. These ranged from the Supreme Court of Canada to [Yukon Premier Tony] Penikett's memorable blast of Prime Minister Brian Mulroney on live television at the first minister's conference of the fall of 1987" (Butler 1990, 17).

Tony Penikett's New Democratic government was elected in Yukon in May 1985. Yet Butler observed that "it took the 1988 death of the NDP government in Manitoba for the *Globe and Mail* to stop calling Howard [Pawley's] crew 'Canada's only NDP government'" (Butler 1990, 17). Butler said the *Whitehorse Star* is the only Yukon paper that files stories with Canadian Press (CP), which ended its brief experiment with a Yellowknife bureau in the 1980s. For a time, the *Globe and Mail* ran a Yukon column on its "Nation" page every second Saturday, but the column was cancelled in 1985, "along with columns from other remote areas of Canada, as a cost-cutting measure" (ibid., 17).

The ease of information access seems to have had little impact on coverage of northern issues. This lack of coverage underscores an urgent problem that I think has more to do with power than with technology. Elizabeth Janeway's words seem relevant: "The powerful still retain the power to define what is happening, even when they too are confused and disoriented because their own interpretations of events are based on archaic social myth" (Janeway 1980, 251). Although the process of social mythologizing is discussed at length below, we should consider here one of Janeway's additional concerns: "Beyond the damage that methods of using power as prescribed by the powerful do to the weak is the harm that they do to the powerful" (ibid., 251). There is no such thing as a one-way process, and the damage affects everyone. It is inadequate and distorting, however, to attribute patterns of northern communication solely to the existence of dominant and subordinate social groups. Such differences in power are relevant, but are not sufficient to describe or explain all that has happened.

In terms of northern communications, I am convinced that although "access" is often constructed as meaning simply the availability of technology, it really has much to do with hierarchies of power. Northerners are informationally disadvantaged. Knowing this, they make extensive use of communication technologies to improve their access to what is happening at the country's core – "core" being a political construction that identifies patterns of power reaching outward from Ottawa and the centres of provincial government. Yukoner Adam Killick points out one of the many absurdities in the use of new technologies. In 1995 YukonNet, a Yukon Internet link, joined the information universe. It enabled Yukoners to get access to the World Wide Web, and ensured that the twice-weekly *Yukon News* could be found on-line anywhere in the world before it hit the local newsstands. Commented Killick, "I find it ironic that even though I live in a small community in a remote corner of the planet, somebody in New Zealand can read my local newspaper on the World Wide Web before I can get it from across the street. For information to flow like this in major urban centres may be commonplace; but here in Whitehorse, where people still talk to each other on the street ... the delivery of our community broadsheet via cyberspace seems absolutely Orwellian." He concludes that "Perhaps the most salient benefit from the Internet's arrival here is not that we can access [the Web] but that the Web can access us" (Killick 1996, A20).

It is a truism that Canadians know more about the United States than Americans know about Canada. Steeped in the superpower mythos, American citizens seldom consider it urgent to know much about Canada unless they see a direct impact on US defence, trade, economic, or military policy, or on tourism or politics. Canadians, on the other hand, make it their business to stay abreast of developments in the United States. In a similar way, northern Canadians are marginalized with respect to the Canadian core (and, as Killick points out, much of the rest of the world). Sheer physical distance and conditions of climate and terrain compound the psychological distance between North and South, and the distance between southern economies and the economic realities northerners face.

Northern Political Life

By the early 1960s there were two northern geopolitical units, Yukon Territory and the Northwest Territories, each represented by elected officials in the federal Parliament in Ottawa and each having its own government in the form of a government leader and a territorial council, akin to the provincial government structure providing for a premier and a legislative assembly. Through the process of devolution, territorial administration was gradually transferred from the federal government to the territorial governments. In 1967 the Northwest Territories Council moved from Ottawa to Yellowknife, and the federal government (which at that point retained control of territorial infrastructures) appointed an Inuk and a Dene councillor. These appointments signalled the official start of formal participation by Aboriginal people not only in their own communities but in the regional government and administration, though still overseen by Ottawa. The appointed council would later be replaced by an elected council, giving northerners still more control over their political lives. Apart from changing patterns of governance and administration, the territories themselves underwent a number of geographical changes, the latest of which was the establishment of the territory of Nunavut.

In northern Aboriginal communities, communications and politics have an intimate and interesting history. Their links extend beyond the coverage of politicians and issues by news media that is typical throughout the country. In a sense, the media have been training grounds for Aboriginal politicians and other leaders. I have always been struck by the fact that many, perhaps most, northern leaders have at one time or another worked as journalists. Such a trend seems to go beyond the usual border-crossing seen in many professions, and it bears some relationship to the broader context in which Euro-American journalism evolved.

In the early years of newspaper history – from the 1600s until the early twentieth century – newspaper owners and politicians were often the same people. At the time this dual role was not perceived to constitute a conflict of interest. Although official attitudes and principles have changed, journalism careers are seldom as pure as some would have us believe. Before and after (and, less often, during) their journalistic lives, journalists are employed as speech writers, political advisors, and sometimes even politicians. Former politicians become journalists or owners of media organizations. Apart from this general pattern, it is also the case that a number of Aboriginal leaders in southern regions have backgrounds in journalism. However, I do not think this occurs on the same scale as in the North; more often, southern leaders have legal rather than journalistic training.

Among the prominent northern leaders who are also journalists are Rosemarie Kuptana, former president of the Inuit Circumpolar Conference (ICC) and Inuit Tapirisat of Canada (ITC); Mary Simon, the former ICC president who in 1994 was appointed Canada's first ambassador for circumpolar affairs; Jose Kusugak, a Nunavut Implementation Commission (NIC) commissioner and president of Nunavut Tunngavik Incorporated (NTI, formerly TFN, the organization set up to administer the Nunavut land claim); and Peter Ernerk, a former legislator and current NIC commissioner. Among other common experiences, all of them have worked for CBC.

The significant number of indigenous journalists in positions of leadership is not merely a coincidence. Leadership requires communication skills, and the job of getting elected and staying in office requires learning to manipulate mass media and public opinion. I suspect that the increased proportion of communications experience to leadership is related to the relative disadvantage northerners experience in gaining access to the machinery of politics and public policy. Communications, especially broadcasting, provides access to news and information on a national and global scale. It also provides access to crucial networks of policy and power.

Access to communication diminishes geographical and intellectual remoteness. Because of its isolation, the North has often been ahead of the rest of the country in developing and exploring new communication technologies – a fact that is seldom communicated to Outsiders. On my first trip

North in 1984, I was surprised to find that people in small Baffin communities were far more skilled at using long-distance computer linkages than the people I knew in Toronto (myself included). Adult education and other programs often relied on community-to-community computer hookups. In retrospect, I wonder why I was surprised.

The following chapters explore the history, development, and current state of Aboriginal media in the North. Chapter 1 looks at portrayals of northern people, issues, and land by people from inside and outside the North. Chapter 2 examines the relationship between communications and language, literacy, politics, and education. Chapter 3 is a historical survey of northern communications in Canada. Chapter 4 looks at the impact of technology on "the circumpolar village," the development of television and Internet resources, and the directions in which northern communications are headed. Chapters 5 and 6 are, respectively, case studies of communications in Yukon and of newspaper coverage of northern people and issues.

The Yukon case study was undertaken for several reasons. First, I wanted an opportunity to observe one region at close hand, over time. As Yukoners are often heard to say, Yukon is almost always given short shrift (and is sometimes omitted entirely) in studies that purport to cover the North. It is doubly marginalized – as a northern region, but also as a region that is not considered a significant part of "the North," perhaps because of its small population and its location in the extreme west of the Canadian North. Yet it has produced a disproportionate number of Aboriginal and non-Aboriginal leaders and leading programs in politics, journalism, film, literature, and the arts. It has developed a government with close ties to Aboriginal communities and to Ottawa. Unlike those in the Northwest Territories and Nunavut, the Yukon territorial government is strikingly like the provincial governments. The Council for Yukon First Nations has been a leader in coalition building between First Nations and Métis people. Northern Native Broadcasting Yukon has produced some of the most creative and influential programming in the North, and its leaders (among them, Ken Kane, Joanne MacDonald, and George Henry) have been at the centre of the development of the ground-breaking coalition Television Northern Canada.

Finally, Chapter 7 offers some concluding thoughts on the issues surrounding Northern indigenous media and briefly speculates about where northern communications might be going.

1
Southern Exposure: Portrayals of the North

The early history of communications about the North is steeped in the language of conquest and colonization. Despite centuries of change and decades of progress, that language persists in many of today's communications. This chapter reviews the history and nature of portrayals of the North and of Aboriginal people in film, television, radio, and print. It begins with a look at the impact of colonial relations on portrayals of the North and outlines some of the players in the North-South drama. It considers the ways Outsiders have portrayed the North, the ways non-Aboriginal people have portrayed Aboriginal people, and, finally, the ways Aboriginal people have taken increasing control over the analysis and production of their own images.

The Vocabulary of Colonization

Although no specific military goals in the North emerged until the Second World War, the language of exploration was littered with quasi-military expressions. Explorers were depicted in their own accounts and in the media as conquerors who launched assaults on the Pole. Polar people were viewed only in terms of their ability to aid those assaults and to increase the comforts of the conquerors. The language of invasion did not provide a tool for analysis of the colonial relationship between the northern peoples and their cultures and the explorers who had invaded northern lands and waters.

Explorers, missionaries, traders, and governments, whose interests were all intertwined, all had similar attitudes toward the North and northern peoples. Some ignored indigenous northern peoples. Others treated them as exotic items for study or observation or as malleable (and infantile) subjects in desperate need of "civilization." Throughout the 1800s and early 1900s Inuit were seen in Europe and North America as live "exhibits" – in circuses and expositions such as the World's Columbian Exposition in Chicago in 1893 and Seattle's Alaska-Yukon-Pacific Exposition in 1909. In Chicago, anthropologist Franz Boas supervised the display of "fifty-nine

Labrador Inuit and their thirty-five dogs" (Fienup-Riordan 1995, 39). The "exhibit" was of sufficient interest that Exposition organizers tacked on an additional twenty-five cents to the regular fifty-cent admission price.

In 1885, before he began his obsessive Arctic adventures, the explorer Robert Peary wrote, "If colonization is to be a success in the polar regions let white men take with them native wives" (Herbert 1989, 15). Peary's comment made a covert case for the two-wife system that has often characterized European-Aboriginal relations. Peary already had a white wife, whose awareness of his Inuit family would engender a complicated mix of tolerance and tension. He made the idea of a second Inuit wife look like a public service. Such a union would result in "a race combining the hardiness of the mothers with the intelligence of the fathers," and the offspring of this fortuitous union would "surely reach the Pole if their fathers did not succeed in doing it" (Herbert 1989, 15). Apart from the problematic question of whether reaching the Pole (or any location) was a valid goal in and of itself (a question asked with surprising infrequency, even today), Peary's proposal contained a remarkable dismissal of cultural complexity and a proclamation of essential "racial" characteristics. In Peary's scheme, cross-cultural understanding was simple: Inuit were "hardy" and Europeans "intelligent."

The news media jumped right on the bandwagon. Newspapers helped publicize Peary's unquestioned distinction as well as his "need" of equipment and financial assistance. His explorations were financed, rewarded with formal prizes, and well publicized. Some of the most helpful publicity for Peary's cause came from the National Geographic Society. Its *National Geographic Magazine* was probably the first magazine to exoticize "natives" around the globe for a mass-market readership. The daily newspapers were equally enthusiastic. "Peary Awarded First Gold Medal" read the headline in the *Sunday New York Herald* for 16 December 1906. The item that followed included an elegant portrait of the photogenic explorer and an elaborate description of the prize, the ceremony, the notables, and the ambience. Although several scientists, diplomats, and politicians were also honoured at the annual banquet of the National Geographic Society in Washington, DC, Peary was the star. US president Theodore Roosevelt was on hand to bestow the gold and sapphire Hubbard medal (endowed by Gardiner Green Hubbard), for the farthest north Arctic exploration (Herbert 1989, 21-2). Moving from reportage to a blatant show of support, the *Herald* also published Peary's plan to "conquer" the Pole (ibid., 260).

To be fair, the media sometimes attempted to break the mould. Although full of condescension and noblesse oblige, the *New York World* made a bold gesture of support for Minik, the young Greenlandic man whom Peary had "collected," along with other human and non-human specimens of Arctic life. Minik was one of two survivors of the six Inuit Peary brought from the Arctic to New York in 1897 (Herbert 1989, 204-5; Harper 1986). In one of the scientific community's most shameful moments, one that tainted the image of even the esteemed Franz Boas, Minik discovered his father's bones in the American Museum of Natural History. His efforts to retrieve his father and take him home made sensational news copy. Photographs showed him in furs. A drawing showed him kneeling, arms outstretched toward the museum. Accompanying the images was the headline "Give Me My Father's Body" and a lengthy sub-head: "The pathetic story of Minik, the Esquimau boy, who is growing up in New York and is going to find the North Pole some day, but who now wants most the bones of his father from the Museum of Natural History" (Herbert 1989, 205).

Whether ignored or objectified by non-Aboriginal southerners, indigenous residents of the North could count on having their interests shunted aside to make way for "civilization" and "progress." But in the third decade of the twentieth century, a new invader arrived on the scene, intent more on recording than on "civilizing." The newcomer carried a movie camera.

The North on Film

Like other media, film first looked at northern people from an ethnocentric, "Outside" point of view. On film, northern people first came to the attention of Outsiders in the early 1900s, beginning with Thomas Edison's depiction of Inuit playing games and racing a dogsled (Fienup-Riordan 1995, 40). Shown at the 1901 Pan-American Exposition in Buffalo, New York, Edison's film echoed the live exhibits to which the public had become accustomed. The focus was on human "specimens" as performers – as entertainers brought into the "civilized" world for the pleasure of the non-indigenous public. But it was not the first time that indigenous people had been seen on film.

In his own hands, Louis Lumière's "magic box" movie camera/projector/printer was used only to record the urban, industrialized world. But Alfred Cort Haddon, a Cambridge zoologist, carried a Lumière camera on his 1898 expedition to the Torres Straits Islands, in the South Pacific. According to Fienup-Riordan (1995, 40), the result was the world's first ethnographic film. The trend continued with the extension of "scenics" – travel films – into the ethnographic and expedition arena. Footage was taken on expeditions to South Africa, Antarctica, and then Alaska and Siberia.

Captain Frank E. Kleinschmidt headed the 1909-11 Carnegie Museum Expedition, which produced 10,000 feet of film: "Running four reels longer than Robert Flaherty's *Nanook of the North,* it is considered by some the first feature-length documentary" (Fienup-Riordan 1995, 41; Brownlow 1979, 473). The footage provided glimpses of daily life in an Alaska Eskimo village. First shown in 1912, Kleinschmidt's film was later enhanced by Alaskan footage taken from aboard the aptly labelled submarine-chaser ship, the *Silver Screen.* According to Hollywood's *Variety* magazine (1923), the revised film was a box office success. Still, it did not achieve the lasting, worldwide

This 1998 cartoon shows that seventy-six years after the release of Robert Flaherty's film *Nanook,* it remains an emblem of northerners and the North, and Inuit are still portrayed as exotic objects of derision. I doubt that an equivalent treatment of, for example, African American or Jewish people would have made it past the editor's desk.

success that would continue for *Nanook.* Even today, Nanook is a familiar name and an emblem for things indigenous, "primitive," and "Northern."

Between 1912 and 1919, teacher and expedition leader William Van Valin made a series of six twenty-minute films, which accompanied his lectures and were collectively titled *The Top of the Earth.* The films depicted early experiments in which government and scientists brought Sámi reindeer herding families to Alaska to teach Alaskan Inuit to herd reindeer (which are domesticated caribou) instead of hunting wild caribou.

At the same time that Van Valin was preparing his Alaska films, Robert Flaherty was at work in the Canadian North on the Ungava Peninsula in Hudson Bay, shooting *Nanook of the North*, the work commonly, and retroactively, referred to as the world's first documentary. (John Grierson actually coined the term "documentary" for *Moana* (1926), Flaherty's second feature [Rhode 1976, 246].) Initially, Flaherty was encouraged by Sir William Mackenzie of Mackenzie and Mann, an employer of his father's, to take a camera along on his expeditions exploring for iron ore on the east coast of Hudson Bay, which started in 1910. Flaherty soon became more interested in the Inuit and their lives and land than in iron ore. With the intention of producing a travel film, he assembled rushes shot in 1914 and 1916. The result became known as the Harvard print. The negatives, which could not be duplicated, were lost in a fire, and the single print that remained has since been lost. According to the film historian Eric Rhode (1976, 246), friends of Flaherty who saw the original film found his Outsider's view uninformative, and Flaherty "recognized that if he wished his subject to take on its own life" he would need a new approach. Resolved to continue the project, Flaherty returned to Ungava in 1919 and 1920 to re-shoot. This time his goal was more ambitious: to involve Inuit as both filmmakers and actors and to portray the North as a "day in the life of" an Inuk whom he called Nanook.

Released in 1922, the film was an immediate popular success. It was praised by French critics for its "purité" (Rotha 1983, 47), and US critic and playwright Robert Sherwood included it in his annual "best films" volume for 1922. He said that it was "rendered far more vital than any trumped-up drama could ever be by the fact that it was real ... Nanook was ... an Eskimo struggling to survive. The North was no mechanical affair of wind machines ... It was the North, cruel and incredibly strong" (in Rotha 1983, 41).

Flaherty's attitude and approach were filled with contradictions. He "saw himself as the servant of his material," declining to be "a God-like creator" and admitting his dependency on his Inuit colleagues and assistants (Rhode 1976, 247). Yet he portrayed himself as having filmed "essential truths" (Manwell 1950, 18), while giving the rest of the world a vision of Inuit "not from the civilized point of view but as they saw themselves" (Griffith 1953, 36). Essential truths or not, the film does reflect Flaherty's practice of showing rushes to the Inuit as the work progressed, so that they could see the footage and check for mistakes (Leyda 1977, 137-8). John Grierson praised Flaherty's sense of social responsibility and dedication to deriving the story from its location (ibid., 176-7).

Moana, which aimed to portray and publicize Samoan life much as *Nanook* had presented the lives of Inuit, never attracted the same level of interest (Rhode 1976, 249). Although the film predated the coining of the term, *Nanook* is still generally considered to be the first extended "documentary" narrative. The films of Edison, Haddon, Kleinschmidt, Van Valin, and others who filmed outside the North could be called pre- or mini-documentaries – more disjointed and abbreviated images of life and land.

Much has been made of the fictional elements of *Nanook*. However, those who see Flaherty's staged scenes and constructed sets as a betrayal of "true" documentary ignore the evolution of the meaning of the term. If Flaherty made the first in the genre, he set the tone for future work in which people, land, and events are at least made to *appear* to be real. His method drew from early ethnography – the description of cultures, primarily by participant observers from other cultures. Today, the production of ethnographic texts is widely acknowledged to be subjective and narrative, not the "scientific" and objective exercise it was considered in earlier years (Malinowski 1922; Dietz, Prus, and Shaffir 1994).

If, these days, it is fashionable for anthropologists and sociologists to proclaim their subjectivity, it is less in fashion in the world of documentary television and film. One of the major differences between *Nanook* and the documentaries of today is that Flaherty's fictionalization was more transparent (and even more so in retrospect). The tendency in contemporary production and commentary is to pretend distance, objectivity, and the representation of "fact." Rhode (1976, 247) considers the "notion of fabrication" essential to Flaherty's project. He says that those who dismiss the film as a "fake" miss the point, that Flaherty "was not trying to be the clinical and detached observer but was trying to show how filming was something else than the record of fact." He also reminds us that the definer of documentary film, John Grierson, called the medium "the creative use of actuality" rather than the complete and accurate rendering of real life. In truth, all documentaries present subjective realities from their makers' points of view and therefore continue, rather than alter, Flaherty's inventive mingling of fiction and fact, which Grace (1996) contends has more in common with fictional romance than with anthropological documentation. I find this dichotomy problematic, because it can be argued that anthropological documentation is itself a form of fictional romance.

There is a tendency either to sanctify or to demonize Flaherty's work with, and portrayal of, Inuit. Yet, he is neither saint nor devil, but a complex man of his times, an innovative experimenter in a relatively new medium, and an observer of Inuit life. In Flaherty's written and filmed work – and his personal history – we see his limitless patience with northern conditions, his creativity, and the limits to his respect for Inuit people and his interest in Inuit lives. He went on from *Nanook* to other things, leaving the Inuit to live out their (often brief) lives and also to care for the Inuit family that he left behind.[4]

Flaherty expressed genuine respect for Inuit and their accomplishments; he also betrayed paternalistic, racist assumptions about their "primitiveness"

(Flaherty 1924). He apparently regarded his Inuk partner, Alice Nuvalinga (Nyla in the film), as some sort of charming property and no threat to his "real" wife, but he also expressed respect and admiration for her and the other Inuit actors and assistants he engaged. In contrast, some twenty years later Robert Peary portrayed his own Inuit assistants and companions as mere childlike servants (Alia 1987, 64). Flaherty's detractors have focused on *Nanook*'s failure to reproduce life literally, but its ability to convey the spirit and culture of Inuit must also be acknowledged.

It is difficult to separate "life" from "art" in *Nanook*. What is important for our purposes in examining the evolution of northern communications is the role of this and other films in communicating northernness and northern people to those Outside.

Nanook continues to reach contemporary audiences and thus to represent and misrepresent Inuit. The version usually seen today was restored by David Shepard and reprinted under the auspices of the International Film Seminars in 1975, with a newly commissioned soundtrack by Stanley Silverman. Perhaps because most discussions of representation concentrate on visual and written portrayals, scholars have not commented on the *Nanook* soundtrack. Rather than provide an unobtrusive backdrop or recreate the style of silent film accompanists (two appropriate possible approaches), the musical score intrudes on the images and perpetuates misrepresentation of Inuit. Performed by the respected Tashi Ensemble with conductor Peter Serkin, it features violin-dominated Western classical instrumentation and a repeating theme evoking the fake "Indian tom-tom" rhythms prominent in popular and "serious" music of the past century. (Composers in the 1990s continue to use this tom-tom cliché.) The result is double misrepresentation: of the heartbeat drumming of some Native North American cultures; and of the Inuit, who never drummed that way in the first place.

As Sherrill Grace (1996, 126) puts it, Robert Flaherty is a sign in the "semiotics of North." Spinoffs from his film included "Eskimo Pie" ice cream bars, popular songs, and a multitude of books. Flaherty's own "real life" has been reinvented to the extent that, according to Grace, none of the books or articles on his work and life mentions the existence of his Inuit family, despite their continuing prominence – the noted interpreter and former Pauktuutit president Martha Flaherty is his granddaughter. Just before its final credits, the 1994 film about Flaherty, *Kabloonak* (Massot 1994), makes passing reference to his Inuit family, but in the past tense, saying that "Nyla's" (Alice Nuvalinga's) son is no longer alive but neglecting his living relatives.

The reconstruction of Martha Flaherty's grandmother as a romanticized sex object by both Flaherty and Massot is reminiscent of the "Indian princesses" documented by Gail Guthrie Valaskakis in her exhibition and book with Marilyn Burgess, *Indian Princesses and Cowgirls: Stereotypes from the*

Frontier (Burgess and Valaskakis 1995). According to Valaskakis, "Near Sitting Bull's grave, there is a bullet-ridden obelisk raised in memory of the Indian woman who accompanied Lewis and Clark on their expedition across the West ... Sacajawea" (Valaskakis 1995, 11). As her history was recorded and popularized, her name was reconstructed as "Sakakawea," an Hidatsa word meaning "bird woman." The "bird woman" label was then applied to various representations of Sacajawea. Her face and body were transformed in popular imagery (for example, a 1920s advertisement for Oriental Dyeing & Cleaning Works) into an "ageless," "shapely Indian princess with perfect caucasian features, dressed in a tight-fitting red tunic, spearing fish with a bow and arrow from a birchbark canoe suspended on a mountain-rimmed, moonlit lake" (ibid., 11).

More recently, the Native American woman has been remade in the style of "Barbie." The cartoon image of Pocahontas in the eponymous 1995 Disney children's film looks strikingly akin to the Sacajawea of the 1920s, although her slightly less Caucasian features include Oriental-looking eyes. The lyrics to one of the main songs, "Savages," contain what are supposed to be parallel stereotyped images of whites looking at Native Americans and vice versa. But the realities of colonial history and persistent, current representations (sports teams called Redskins and Indians and brand names such as Redman fruit, which are currently visible in flaming red logos on fruit boxes in my local Bellingham, Washington, supermarket) make it likely that these "Indian" stereotypes will stick with children who view the movie: "What can you expect from filthy little heathens? /Their whole disgusting race is like a curse / ... Savages, Savages ... "

It should not take Buffy Sainte-Marie to tell us that "First Nations people do not typically feel flattered by Disney's *Pocahontas* or mascots like the Washington Redskins." Sainte-Marie lays the blame on everyone who buys into the system, including some Aboriginal people: "It is with great embarrassment that I ... [express] my regret at having participated in the National Aboriginal Achievement Awards this year, even though a part of the show is dedicated to 'honoring' me and my work ... I feel I must divorce myself from certain offensive and exploitive aspects of this production." She protests the inclusion in the evening's entertainment of "Indian 'devils'" – "a corps of young dancers in renditions of sacred religious costumes of the holy people of Zuni, the Hopi, and the Apache cultures," who leapt about "in menacing postures" and were followed by actors Graham Greene and Tom Jackson performing a comedy routine in "devil" hats, standing on "a huge inverted replica of a Pueblo bowl." She calls for greater consciousness of the inconsistency of honouring Aboriginal arts and scholars "while defaming and exploiting the cultures they seek to serve" (Sainte-Marie 1998, 7).

Two relatively recent television series, while both managing to capture something of the reality of the North, reveal the challenges of fiction media. I am one of the many who mourned the death of the American television program *Northern Exposure* and treasured its many wonderful moments. The show managed to communicate an essential northernness and promote intercultural awareness despite its often casual approach to accuracy. It was rare among television programming for its fine writing and "high-culture" connections (great music and art, elaborate literary allusions). Nevertheless, the show perpetuated some of the myths that many of us are trying to challenge – including the persistent metaphorizing, exoticizing, and poeticizing of the North itself.

I have often turned to the Canadian television drama *North of 60* for my northern "fix" during the months of confinement in the South. The requirements of collapsed time and place and dramatic device notwithstanding, I feel a great affection for this Canadian-produced show, with its predominantly Aboriginal cast and impressive roster of respected northern Aboriginal advisors. The fictional community of Lynx River (really a mock-town built in a northern-looking part of Alberta not far from metropolitan Calgary) resembles communities I have visited in Yukon and the Northwest Territories. The characters, too, are recognizable. Most are well drawn and they come alive thanks to solid writing and fine acting. The advisors help keep the representation of people and locale honest, and an increasing number of Aboriginal writers and directors are making their mark on more recent episodes. Unfortunately, at the time of this writing, the show appears to have been cancelled. It's not dead yet; its loyal supporters are lobbying for a resurrection.

The poet and playwright Daniel David Moses made me rethink my unquestioning adulation of the show. Having interviewed him for the *Globe and Mail,* Kate Taylor wrote, "He knows many of the native actors ... and says they don't feel it's a realistic depiction of a town in the Northwest Territories: 'What northern community doesn't have laughter or dogs?' he asks" (Taylor 1996, C5). Moses is right. Humour is the lifeblood of Aboriginal communities and the survival tool of northern winters. And dogs are everywhere.

Despite Moses's criticism, I will probably go on loving *North of 60,* although I seldom watch it when I am *in* the North – which may be part of Moses's point. While living in the South I yearn for the brief, fast-action glimpse of the Northern Lights and the vignettes of pseudo-northern life. Because so little information comes from North to South, the inaccuracies can be dangerous. Certainly, the lack of humour (corrected in some of the later scripts) does northern people a significant disservice. The perpetual-angst, perpetual-crisis mentality is a serious distortion.

That said, I am not sure that *North of 60* distorts reality any more than other television programming – which by its nature must collapse, distil, and distort "real life" due to constraints of time and dramatic expediency. This speeding-up of life, which today is considered an inherent characteristic of television production, was not so pronounced in the earlier days of television drama. It is partly a product of the fast-forward, channel-surfing, music-video generation that has come to expect powerhouse perpetual-motion imagery and sound. I would add this criticism to Moses's list: As much as humour and dogs belong in northern communities, speed does not.

Alex Karoniaktatie Jacobs refers to the rampant appropriation and (mis)representation of First Nations identity and culture as "the politics of primitivism" (Jacobs 1986). In *Freeze Frame*, her study of the depiction of Alaska Eskimos in the movies, Ann Fienup-Riordan (1995, 4) dissects this politics of primitivism. She notes that "primarily, Eskimos appear as 'primitives,' noble survivors in a hostile land." Her interest in the subject began with the "disjunction between how life is lived in Alaska and how it is represented in film."

Through the years, the actors in films depicting indigenous northerners have been drawn from every cultural group except the actual people being portrayed. There has been some improvement in the 1990s, but the general pattern remains. The 1932 film *Igloo* purported to portray Canadian Inuit but featured Iñupiat Ray Mala and an all-Iñupiat cast (Fienup-Riordan 1995, 4). Other films have featured such "Inuit" as Anthony Quinn, Yoko Tani, Gloria Saunders, Lotus Long, Carol Thurston, and, more recently, Joan Chen, Meg Tilly, and Lou Diamond Phillips. Such casting is not limited to films about Alaskan Eskimos. Among other recent examples of Hollywood's depictions of first peoples is the 1996 movie *Smilla's Sense of Snow*, with English actor Julia Ormond portraying the Greenlandic lead.

It was not until the 1960s that Aboriginal filmmakers entered the Canadian picture and began to make their own representations of Aboriginal experiences and people. In 1969 the National Film Board (NFB) produced a work that was created primarily by Aboriginal people – *These Are My People*, directed by Michael Mitchell, who was trained and sponsored by the NFB's Challenge for Change program. That same year, the Anik satellite system was launched. It would permanently change the shape of northern communications and would pave the way for TVNC, the television service that is continuing to develop the work of Aboriginal filmmakers and videographers. The first Aboriginal national television documentary, *Sharing a Dream*, produced by the Native Communications Society, would not appear until 1988. Today, there is a strong body of works by Aboriginal filmmakers in Canada and other countries, and an international network, the First Nations Film and Video World Alliance, which includes members from Canada, Australia, Greenland, Mexico, New Zealand, the Solomon Islands, the United States, and Vanuatu (First Nations Film and Video World Alliance 1993).

The roster of indigenous filmmakers is rapidly growing, and northern Canadians continue to have a strong presence. Several of the leading actors in Sherman Alexie's 1998 American feature film, *Smoke Signals,* are Canadians (Tantoo Cardinal, Adam Beach, and Gary Farmer, whose acting career continues to parallel his career in journalism). Also released in 1998 was a four-hour made-for-TV movie, *Big Bear,* based on the life of Cree chief Big Bear (played by Gordon Tootoosis). The movie also stars Tantoo Cardinal and dancer and actor Michael Greyeyes, and is directed by the distinguished Métis director, Gil Cardinal. The Inuit Broadcasting Corporation (IBC), the National Film Board, and Words and Pictures Video co-produced the 1998 documentary *Amorak's Song.* The film – narrated by Martin Kreelak, an IBC producer whose eighty-year-old father is at the centre of the film – had its world premiere in Baker Lake, Nunavut, in June 1998 (Robinson 1998, 52; Shaver 1998, 52-3).

The Persistence of the Exotic: Current Non-Aboriginal Publications

The exoticizing of northern land and people, which began with the early explorers and continues in films and television shows, also persists in many of the publications produced for consumers of the news and of the North, as Ann Fienup-Riordan (1995) documents. Although they publish thoughtful and informative articles with increasing respect for indigenous northern people (sometimes by indigenous authors), non-Aboriginal northern magazines often continue the portrayal of the North as a place for Others to visit, a place of exploration, tourism, and trade.

It is no coincidence that the 1995 Annual Report of the Arctic Institute of North America (AINA) reveals that the overwhelming majority of AINA's largest funders are resource-based corporations such as Alberta-Pacific Forest Industries, Amoco Canada Petroleum Company, and TransCanada Pipelines (Arctic Institute of North America 1995, 17). After centuries of north-south contact, the North continues to be depicted as a place of quaint people and exploitable resources. As Lorna Roth puts it in her essay on "(De)Romancing the North," media portrayals have described the North as both "a despoiled paradise and ... an inhospitable landscape" (Roth 1995, 37).

It is true that many northerners want to increase tourism and trade and become partners in exploration. And there is a growing tendency in non-Aboriginal northern magazines at least superficially to consider social, political, and environmental concerns. However, even today's environmentalists often focus more on land, flora, and fauna than on the effects of environmental problems on northern people. *The Beaver* remains the publication of the Hudson's Bay Company (HBC) and the portrayer of its history, although it has often published work by Aboriginal writers (for example, Ernerk 1987). The writing in the journal tends to reflect Hudson's Bay Company interests or to avoid contradicting them. Ernerk's anti-animal rights piece supports not only Inuit culture and subsistence but the HBC's own interests in promoting the fur trade by which not only Aboriginal people but also "The Company" survived.

Among other mass market magazines that deal primarily with the North, *Above and Beyond* is essentially an airline magazine; *Up Here* is a tourist magazine that occasionally explores current developments or profiles interesting people but seldom reveals conflict or controversy beneath its idyllic surface. Winter hardships, yes, and accolades to bush pilots and trappers; but political or cultural struggles are invisible. The only bright spot among the northern "slick" magazines directed at Outside readers was *Arctic Circle,* which unfortunately ceased publication in 1994. It was the only mass market magazine that dealt in depth with significant issues, and it is greatly missed.

To find greater depth and range, readers must subscribe to *Northern Perspectives,* a cross between a journal and a newsletter, published by the Canadian Arctic Resources Committee (CARC). Although its focus is on environmental concerns, it has published thoughtful papers – thoroughly researched and usually written in accessible language – on the Inuit relocations, cooperative circumpolar projects and programs, circumpolar health, and other topics. However, its authors are almost exclusively non-Aboriginal.

Much as women in male-dominated societies are put "on pedestals," Aboriginal northerners are often treated in the media as "noble savages" who are admired for their intriguing costumes, appearance, and skills but are dismissed as having lesser intellect or fewer accoutrements of "civilization" than non-Aboriginal southerners. Non-Aboriginal northerners get some of this treatment as well. Although in the case of Euro-Canadian northerners the element of racism is sometimes less obviously involved, the idea prevails that northerners in general are quaint and that only social misfits voluntarily move North. It is also important to remember that racism affects more than Aboriginal northerners. In the Canadian North are people of Caribbean, Asian, African, and African-American descent, as well as Euro-Canadians whose first languages and cultures vary widely. Nonetheless, it is undeniable that indigenous northerners are the most vulnerable to patronizing and racist misrepresentation in the media.

Missing the Boat: Trivializing Northern Peoples and Politics

The Inuit Circumpolar Conference (ICC) has been of primary importance in the lives of northern peoples around the world for over twenty years; it celebrated its twentieth anniversary at Barrow, Alaska, in June 1997. Yet it

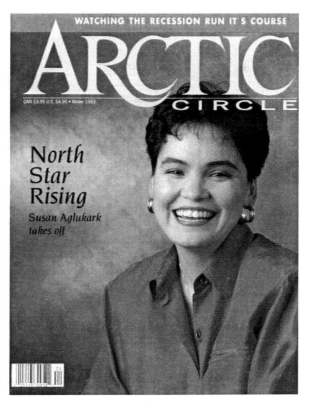

WATCHING THE RECESSION RUN ITS COURSE

ARCTIC CIRCLE

North
Star
Rising
Susan Aglukark
takes off

In *Arctic Circle,* which ceased publication in 1994, both
Aboriginal and non-Aboriginal writers covered politics,
news analysis, society, culture, environment, and science,
with a circumpolar/international focus.

has rarely been accorded the media coverage it deserves. In 1987 the ICC
brought the Inuit Regional Conservation Strategy to the United Nations,
the first time that such a strategy had been developed by an indigenous
people anywhere in the world. Despite this momentous occasion, it wasn't
until 1992 that the *Globe and Mail,* which bills itself as "Canada's National
Newspaper," finally decided that the ICC merited serious coverage (Cernetig
1992).

The *Globe* was not alone in inadequate coverage of the ICC. From the
time it was founded in 1977, the ICC has held a general assembly every
three years. At the 1989 assembly in Greenland, I observed a non-Aboriginal
reporter, who had spent much of the week drinking (excessively) and com-
plaining about the lack of four-star hotels in the village of Sisimiut, file
copy that not only missed most of the important political debate but also
made derogatory mention of the drinking habits of a few of the hundreds

of Aboriginal participants. Apart from the obvious hypocrisy, he missed a major international story.

The 1989 general assembly was significant for two reasons. The first was the arrival of an unofficial delegation from the Soviet Union. Covering that occasion for a northern magazine, I wrote:

> I joined townspeople and assembly organizers on the small ferry dock, to await the arrival of the boat with delegates from all the polar nations. The flags of Canada, Greenland, the U.S. and the U.S.S.R. waited with us ... Since its founding in 1977, the ICC has declared itself "under four flags." Until now, Soviet participation was only symbolic – the Soviet flag and an empty chair were placed at the head of each assembly. The flags remained, but no chair was empty. The flags welcomed Inuit from Chukotka Autonomous Region in the U.S.S.R., from Alaska, Canada's Northwest Territories, Labrador, northern Quebec and Greenland. ICC President Mary Simon called the Soviet presence "a milestone in Inuit history." "Our family of Inuit is today complete," said Greenland Premier Jonathan Motzfeldt (Alia 1989a, 19).

In addition to the historic presence of representatives from the Soviet Union, the 1989 assembly was notable for the presentation in draft form of an Arctic policy document that was reported as news by the *Globe and Mail* three years later, in 1992. Copies of the draft document were available to all of the media representatives at the 1989 assembly. The comprehensive policy addressed every aspect of northern life – environmental, social, cultural, and political. It included a set of Draft Principles on Communications, which set out policy for broadcasting, telecommunications, and print services and made Inuktitut-language services and extensive northern coverage a priority.

Also in 1989, the Soviet foreign affairs department invited ICC to Moscow for environmental talks. In 1990 Mary Simon accepted another Soviet invitation to the founding conference of the Arctic Peoples of the Soviet Union. She spoke at the opening session in Moscow, where Mikhail Gorbachev's presence highlighted the support of his (soon to be ousted) government. The urgency of the Moscow conference and the creation of the Organization of Arctic Peoples of the Soviet Union were underscored by information that began to surface during the same period. In 1990 the *Moscow News* began to acknowledge some of the problems confronting Soviet northern peoples, including a cancer rate among indigenous people on the Chukotka Peninsula two to three times the national average. In Moscow, Simon and others from ICC met Vladimir Sangi, a distinguished poet and president of the new organization, which was helping to publicize such concerns as the need for better education and the link between industrial pollution and poor health. Also in 1990 Sangi came west, to the Inuit Studies Conference in Fairbanks, Alaska, where I met and interviewed him. He told me that his struggle to establish this organization spanned three decades (Alia 1992a).

By failing to report on the meetings in Moscow and the Soviet participation at the Fairbanks conference, the southern news media missed an opportunity to report northern news accurately; they also missed an important perspective on the impending demise of the Soviet Union. Sangi predicted that "this movement of Arctic minorities" would help to "stimulate the whole destruction" of "this ugly [Soviet] federation" of Soviet society and would help to "create within the borders of Russia a state of equal peoples" (Alia 1995, transcript 21, translated by Igor Krupnik).

Although more media coverage of the North is needed, a 1992 article on the ICC assembly in the *Globe and Mail* was a mixed blessing. Under a front-page photograph it ran the caption "The lifting of the Iron Curtain is redefining the Arctic." The article itself offered some interesting observations and provided the substantial service of informing readers, however belatedly, that important things were happening in the circumpolar North. But such coverage not only informs; it also shapes public understanding of the people and the issues. It is important therefore to get the facts straight – that while the 1992 assembly may have been the first with an *official* Soviet delegation, an unofficial delegation had attended the 1989 assembly, greeted with much fanfare in the North but uninterested silence in the South. Why pass off an opinion piece as reportage? And why patronize Inuit, whom you have just called politically astute, with ethnocentric observations, such as, "When the Russian Inuit arrived in Inuvik, they were a heart-rending sight, more like figures from grainy photographs in an archive than citizens of a former superpower. They walked the sidewalks of Inuvik, dressed in ill-fitting clothes ... [and] carried bulky Soviet cameras"?

Such writing is problematic on many levels. First, if not blatantly inaccurate, it at least displays questionable value judgment. The Russian Inuit I met at the 1992 assembly were dressed just fine, if not like the folks in downtown Vancouver or Toronto. Second, in noting the perceived inadequacies of dress and accessories of the Russian Inuit, it ignores widespread poverty among circumpolar peoples. Third, the use of language is overblown and misplaced. What does one make of a story that characterizes the sartorial style of the Soviet Inuit delegation as "heart-rending" but ignores the truly heart-rending story – the environmental and social destruction that continues to kill Aboriginal people in the Russian North?

The reporter goes on to apply words such as "fashionable" to North American participants at the conference and "sophisticates" to the Greenlandic participants. He attributes the sophisticated appearance of the Greenlanders to their "ties to Denmark" and their consequent "European flare," not their own fashion sense. Such imperialist assumptions aside, one has to ask why fashion sense is relevant in the first place. News coverage of non-Aboriginal Canadian politics mentions fashion only when describing women. This trend, coupled with the observations on the delegates to the ICC assembly, is evidence of a hierarchy of discriminatory coverage that affects women in the dominant culture and both men and women in the subordinate culture. In the classroom, I ask journalism students to apply what I call the "test of parallels" to measure equality of coverage. To clarify the point, I bring in news stories that describe female politicians (their clothes, hair, deportment) and ask if a reporter would provide a similar description of a male politician's clothes or hair.

Despite such shortcomings in its story, the *Globe* at least paid some attention to the ICC assembly. More often than not, news of the North is simply ignored. In 1995 a political scientist chided the paper for yet another missed northern story.

> Shame on Canada's self-proclaimed "national newspaper" for completely ignoring an important and innovative constitutional conference in Yellowknife.
>
> With division of the existing Northwest Territories slated for 1999, the people of the Mackenzie Valley are engaged in an unparalleled exercise in determining how they are to govern themselves.
>
> The 150 delegates to the conference called to work out guiding principles for a Western NWT constitution included cabinet ministers, leaders of aboriginal organizations, representatives of women's groups, youth delegates and unaffiliated private citizens ...
>
> All this the *Globe and Mail* ignored ... As former prime minister Joe Clark, the conference chairman, observed, Canadians "south of 60" have much to learn from this unique exercise in creating a constitution from the bottom up. Too bad your readers missed it (White 1995, A18).

Yet even in those instances where the southern media deem a northern story worthy of coverage, editors of mainstream media have made little progress in their knowledge of the North and of Aboriginal and other minority peoples and issues. Thus, they are unable to catch the kinds of errors most editors would quickly correct in other stories. Sometimes the problems are rather mundane inaccuracies and misrepresentations. For example, whoever wrote the cutline for a photograph of Ludmila Ainana in the *Globe* coverage of the 1992 ICC assembly neglected to consult the newspaper's own style book, which explains the proper use of "Inuit" (plural) and "Inuk" (singular). The unfortunate Ainana was pluralized as "a Russian Inuit."

Journalists who generally take care to learn the spellings of non-Aboriginal names do not apply the same care in reporting about the North. I have grown weary of counting the times I have seen the Baffin Island community of Iqaluit written Iq*u*aluit – a word with an obscene meaning in Inuktitut. The Media Coordinator for the Baffin Emergency Response Committee was so incensed by the misspelling in a 1994 *Globe and Mail* article, he asked to have his letter to the editor of the *Globe and Mail* reprinted in *Nunatsiaq News*. He wrote, "It is surprising that your paper has not yet adjusted its SpellCheck program to include the proper spelling of Iqaluit, the largest community in the soon-to-be created territory of Nunavut. [*Globe and Mail,* "Two Hunters Rescued from Frigid Sea," November 2, 1994]. 'Iqaluit,' when properly spelled, means 'the place of fish,' whereas 'Iqualuit' means 'unwiped buttocks'" (McBride 1994, 7).

At other times, the problems with the coverage are more serious. Marion Soublière, a northern magazine editor, published a long "open letter" in *Nunatsiaq News* to *Globe and Mail* editor-in-chief William Thorsell. In her response to *Globe and Mail* coverage of northern animal-harvesting practices, she cited numerous factual errors, and "several very irresponsible editorial decisions" that have "incited racism against aboriginal Canadians ... and uneducated finger-pointing in letters printed in newspapers (including your own) and messages posted on Internet discussion groups. The one stunning achievement ... is that you have finally made it crystal clear to me why northerners feel marginalized by southern Canada" (Soublière 1998, 25).

Soublière argues that if the *Globe and Mail* is taking an editorial position against animal harvesting, it should cancel its lucrative fur-industry advertisements. At the same time that the newspaper demonizes Aboriginal hunters and trappers, it glamorizes the industry they serve, running elegant ads for luxurious Toronto furriers. Moreover, she notes that the reporter on the wolf hunt story failed to interview any northern Aboriginal leaders or others who are involved first-hand in a practice that was criticized not only in the "news coverage" but in editorials by the editor-in-chief himself. The failure to present the perspectives of northern Aboriginal peoples on a story in which they are so immediately involved is a travesty of "fair" journalistic practices. It also leaves the Aboriginal people vulnerable to criticism based on stereotypes and incomplete information. Soublière is particularly concerned with the effects of such stereotypes. As she admonishes the *Globe,* "Your story should have been the size of the ... news brief that ... appeared the same day the wolf hunt story broke, on the Federation of Saskatchewan Indian Nations poll that found 80 per cent of people surveyed reacted negatively when they heard the word 'Indian'" (Soublière 1998, 26).

In the same way that the *Globe and Mail* misrepresented the northern wolf hunt by neglecting to include the perspective of the Aboriginal participants, the daily newspaper in London, Ontario, depicted a powwow that included a sacred memorial grassdance as an exotic carnival. The powwow organizers had taken steps to prevent such misunderstandings by providing each visitor with a carefully written leaflet explaining meanings and proto-col. This was further clarified and enhanced by spoken commentary through-out the ceremonies and events. The reporter apparently neither read nor heard the information that was provided (Alia 1991f).

A recent *New York Times* article carried in many American and Canadian newspapers described "Siberia's mystery nomads ... reindeer herders who dress in skins, practice ritual sacrifice ... eat raw fish ... and live year-round in reindeer-skin teepees" (Alia 1995, 20, transcript). Apparently, the reporter had not heard of the Jewish laws for ritual slaughter, the Christian tradition of symbolically eating the body and blood of Christ, or the Japanese culi-nary art of sushi. The reporter forgot to mention that Aboriginal Siberians have highly developed cultures, suffer from unprecedented levels of pollu-tion and poverty, and rarely live past forty (Alia 1995).

Such questionable reporting is not limited to North American newspapers. In 1991 the English newspaper the *Daily Telegraph* sent a team for a brief visit to Holman Island, then published in its magazine supplement a photo essay that infuriated members of the Holman (Uluqsaqtuuq) community. Headlined "Dressed to Kill: Hunting with the Eskimos of Holman Island," it presented a picture so distorted that many observers called it racist. In a letter to the editor, which the *Telegraph* declined to publish, Holman Mayor Gary Bristow, Holman Community Corporation chair Robert Kuptana, and anthropologist Richard Condon wrote that "thousands of ... readers have had their opinions and attitudes about the Canadian Arctic falsely influ-enced by individuals with no understanding of even the most basic aspects of Canadian Inuit culture, much less the modern complexities of northern life" (Condon, personal communication, 6 November 1992). They pointed out "a few of the more grotesque errors" in the article: "'Among hunters there is no code of honour,' the article proclaims ... apparently measuring Inuit hunting against aristocratic English fox hunts. 'The hunter who kills by stealth rather than confrontation feels all the prouder: he considers he has shown not cowardice, but cunning. He is merciless and self-interested, gathering food only for himself and his family. The unsuccessful hunter and his family could go hungry only steps away from someone else's well-stocked tent'" (Condon, personal communication, 1992). In response to such misrepresentation, the letter from the Holman citizens noted that Copper Inuit, "like most other Inuit groups throughout the North Ameri-can Arctic," have long had an extensive food-sharing system. The letter also criticized the *Telegraph*'s writers for characterizing subsistence hunting as more "merciless and self-interested" than elaborately ritualized fox hunts in Britain, in which foxes are terrorized for no purpose other than aristo-cratic amusement.

The *Telegraph* story absurdly declared that snowmobiles have supplanted dogs as the primary mode of transportation but that "during the summer migration at least, the dogs come into their own." The reality is that dog teams are never used in summer but are used almost exclusively in winter to guide polar bear sport-hunters. The *Telegraph*'s readers read about "Eskimos" who eat "boiled duck and grease soup flavoured with feathers," an assertion with no basis in fact, although the occasional feather might inadvertently land in someone's duck soup!

There were many other inaccuracies in the essay, which claimed that "caribou are tracked by satellite and shot with M-22 rifles." The Holman representatives replied: "Perhaps the author is of the opinion that each snowmobile includes a satellite dish and computer screen? ... Wildlife biologists ... track the wanderings of caribou on Victoria Island, making use of satellite technology. This technology is *not* used by Holman hunters ... Caribou [and] musk ox are more likely to be shot with .222 and 22.250 rifles."

Bristow, Kuptana, and Condon also took the *Telegraph* to task for failing to identify the subjects of its photographs. Noting sarcastically that this practice follows "in the fine tradition of *National Geographic* ... [of photographing] nameless 'primitives,'" their letter states that the *Telegraph*'s failure to affix names to people "is especially disturbing in the photograph of two of Holman's most respected elders, Jimmy and Nora Memogama" (Condon, personal communication, 1992). To add further insult, the cutline indicated that the (unnamed) Memogamas had been photographed in front of a government-subsidized house in Holman, when in reality they were standing in front of their (private, unsubsidized) hunting cabin, which Jimmy Memogama had built, several miles from town.

Some of the *Telegraph*'s errors were downright funny. "All of us in Holman were amused to hear about the community's 'richest villager' who ... decided to order a steam roller ... One does not purchase a steamroller to make gravel roads in the Arctic" (Condon, personal communication, 1992). The *Telegraph* reported that "locals used to tell the story about a young white man who stepped off a train to stretch his legs; his frozen body was discovered the following spring." The Holman writers replied: "We know of no 'locals' who would tell this story. There is no train even close to Holman. In fact, the nearest railhead is over 1,000 miles away near the Alberta border ... Perhaps, in the author's imagination, this is the same train which brought the steam roller and the satellite equipment for hunting caribou?"

Such absurdities aside, the photo-essay is not just an amusing example of journalistic ignorance. The Holman writers saw it as "representative of a disturbing trend in journalistic coverage of the North ... Each year ... Holman is visited by journalists who desire to write or photograph the definitive article about an isolated Inuit community ... The community has no way to ... monitor or comment upon their finished works ... [The] worst harm is not the offence they give to northern residents but the distorted view they present to thousands of readers about northern life and northern people. In an age when Inuit culture is being attacked by numerous animal rights groups, articles like 'Dressed to Kill' ... perpetuate prejudice" (Condon, personal communication, 1992).

Political Coverage: From the Outside, Looking In

In 1991 I conducted a study of media coverage of Aboriginal and northern issues, campaign and election coverage for the Royal Commission on Electoral Reform and Party Financing (Alia 1991a). The study revealed several unwritten rules. First, only nationally prominent leaders (for example, people such as former Yukon member of Parliament and national New Democratic Party leader Audrey McLaughlin or NWT Liberal MP Ethel Blondin) merit coverage in national, regional, or urban media.

Second, Aboriginal people and issues are covered in national, regional, or urban media only in times of crisis (for example, during the confrontation at Oka/Kanehsatake) or when negative issues are involved. If a crisis does not exist, the media sometimes make one. A newspaper wire feature on Eva Deer, the mayor of Quaqtaq, Quebec, was so full of stereotypes, it was easy to lose count. The portrait focused on Deer as female, Inuk, and challenger of drugs, alcohol, and men, in that order. Packaging distorted further: "Drug problem 'epidemic,' female Inuit mayor says" (Abramovitch 1990). In a single line, the reporter gratuitously identified a politician by gender and culture, mistakenly used the plural Inuit, and identified her with a negative subject (drugs). No one would suggest that people's problems and politician's agendas should be censored, but Aboriginal politicians and communities tend to receive disproportionately negative coverage. Euro-Canadian communities and politicians are seldom covered in comparable ways (de Uriarte and Balough 1990).

Third, northern and First Nations elections merit coverage when they directly affect concerns of southern Canadians. Similarly, northern topics are covered when southern economic development (oil, gas exploration) or tourism is involved, or when southern Canadian, national, or international interests are at stake.

In general, the politicians, political workers, and news consumers who were canvassed were least critical of radio and most critical of television. They also had harsh words about the quality of print coverage. The Aboriginal leaders we interviewed identified several serious problems: the media continue to reinforce rampant ethnocentrism; journalists' fears of travelling to remote communities and the more general fears of Aboriginal people are projected to news consumers; ignorance of Aboriginal political priorities, traditions, and values continues to abound. In addition, they said the non-Aboriginal media had a tendency to assign low priority to Aboriginal issues.

Television was criticized for being largely absent from northern elections coverage. Criticisms levelled at both print and television have some foundation in economics. The lack of on-the-spot coverage and, in some cases, availability of any television or print media, is often connected to budget cuts or restrictions. Some Aboriginal newspapers and magazines on which candidates had relied in previous elections were not expected to survive into the next election.

Trivializing Northern Art
Northern politics and ways of life are not the only victims of poor media coverage. A major feature on the front page of the *Globe and Mail* weekend arts section headlined "The mainstreaming of Inuit art" contends that "many Canadians" have long considered the work of Inuit artists "an essential part of the country's cultural identity." Yet the emphasis of the article is on the "substantial prices" these works command "on the international scene" and not on their influence and impact on the imagery and cultural production of Canadian art and consciousness. When the writer does refer to the content of the works, they are discussed as a unit – not in the way the Group of Seven are linked as mutually influential collaborators, but as if all works by Inuit artists belonged to a single opus.

The big questions for the writer of this article were not what kind of art is emerging in the North today, but the oft-repeated colonizer's lament, "Has commercial success and contact with the outside world degraded the work?" And in this context, "Where is the boundary between craft and art?" (Ross 1996, C1).

Such questions have little relevance for most Inuit artists. First, "commercial success" is an elusive concept for artists, who see precious little of the profit from the sale of their works and who tend to care more about performing their primary roles as parents, spouses, hunters and providers, and makers of homes and clothing than about the performance of their art on an international market (Alia 1991d). Second, when have we seen comparable discussions of the work of Euro-Canadian, American, or European artists that insist that their work is inherently "degraded" by "commercial success"? Few artists of any cultural background enjoy the rewards of such success, and even fewer during their own lifetimes. Even when their works command high prices, artists' fees are diminished by the time and labour-intensive nature of their work, the high cost of materials and preparation of exhibitions, and the substantial fees charged by galleries and agents. When an artist does achieve some economic success in his or her lifetime, we are unlikely to read that it might diminish his or her work. In fact, such success is likely to simply get the artist more press.

As for the suggestion that "craft" is somehow related to economically and Outsider-generated ideas about degradation of "art," the use of those terms is spurious. In an earlier discussion of northern art, I rejected the art/craft dichotomy and suggested that conventional distinctions between "art" and "craft" are grounded in inequalities of culture, class, and gender: "The distinction between 'art' and 'craft' has often turned on the association of objects and skills with women's and men's social roles. Men are most often designated artists and women craftspeople." Moreover the work of minority peoples is more often called "craft" than is that of cultural majorities. "In subsistence societies, art is tied to livelihood and work roles. Practical first and beautiful second, it is usually called craft" (Alia 1991d, 99). I also noted the anthropologizing of artworks produced by minority peoples and the tendency to display this work in natural history museums instead of art galleries. The works of minority artists are depersonalized, essentialized into a single cultural identity, and historicized into past-tense productions of archaic "craft." In that context, media are able to continue the habit of discussing "Inuit art" as a category that can be "degraded" by contact with the "outside world." I used to hear comments like this from people who were either personally and artistically offended, or patronizingly charmed, that distinguished Cape Dorset artist Pudlo Pudlat had introduced airplanes and helicopters into his drawings, sculptures, and prints.

When in 1946 an anonymous government employee wrote the captions to a series of photographs by Bud Glunz that were provided to news media as representations of the North, he or she helped to shape the way readers would understand Inuit people. Each photograph was introduced by the same sentence: "The Eskimo is a happy, childlike nomad" (see Alia 1995). Beneath the surface of the images and words were adults and children from different experiences and regions. Through these misrepresentations of image and text – widely disseminated to an uninformed public – those photographs effectively destroyed Inuit people and Inuit lives.

After forty years, news media still destroy northern and Aboriginal people through misrepresentation, or through failure to provide coverage. I am sometimes shocked at how little we have learned. When the *Globe and Mail* treated the ICC assembly like a costume party, readers had no chance to grasp the ground-breaking political developments. I look forward to the day when the North will be portrayed as a complex and important part of Canada, with newsworthy people, issues, and events that require hard work for reporters to understand. I look forward to the day when the north will be reported, not romanticized, and paternalism will have died. The issue is not just one of higher purposes and commitments. It concerns that value all journalists say they revere above all – accuracy in reporting.

There is a need for continuing analysis, education, and action to change both the content and the people who display paternalistic and ethnocentric biases in their portrayals of the North and of indigenous peoples. Increasing the number of indigenous and northern journalists and filmmakers will not in itself guarantee accuracy or respect, but it will certainly help. So will the increase in cultural collaborative projects and educational programs. The next chapter considers some of the underpinnings of problematic and appropriate portrayals; examines the relationship between communications, culture, language, and literacy; and suggests some ways we might go about developing relevant projects and programs.

2
Communications in Context: Language, Literacy, Politics, and Education

Communications is more than the production and transmission of information. Understanding the subject requires examining the *context* in which information is produced and transmitted. In the case of the North, communications have evolved in an environment enriched and influenced by the cultures of northern Aboriginal peoples.

In earlier times, the communications "media" in all cultures were human voices. Language and cultural traditions were transmitted and maintained through story telling and other techniques integrated into all aspects of everyday life. Oral cultural traditions continue today in northern broadcasting, particularly in the prevalence of radio in the daily life of northern communities.

In oral cultures, literacy was not a "problem," but has emerged as one in the post-orality years, when some people have found themselves disadvantaged with respect to the dominance of written literature, news, and other information media. The whole concept of literacy is problematic, because it is often constructed and problematized as a negative – as illiteracy. Instead of being considered orally *advantaged*, people who have strong verbal skills but who are not facile readers or writers are disadvantaged in a world in which written language is usually considered the only valid form of literature.

We must be careful not to oversimplify these issues. Oral cultures and literacy are not mutually exclusive. Yukon, with its indigenous oral traditions, has the highest literacy rate in Canada. While clearly not ignoring the demands of living in a world dominated by written language, education in Yukon is also grounded in older traditions. Notes Lou Jacquot (1992, 5), "Contemporary elders seem to go to school in their communities and local campuses constantly, where they pass on old skills and learn new skills that maintain and improve the lives of the younger generation."

Jacquot's example illustrates one of the primary features common to Aboriginal cultures in this region: the integration of aspects of knowledge and information that are often separated in Western/Euro-North American society. Education is not a field to study, or a vehicle with which to ensure the acquisition of "basics," intellectual knowledge, or socially accepted behaviours. It is an integral part of daily life. In the same way, politics is not kept remote from other activities, in a rarefied, power-focused separate sphere, but is integrated into the total life experience of the community.

The persistent portrayal in southern media and society of communications, language, literacy, education, and politics as separate though sometimes interrelated entities continues to deeply damage Aboriginal people – in communities, schools, the political arena, in journalism, and in the society at large. We need to develop new ways of examining these elements as components of an integrated communications picture. Without a major shift in the framing of communication questions, we will be unable to make any significant breakthroughs in understanding what does and does not work in northern communications.

The principal task of this chapter is to examine the context within which northern communications is produced. The chapter will consider the relationship between journalism, particularly print journalism, and literacy, and the crucial process of educating future generations of journalists. In addition, it will introduce and address the concept of *cultural literacy:* knowledge of one's own culture and the ability to understand, respect, and accurately depict the cultures of others.

Patterns in Northern Communications
Aboriginal people in Nunavut enjoy linguistic unity and access to print journalism (albeit only one, non-Aboriginal-run, Inuktitut/English newspaper with some Aboriginal staff). In Yukon, roads facilitate access, but there are few remaining print media with significant Native input or control. In some ways, the NWT shares assets and liabilities with both Yukon and Nunavut. It has linguistic diversity, but Aboriginal print media are published primarily in English. Its communities are divided between air and road access. It would be useful to develop ways for the various northern regions to learn more from each other. Despite increased *circumpolar* cooperation among northern nations, the territories and northern regions of the provinces are surprisingly alienated from each other. Such alienation is attributable not only to geographic distances but to a different history in the eastern and western Canadian Arctic and different patterns of media development.

In the eastern Arctic (Nunavut), radio developed first, followed by television. There still has not been an Inuit newspaper, although ITC has published several newsletters over the years, and *Nunatsiaq News* publishes in both Inuktitut and English and has gradually increased the involvement of Inuit as journalists.

In the NWT under the Native Communications Society of the Western NWT (NCS), newspapers were the first to develop, followed by radio and finally television. This order accounts for the relatively poor development of television programming in the region, but it does not explain the inconsistencies in producing and maintaining print media, especially the difficulties with the continuity, consistency, and viability of the newspaper *Native Press* and its alter ego, the *Press Independent*, and the tensions and conflicts among some indigenous media groups.

Barry Zellen, executive director of the Dene-Métis Native Broadcasting Society, says that although Dene in the Northwest Territories are part of the TVNC consortium they have been consistently "under-funded" relative to Inuit in Nunavut. Others say that the lack of broadcast funding for NWT Dene-Métis is related to the failure of NCS to make significant inroads into improving broadcast skills and producing programming. Most of the Dene television programming has been produced by CBC's Yellowknife facility.

Whatever the explanations, the unevenness in funding and programming is likely to carry on, as each region follows its existing path. Nunavut will probably continue to be the leader in northern Aboriginal broadcasting. I hope NCS will manage to survive the continuing threats to its press – persistent economic difficulties, and disagreements among the Dene and Métis communities of the Northwest Territories – which make it hard to maintain a unified communications program. In its most recent incarnation, *Native Press* is primarily a loosely organized collection of community reports published in newspaper form about twice a year.

The other players in the picture are the Inuvialuit, who maintain their own news service in the Northwest Territories, and whose newspaper, *Tusaayaksat*, continues to thrive; and Yukon Métis and First Nations, who have produced excellent newspapers and magazines as well as radio and television, and thus have a more balanced history of print and broadcast media production than the other northern regions.

The newspapers and magazines in the Canadian North are strengthened by maintaining close ties to media in other northern countries. It is not uncommon to see articles informally networked via an unofficial "wire service." For example, a 1997 story about the Inuit Circumpolar Conference (ICC) twentieth anniversary carried by *Nunatsiaq News* originated in the *Arctic Sounder*, one of the eight newspapers in the Yup'ik Native Corporation's Alaska Newspapers group (Adams 1997, 17).

Integrating Politics and Education with Community Life
There has been only intermittent and inconsistent progress in addressing the alienation of northern Aboriginal people from educational or political systems. I think the explanation lies largely in the persistence of ethnocentric thinking in educators' and policymakers' framing of "problems" or questions. Alienation is not just about access to media or to the political or educational process. It is related to maintenance or destruction of cultural

values, and to the acceptance or rejection of a different and equally valid way of doing politics. In many Aboriginal cultures, political information is not relayed *through* media to a remote public, but is part of a forum in which politicians and leaders engage in intimate dialogue with the whole community. Elders do not retire, they are the political centre; children are participants, not bystanders. Bobbi Smith, director of the Yukon Women's Directorate, described the political education of members of her northern British Columbia coastal community: "When we were kids, we were *expected* to be in the longhouse. Around 6:00 [p.m.], someone would come around to all the houses and tell everyone to be in the longhouse for council meeting. Children were expected to be there, and you were expected to be quiet. You might not understand everything that was going on, but you would understand some of it, and you'd be part of it" (Alia 1991a, 109).

Big imaginations and small funds can have innovative results in integrating education and community life. For nearly a decade the Canadian Museums Association has sponsored an array of community-based literacy and cultural literacy programs under the title "Reading the Museum." The project is the brainchild of Montreal educator and art historian Lon Dubinsky, and utilizes existing community resources to link museum programs and exhibitions to literacy. It has funded several programs involving northern museums and Aboriginal communities.

In another innovation, adult educator Richard Lawrence put up a year-round "literacy tent" in Pelly Crossing, Yukon, bent on establishing new literacy programs in culturally relevant ways. Pelly Crossing is home to the Selkirk First Nation, whose members make up about 90 percent of the community's population. In 1990, Jim Tredger, principal of the local school, started special twice-monthly community lunches at the school with the hope of encouraging people in the community to take advantage of the school's facilities. He was not just the "idea person" for this project: he got into the kitchen and did the cooking and serving, alongside a group of students.

The lunches are attended by people of all ages from all parts of the community. They are clearly a success, not only as a way of bringing people together to eat and to talk to each other, but as a way of bringing the community to the school and the school to the community. People stop to read bulletin-board information, pick up leaflets, and visit classrooms and each other. According to Tredger, each successive lunch has required more food and more work in the kitchen, as the number of people attending has increased.

There are many other efforts to increase the relevance of schools to their communities. Chehalis Public School, built in longhouse design and run by the Sumas Band, is one of twelve schools in British Columbia run by First Nations communities. It is part of a growing number of programs grounded in Aboriginal cultures (Shiell 1990). The Kipohtakaw Education Centre in Alexander, Alberta, is another community-run school that combines old and new, Aboriginal and non-Aboriginal programming (Schiller 1987).

Journalism, Literacy, and Cultural Literacy

Penny Petrone writes of the important interrelationship of journalism and literacy. The interrelationship constitutes a major component of the northern communications picture, especially where Aboriginal people are concerned: "As more and more Indians learned to read and write, newspapers, newsletters, and periodicals ... appeared to inform, instruct, and entertain their native and non-native readers" (Petrone 1990, 84).

Cultural literacy has long been a component of Aboriginal communications. Aboriginal people wrote essays and letters for these early periodicals. One of the leading lights was Andrew Paull (1892–1959), the Squamish leader born in Burrard Inlet, British Columbia, who founded the American Indian Brotherhood. A musician and broadcaster as well as a writer and political leader, he founded, published, and edited two newspapers, *The Thunderbird* and *The Totem Speaks*, from 1949 to the mid-1950s (Petrone 1990, 105).

More often, publications were not run by Native peoples themselves, but by missionaries and other newcomers. Such a situation presented some interesting contradictions, at once undermining and supporting Aboriginal cultures. I use the term "missionary" to refer to both sacred and secular "missions": business and government representatives came North to "civilize" (change, assimilate, transform) as strongly as the religious missionaries came North to save souls. It was the specific task of all of these Outsiders to replace the beliefs and practices of indigenous people with their own. At the same time, they provided new outlets for the expression of ideas, customs, and opinions of indigenous people. The founders of pre-1950s newspapers, newsletters, and magazines "recognized the power of the written word and the educational usefulness of print. Indian correspondents and subscribers were encouraged. Unfortunately these early papers had to struggle to survive, plagued as they were by infrequent publication, minimal staff and resources, poor distribution, and low circulation" (Petrone 1990, 84). As we will see, those conditions continue today.

The widespread call by governments, policy makers, social service spokespeople, and community members for increased attention to literacy is undermined by the demise or restriction of print media in regions most affected by illiteracy. The brief and brilliant blaze of *Sweetgrass: The Magazine of Canada's Native Peoples* had many people eagerly anticipating the future of this fine publication. The magazine managed to survive for a year under the expert leadership of editor Lenore Keeshig-Tobias. She and other *Sweetgrass* founders were alumnae of *Ontario Indian* magazine and of the University of Western Ontario's Program in Journalism for Native People

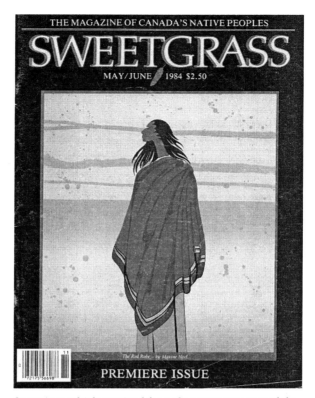

THE MAGAZINE OF CANADA'S NATIVE PEOPLES

SWEETGRASS

MAY/JUNE 1984 $2.50

The Red Robe — by Maxine Noel

PREMIERE ISSUE

Sweetgrass, which survived for only a year, was one of the most beautiful magazines ever produced in Canada and featured work by outstanding Aboriginal artists and writers.

(PJNP), whose first director, Dennis Martel, was also with *Sweetgrass* and *Ontario Indian. Sweetgrass* featured fine writing and art and stunning design. In the premiere issue (May-June 1984) was an article by Bernadette K. Immaroitok and Peter Jull that addressed the language and literacy question, "Inuktitut: Surviving in the Arctic's New Age!" (Immaroitok and Jull 1984, 15-6).

Research reveals widespread concern about northern illiteracy and functional illiteracy. Yet contradictory policies abound. A 1996 issue of *Tusaayaksat,* the Inuvialuit newspaper for the Northwest Territories that has made substantial contributions to literacy in both English and Inuvialuktun, included the following announcement: "1996/97 Community Literacy Projects Fund: Organizations are invited to submit proposals for community-based literacy projects. Financial assistance is available to support projects which promote awareness, literacy outreach services, the development of learning materials or innovative approaches to literacy development at the community level" (*Tusaayaksat* 1996, 19). The Literacy Projects Fund is administered by the Literacy Office of the Northwest Territories Department of Education, Culture and Employment. Unfortunately, this office (and offices like it in other territories, provinces, and regions as well as at the federal level) has been unable or unwilling to coordinate its literacy efforts with those who control public funding of print media. The effect is that funding for literacy, cultural literacy, and language programs is on the rise at the same time that funding for print and broadcast media – which play a crucial role in promoting literacy – is rapidly and substantially declining.

In 1990 the Northwest Territories government enacted historic legislation amending the Northwest Territories Official Languages Act. It was "the first time a Canadian jurisdiction has recognized aboriginal languages as equal to English or French. Under the ... law, Chipewyan, Cree, Dogrib, Slavey, Gwich'in and Inuktitut (which includes the Inuvialuktun dialects and Inuinnaqtun) ... share the same status as French and English ... which have always represented the minority of northerners" (Smellie 1990).

Canada is not the only northern nation to address the question of the survival of Aboriginal languages and cultures. Elsewhere in the North, there is an escalating demand for increased availability of Aboriginal language materials of all kinds, including political and policy materials, broadcast and print news, speeches, public meetings, and workshops. In the former Soviet Union, northern indigenous peoples are organizing their own cultural revitalization projects. Addressing the first Congress of Small Indigenous Peoples in 1990, Chuner Taksami, a professor and member of the organizing committee, stressed the connection between journalism, language, and culture. "There is an urgent request to establish local national publishing centres ... The journal *Severnye prostory (Northern widths)*[5] ... propagates the culture of our peoples ... I think the time has come to raise the question of founding a special series for literature written in the Northern languages ... We must publish books about each people that must serve as a depository of memories" (Taksami 1990). In the short time since the congress, the Soviet Union itself has been transformed, and northern indigenous peoples must now renegotiate with the government of Russia: "Today we are still waiting for a new law that should be passed by Russian Parliament regarding the legal status of small nations of the North, Siberia and the Far East. This unfortunate bill has been wandering through the corridors of the authorities for five years" (Achirgina 1994, 3). Despite the delays, the cause of cultural survival and political self-determination is promoted in an increasingly vocal indigenous press. It includes the newspaper *Far North*, published by members of the Chukchee nation at Anadyr, Chukotka (Achirgina 1994, 7). It is no coincidence that Svetlana Taliok, the new president of the Council of Elders of the Small Nations of Chukotka, is a journalist.

The transformation of the former Soviet Union has presented unique challenges for northern people of that region, but even normal changes in government leadership can jolt the negotiations of northern indigenous peoples. Poor communication and coordination among agencies, programs, and policies exacerbates the lack of continuity or consistency in government policy. As we have seen, at the same time that the demand for materials in Aboriginal languages has increased, with the support of the Ministry of Culture and Communications, funding cuts from the Secretary of State have cancelled or curtailed print and broadcast media that could have strengthened the northern Aboriginal language programs.

An Aboriginal Yukon politician interviewed in the course of research for this book noted, for example, that elders were the biggest losers when CHON-FM, the radio outlet of Northern Native Broadcasting Yukon, responded to budget cuts by curtailing translation from English into Native languages during political campaigns. Many elders speak little English and, consequently, are ill informed when Aboriginal language programming is cut. He said that leaving elders out of the loop through withdrawing translation services not only removes a substantial portion of the population from the wider information system but also undercuts their traditional importance as political leaders and contributes to the decline in Aboriginal language use that he has observed in the past thirty years.

The bilingual English-Inuktitut news media received widespread public and government praise for meeting the needs of a largely Inuktitut-speaking population in Labrador. Yet instead of continuing, and expanding, bilingual communications, the federal government imposed major funding cuts that made it nearly impossible to continue the bilingual services.

One of the most destructive waves of budget cuts to indigenous media in recent history came in 1990, the same year that violence erupted in the Kanehsatake Mohawk Territory near Oka, Quebec. Many people believe that the cuts were punitive, directly related to those events, and aimed at silencing Aboriginal voices. Regardless of whether this was the case, the cuts exacerbated tensions and contributed to the difficulty of assuring accurate coverage of the Oka crisis. The combination of sudden cuts to Aboriginal media, poor preparation of many non-Native journalists, and resistance to hiring Aboriginal journalists in mainstream media resulted in coverage both ill informed and incomplete. The cycle of mistrust that helped create the crisis was perpetuated in relations between government, police, media, and first peoples. When Aboriginal journalists and filmmakers took matters into their own hands and produced, on shoestring budgets, their own interpretations of events, the public was slow to gain access to their work.

In one of the First Nations newspapers that would eventually fall victim to funding difficulties, *Nativebeat* co-founder and editor Miles Morrisseau wrote, "[Filmmaker Alanis] Obomsawin was working on another film when the shots rang out that early morning on July 11. She found out [about Oka] like we all did, through the newspapers, the radio and the television cameras of the mainstream media. But that was the last time she would see any of it through their eyes. She packed her crew and was in Kanehsatake that evening. She would not leave until it was over and what she saw now stands as her record of the truth" (Morrisseau 1994, 3).

At first, the CBC refused to show the resultant film, *Kanehsatake: 270 Years of Resistance*. The network aired it only after the film received rave reviews in England following showings on BBC and then was chosen best Canadian film at Toronto's Festival of Festivals. The Oka confrontation came to a head over plans to extend a golf course into The Pines, a sacred Mohawk burial ground in Kanehsatake. The armed confrontation led to a blockade, with Kanehsatake cut off from the rest of Canada and journalists locked either inside the community or out. Trapped in the Kanehsatake radio station, Mohawk journalists Marie David and Bev Nelson produced courageous on-the-spot broadcasts. Disbelief that an armed showdown could happen in Canada, with its international peacemaker image, was expressed by Aboriginal and non-Aboriginal people alike. The theme echoes throughout Obomsawin's film like a refrain. "This is *Canada*," the Mohawk people she interviews keep saying (Obomsawin 1992).

The Oka/Kanehsatake conflict erupted in southern Canada but its repercussions were felt throughout the country. Members of Yukon First Nations went to Kanehsatake, organized demonstrations, radio and television phone-ins, and other events to provide forums for dialogue and public education. I was in Whitehorse for the lighting of a sacred fire in support of the people of Kanehsatake. Standing in a large circle with people from many cultures and backgrounds, we felt next door to southern Quebec, even in Yukon. Apparently, that feeling did not extend to the department of the Secretary of State, which went right on hacking funds – and journalism – out from under Aboriginal people.

Journalism, Literacy, and Inuit

Reflecting on the evolution of language and literacy programs in Nunavut, the Inuit leader John Amagoalik emphasized the links between language, literacy, and print media: "What is not written down or stored in the memory bank of a computer has a sad habit of fading away. A spoken word not spelled out on a page ... may not survive. This is the challenge the Inuktitut language faces" (Amagoalik 1994, 9). When Inuktitut was the only language around, it was not threatened. Once other languages arrived, spoken by members of newly dominant European and North American cultures, Inuktitut was in danger. Inuit "have been very resilient," and their language has survived despite "a tidal wave of other languages." But the challenge continues to grow. Instead of promoting or strengthening Inuktitut, "the mass media, which operates mostly in English, continues to seep into almost every part of our daily lives ... In order for Inuktitut to compete with English, it must continue to expand its presence in the mass media." Amagoalik notes that the Inuit Broadcasting Corporation is doing "a commendable job in presenting the Inuktitut language on television." He also credits CBC Radio and community-run stations for respecting Inuktitut over the decades, but declares that "the print media is a different story" (1994, 9).

Amagoalik advocates not only strengthening Inuktitut print media but also abandoning the syllabic writing system currently in use in most of Nunavut in favour of the Roman orthography used by Greenlandic and Alaskan Inuit. He reminds the syllabic "traditionalists" that the syllabic system is not, as some imply, indigenous to Inuit: "It was ... given to us by the missionaries who first gave it to the Cree ... It arrived with the white man. Many people forget that. So, what do we do? We create our own writing system ... which will be used by all Inuit in the circumpolar world" (Amagoalik 1994, 9). One result would be access for Canadian Inuit to the scores of books published in Greenland. Greenlandic can be read and understood by many Canadian Inuit, as it is close to Inuktitut dialects in various parts of the Canadian Arctic. A unified writing system would therefore increase the access of most Inuit to most of the literature.

His is not the only, or necessarily the dominant, position among Canadian Inuit. At the 1989 ICC General Assembly in Sisimiut, Greenland, emotions ran high during debate on orthography because many Canadian Inuit feel a deep emotional connection to the syllabic writing system. Some of them directed accusations of cultural imperialism at the Kalaallit (Greenlandic Inuit), who advocated that ICC officially adopt their version of Roman orthography across the Arctic. The Kalaallit government publishing house has been publishing books in Greenlandic for many years. Other publishers have emerged in recent years, and as of 1995, Greenland's private publisher, Atuakkiorfik, had published over ninety books in Greenlandic, Danish, or English – sixty-five of them textbooks distributed through the schools and postsecondary institutions, and twenty-five of them Greenlandic literature for children and adults distributed through private booksellers. John Amagoalik is one of those who want Nunavut residents to have access to these resources.

Amagoalik points to the case of Greenland, with its thriving book list and wide use of Greenlandic in print media, and says that like the Inuit themselves, Inuktitut "must adapt to changing times" (1994, 11). That is only part of the story. However well Inuit adapt their language, there must be print media – books and periodicals – to carry that language to the people. Recent funding decisions have turned Canadian communications policy in precisely the opposite direction.

There is more to literacy than reading, and more to "reading" than the printed page or computer screen. John Amagoalik eloquently clarifies the cultural core of literacy – what I have called cultural literacy – while unravelling some of the layers of colonial thinking.

> We must teach our children their mother tongue. We must teach them what they are and where they came from ... [and] the values which have guided our society over the thousands of years ... our philosophies which go back beyond the memory of man. We must keep the embers burning from the fires which used to burn in our villages so that we may gather around them again. It is this spirit we must keep alive so that it may guide us again in a new life in a changed world (Amagoalik in Petrone 1988, 210).

Amagoalik considers the adoption of a universal writing system an important component of cultural literacy programs for Inuit. He seeks a broadening of access to both the spoken and the printed word, across regions and generations: "Radio and television have helped [Inuit] get to know each other's dialects" (Amagoalik 1996a), he says. The linguistic similarity among Inuit dialects across the international Arctic makes this a possibility. Amagoalik's position emphasizes the complexities in colonial relations.

Stephen Riggins takes on these complexities in his analysis of the "unexpected paradoxes" in the interrelationship of mainstream and ethnic minority media. He argues that "minority empowerment is in itself paradoxical. On one hand, the unique group identity of a relatively marginal population is revitalized from within and the politics of multiculturalism are advanced. But on the other hand, at the same time, the minority is likely to become more integrated into national life, because short of reaching total political independence, a high level of assimilation seems to be a prerequisite for achieving empowerment" (Riggins 1992, 17). For all his good intentions, Riggins is in danger of adopting too simplistic a view of assimilation. While we must acknowledge power inequities, it is probably more accurate to look at cross-cultural reciprocity than "assimilation" or "non-assimilation." Amagoalik reminds us that northern political culture has much to offer the Outside: "The Nunavut Agreement is unique in the world. It creates a different political landscape. It has made some people quite nervous in Ottawa, especially the proposal for gender parity [in the Nunavut legislative assembly]. The idea of electing a government leader by direct election is unique in Canada. It's happening in other places. The Israelis are moving toward the Nunavut system of direct election of the government leader and Knesset members" (Amagoalik 1996a).

John Amagoalik and Martha Flaherty were among the most vocal proponents of the principle of gender parity, a policy – narrowly defeated by a

Nunavut-wide vote in 1997 – that would have guaranteed an equal number of female and male representatives in the new legislative assembly. According to Amagoalik, such a policy was needed to remedy the damage done through colonization, which has left Inuit women with "less voice." For him, parity is about fairness and political responsibility; it is "not a women's rights issue. Women make up 50% of the population. Decision-making should reflect that population" (Amagoalik 1996a). With the defeat of gender parity, Inuit went back to the political drawing board to address equality issues.

As the Nunavut government evolves, Inuit will look for ways to bring cultural and political literacy together. As we will see in more detail in Chapter 4, the media play a key role in this process.

Educating Journalists

Journalists of all backgrounds must take responsibility for the power and impact of their work. After twenty years in journalism and journalism education, I am extremely frustrated with the inadequacies of conventional training and practice, which remain grounded in ethnocentric principles of "expert" authority and "balance." Most of us know that two or three "sources" chosen in the haste to meet deadlines do not constitute adequate "research," and that two "sides" are a small part of the many facets of a news story. The journalistic tradition of aggressive information-gathering is not only ethnocentric and often androcentric but is not always the most effective way to get the story. Softer approaches such as "hanging around" (now considered a bona fide research technique in social science), quieter and less obtrusive ways of presenting the journalistic self in the world that is being observed, sometimes result in greater trust and information access.

There is a need for better journalism in all directions – by southerners covering the North; by northerners covering the North; by Aboriginal journalists covering their own communities, each others' communities, and those of non-Native people; by non-Native journalists covering Aboriginal people and events. Perhaps it will seem simplistic to say that the improvement of journalism requires improvement in the training of journalists. It is unfortunate that many journalism educators ignore that truism.

Funding for educating Aboriginal journalists is even scarcer than funding for Aboriginal media. Moreover, if Aboriginal journalists do manage to find education programs, they encounter double standards in the workplace when they leave school. They are seldom hired but are often called upon to comment in pieces for which non-Aboriginal journalists receive bylines and payment. They are considered members of a fictional, monolithic culture of "Natives" rather than members of many socially, politically, and geographically distinct cultures. They are told they are "too biased" to provide accurate coverage of Aboriginal issues, or are ghettoized into reporting only on those issues. Yet no one considers francophone journalists too "biased" to cover francophone issues or Anglican journalists too biased to cover the Church of England.

Journalist Bud White Eye writes that even when news organizations hire First Nations journalists and advisors, there is "no guarantee that news outlets will get their reporting right" (White Eye 1996, 92). He recalls an exchange at CBC in Windsor, Ontario:

> The first story I tried to sell was about Walpole Island ... The producer said ... "We've already done two Native stories this week." When I asked how many "white" stories we had done so far, she slipped right off the handle ... Media say their budgets are tight. But if you stand by the door long enough, you'll see a new face come in, and it won't be Indian ... When the London Free Press asked me to review the ... Harry Rasky documentary, "Wars Against the Indians" I thought this was great ... They didn't tell me they had also asked a white journalist ... They put his review on the front page of the arts and entertainment section ... [and] stuck mine on the third page ... I thought, "They didn't trust me enough" ... But I don't think it's just about trust ... it's also about the authoritative voice (White Eye 1996, 92-7).

A 1995 article in *Editor and Publisher,* the trade magazine for North American newspapers, is headlined "J-School faculties get F in diversity" (Hernandez 1995). The article cites a survey of North American journalism programs that showed little progress in recruiting minority students or faculty. The gender equity picture is a bit better, at least in terms of student enrolment if not in the hiring of faculty. When I arrived at the University of Western Ontario's Graduate School of Journalism in London in 1989, the class was evenly divided between women and men, but only two or three women had been hired as full faculty members in nearly two decades since the founding of the school. There was a scattering of "visible-minority" students over the years, but not one faculty member. The record for educating indigenous journalists in "mainstream" institutions and programs is poor. Aboriginal journalism programs are scarce, and are fragile when they do exist. There is an urgent need to develop more bridging programs, such as the University of Toronto's Transitional Year Program, which prepares educationally disadvantaged students for full-scale university programs. There is also an urgent need to improve access to communications training.

In the early 1970s Grant MacEwen Community College in Edmonton, Alberta, started the first academic program in Canada for indigenous journalists, the Native Communications Program (which continues to offer courses on Native and communications issues, print journalism, radio, television, photography, layout, and design). Grant MacEwen's program was in place nearly a decade before the University of Western Ontario created its own Program in Journalism for Native People (PJNP) in 1980. These programs were followed in 1983 by the establishment of the Department of Indian Communications Arts (INCA) at Saskatchewan Indian Federated College (SIFC) in Regina (Chrisjohn 1986), which is probably the strongest of the programs operating today. In addition to its year-round curriculum, SIFC started an annual Summer Institute in Journalism in 1993 (SIFC 1993, 10).

In 1992 the Gitksan Wet'suwet'en Education Society founded the Gitksan Wet'suwet'en School of Journalism in Hazelton, British Columbia, and issued the following statement of philosophy: "In recognizing the power of mass media in society, the program is designed to provide the opportunity for people of First Nation ancestry to acquire journalism training so their perspective is represented better in print and broadcast media so that there is an improved awareness within First Nation cultures and an increased understanding between those cultures and Western society" (Gitksan Wet'suwet'en Education Society 1992, 2).

Allan Chrisjohn, the last person to head PJNP, placed the need for such programs in perspective: "Despite increasing pressure by the federal government for racial equity in hiring, and requests by organizations, such as the CBC, for qualified Native applicants, most mainstream placements have been primarily in technical fields and have had little impact in policy areas or on the 'face' of journalism. Potential Native journalists continue to avoid mainstream Canadian journalism schools" (Chrisjohn 1986). More than a decade later, his words still ring true.

In Memoriam: The Program in Journalism for Native People

Accurate representation of northerners is only one of the important issues. Northern and Aboriginal journalists must be able to do their work, and this means having access to jobs and education. For a decade, PJNP provided the important service of improving that access. Then, in 1990, the University of Western Ontario closed the program – not at a moment of failure but of success. Thanks to directors such as Allan Chrisjohn and Dennis Martel, PJNP produced a steady stream of fine journalists. Many of them – including Dan David (Mohawk), Bud White Eye (Delaware), Miles Morrisseau (Métis), and the Inuvialuit writer and journalist Mary Carpenter Lyons – achieved national or international recognition. In 1997 Morrisseau's achievements were recognized by his appointment to the Canada Council.

I was a direct witness to the process that led to the closing of PJNP. I had joined the faculty of the University of Western Ontario's Graduate School of Journalism in September 1989, under the impression that the program was closely tied to PJNP (which shared some faculty and curriculum and had its offices down the hall from ours). I was dismayed to learn shortly after arriving that ties between the two programs were virtually non-existent.

According to several PJNP graduates interviewed, many people treated PJNP from the start as a stepchild of the university's "real" journalism program. "Nobody wanted to teach us," a PJNP graduate recalled. "No one ever spoke to us even though we were using the same facilities and were just down the hall from them."

While Andrew MacFarlane was dean of the Graduate School of Journalism, he worked to raise and maintain PJNP's funding structure, which for the first five years had come from private sources, and later from the federal Department of Indian Affairs and Secretary of State. From one perspective, PJNP was one of many victims of the 1990 wave of cutbacks to Aboriginal communications, under Secretary of State Gerry Weiner. However, many people believe the program would still be alive had MacFarlane's successor, Peter Desbarats, fought for it. Before the official announcement of its closing came, he told the media that there was "'no glimmer of hope' for the native journalism program ... Frankly, the applicants [for the coming school year] shouldn't count on the program being there" (MacArthur 1990, B3).

Desbarats's brief statement on the demise of PJNP contained none of the passion that emerged three years later when the university threatened to close the Graduate School of Journalism. In that instance, he mounted a long and costly campaign to save the school, which included asking prominent journalists to join the campaign and alumnae/i for money and letters of support. The inclusion of PJNP alumnae/i and other indigenous journalists in the fund-raising campaign after their own program had been cancelled was insensitive, to say the least. Several people were stunned that the same dean who had cancelled PJNP was sending them letters of solicitation asking them to help save the graduate school.

In the period during and after the closing of PJNP, the voices of its faculty and students were seldom heard. Until it ceased publication with the end of the program, *Tellum ... As It Is,* the PJNP student newspaper, provided Native students with a rare vehicle for their words, even though its readership was limited to PJNP students. *Tellum* is a unique source in which to find PJNP students' defence of the threatened program. To enter their version of the story into the record, I have reproduced much of Kate Powless's powerful and poignant editorial from the newspaper.

Editorial
PJNP: Dying a slow death
By Kate Powless

The fight for more funding for the Native Journalism Program has ended. "Battle fatigue" has meant that the Program in Native Journalism at The University of Western Ontario is no longer [considered] necessary ...

For the past 10 years, rumours of the program's demise have been whispered through the halls. Most years the rumours weren't taken too seriously and proved to be false with another class of new students each Fall. Again this year the rumour raised its ugly head, but this time it's different ... A meeting of the advisory board for the journalism school put an end to the rumours with a decision to end the PJNP program ...

When asked why, the Dean of the Graduate School of Journalism, Peter Desbarats, says "It is basically because of two reasons. We were aware of the funding climate in Ottawa. With the funding climate the way it was, I knew it would be a real long shot if we went up this year and that we would probably be turned down." Desbarats also went on to explain, "We haven't got quite the crisis situation that this program was designed to respond to ... We had reduced the crisis to some extent and [we believed] that it was probably for other people to take up the work that we had been doing."

But has the program run its course? Has the demand or need for native journalists been fulfilled? Who decides on this need for native journalists? And just how many native journalists are needed? ...

This program has filled certain positions in the media field. Most of the graduates who have applied for work in the media are doing well. A few of the graduates in the media field now are: Miles Morrisseau, national native broadcaster for CBC Radio; Bud White Eye, associate producer for CBC Morningside; Keithera Riley, production assistant [for] Global TV; Rob Belfry, co-ordinator of [the] National Aboriginal Communications Society in Ottawa; and Scott Smith, editor of the *Tekawennake* [the newspaper at Six Nations].

I asked Dean Desbarats where do we go from here? What about the applicants for next year? He replied that there are other journalism programs for natives, and that the native people have proven they can master the same channels as the non-native journalists.

That's fine for the young natives, but what about the mature native person who decides to make a career change, or who finally has the time to devote a year to pursue such a career? Where do they go? As a mature student myself I can understand the hesitation of re-entering the academic field. The majority of PJNP applicants are mature students, their ages ranging between early twenties to late forties. These students have had to re-arrange their lifestyles, some transferring families across provinces, other leaving their families behind at home. These people committed themselves to PJNP.

Entering the program challenged me and the decision to leave my family didn't come easy. This program is by no means easy. It provides graduates with entry level skills required by the Canadian news media.

The course is strongly geared to practical training with several academic subjects as well. But having classmates who are natives provides support and a sense of community; we each know we can depend on one another. I'm sure I speak for the other students when I say I really don't think I could have made it as well as I have in a non-native environment. My classmates are natives from across Canada. One classmate said, by being with other natives [it] was less intimidating. In an all native class, it was easier to be ourselves.

I'm not saying we couldn't be journalists, but by being with our own people who understand our backgrounds and lifestyles, we can succeed on our own terms.

When I realized the course would end, I became emotional and still mourn the slow death of the PJNP. If the PJNP course wasn't meant to be a continuing option for natives, why was it started? Why offer a necessary and functional journalism program and then snatch it away?

To me it's like offering a glass of water to a man who has just crossed a barren desert. When he finally reaches for that glass, you drop it and spill every last drop. Can you imagine the feelings of frustration?

I am thankful for the opportunity I have in attending this program. And I'm glad I finally took the initiative to enrol in the PJNP program; just imagine if I had waited another year.

Many news organizations have turned their attention towards the PJNP closing. Is it because there is a genuine concern here or is this just another story to fill space? Will these other media show the emotional impact of the speakers, the students that have been interviewed? My concern here is, what will the public finally see, hear, or read?

There is still a need for this program ... One of the major concerns of the native peoples is the lack of coverage and the misinterpretations by the non-native press on native issues. How can we train qualified native journalists with the skills and education if this program ends? I'm angry because of the government's intervention towards [the] goals that natives set for themselves, recent cuts to native communications, caps set on native education funding, and now the closure of the native journalism program. Native issues are escalating ten times stronger and those voices want to be heard. We need our own media. We do need native journalists. We need PJNP (Powless 1990b, 6).

Perhaps to soften the blow of closing the program, the University of Western Ontario set up a $2,000 admissions scholarship for indigenous students who could qualify for admission to its Graduate School of Journalism. However, the scholarship could not disguise two facts: the graduate school made no outreach effort to attract Aboriginal or other minority students, and the whole point of PJNP was to increase accessibility of education to qualified but differently credentialed students. In my six years on the Graduate School of Journalism faculty, only two Aboriginal students were admitted to that program. One of them, Carla Robinson, was hired in late 1998 as a CBC Newsworld anchor.

Although journalism education is available at institutions such as the Saskatchewan Indian Federated College in Regina, and a few new programs are being developed, the demise of PJNP inflicted permanent damage on Aboriginal journalism education in Canada. In the same issue of *Tellum* in which Kate Powless mourned the death of PJNP, Andrea Simon, a Mik'maq alumna of PJNP with strong ties to the North, wrote a piece lamenting the death of yet another journalism program. The program at Arctic College closed just two years after it had begun the extremely important task of training northern journalists in the North. It had taken four years of careful planning, program development, and negotiations between the college and media organizations. As in the case of PJNP, the program was closed at a point of success.

In an article headlined "Another Journalism Program Bites the Dust," Simon wrote that despite "a 100 percent student success rate," the Arctic College journalism program was being cancelled (Simon 1990, 6). According to Arctic College senior instructor Kandice Karr, the program had been founded because northern media organizations had tired of dealing with the "steady stream of journalists going North, who thought the North was a good place to get training, then go back south" (Simon 1990, 6). They were often inexperienced and had "little sensitivity or understanding of northern communities."

The program was intended to encourage northerners to enter print and broadcast journalism. "Northerners needed a journalism program of their own. Going south to school far from their homes and traditional lifestyles meant loneliness, alienation and culture shock" (Simon 1990, 6). In December 1989, Arctic College graduated the program's first four students. Within a year, all four had obtained work in the field: two were freelancing, while Rosie Simonsalvy and Livete Atagoyuk were both working for CBC in Iqaluit, the former as an announcer and program host, the latter as a reporter in the newsroom.

I do not have a clear sense of precisely what happened at Arctic College. My feeling is that it was a mix of weak leadership, interpersonal conflict among faculty and administrators, misguided short-term financial concerns (there was not a large initial enrolment), and a trend toward increasing business and technical skills without the wisdom to see the relevance of journalism. Nevertheless, early in 1999 Arctic College announced a new program in communications, to begin later in the year. This will give Nunavut a training ground for communicators, which it increasingly needs.

Perhaps eventually, Nunavut will follow Greenland's lead. The Greenland Home Rule Government has established a school of journalism that offers a combination of theoretical education and practical training (Statistics Green-land 1997, 96). Meanwhile, in 1996, the Inuit Broadcasting Corporation (IBC) started training sessions in new media at its New Media Centre in Iqaluit (Bell and Mattson 1996). TVNC has also started to help people locate appropriate training programs.

Cross-Cultural Training: Some Beginnings

The First Nations Intensive Seminar
The IBC program in Iqaluit, Nunavut, and the Greenland journalism school will help to improve media representation from the inside and strengthen cultural literacy within the Inuit community. Those programs address only part of the misrepresentation problem. The existing college and university training grounds for non-indigenous media have tended to perpetuate mis-representation and intercultural misunderstanding. Changing the media means changing the journalists' attitudes and knowledge base, a process requiring what might be called *cross*-cultural literacy.

A few years ago, I helped to develop a pilot project in cross-cultural lit-eracy: the First Nations Intensive Seminar. For years, I had heard that non-Aboriginal journalists were afraid to go into Aboriginal communities to research stories first-hand, a fear derived from stereotypes that were often perpetuated by the news media themselves. While living in Yukon I was repeatedly warned not to go into First Nations communities. Yet my experi-ences in these communities were both positive and crucial to the accuracy of my understanding of people and issues, as a researcher and a journalist.

In 1990, after years of feeling frustrated by poor media coverage and by the apathy and fear of journalists, Bud White Eye (an alumnus of PJNP and a member of the Moraviantown Delaware First Nation in Ontario) and I brought students in the Graduate School of Journalism at the University of Western Ontario and members of nearby First Nations together for a day-long seminar. Our sense of urgency was increased by the ill-informed cover-age of the 1990 confrontation between government, police, and members of the Kanehsatake Mohawk community near Oka, Quebec. With PJNP gone, we saw an immediate future with even less training for indigenous journal-ists, which would mean continuing the pattern in which most of the peo-ple covering Aboriginal communities were non-Aboriginal journalists who seldom had any relevant background or preparation.

Wanting to turn our anger and disappointment to constructive action, we designed a one-day "intensive" seminar that would introduce future journalists to the history of first peoples in northern and southern Canada; to some of the current issues they might eventually cover; and to the diversity of First Nations languages, cultures, and concerns. We chose speakers from several cultures, communities, and professions and brought in newspaper stories and videos such as the Northern Native Broadcasting Yukon documentary *The Mission School Syndrome*.

The seminar ran for several years, despite continuing resistance from some of my academic colleagues. Most students said it was extremely valuable. A minority (along with some faculty members) complained about the introduction of what they called the "irrelevant" or "marginal" issues of diversity and equality into the journalism curriculum. The irony is that, during this period, universities throughout North America were increasing their commitments to "diversity" in their faculties, student bodies, and curricula. Especially after Kanehsatake/Oka, Canadian educational institutions were paying particular attention to First Nations. Nonetheless, the lack of support persisted. Even though the seminar cost only a few hundred dollars, and a few hours, to run, the budget and schedule were cut incrementally each year. Finally, we were able to continue only because we shortened the seminar and moved it into my ethics course, and because the First Nations organizers and participants were willing to accept lower fees, or none at all (and when necessary, I subsidized their participation myself).

In their written evaluations, many students said they had never met any Aboriginal people before. They expressed surprise at the "friendly," "fair," and "open" exchange and the widely divergent points of view. They said they had been led to believe (by journalists, among others!) that any dialogue with First Nations people would be driven by specific (and predictable) political agendas.

While this seminar was an important beginning and had many strengths, it was not without its flaws. Some are inherent in any program of this kind; some were particular to this specific seminar. Despite the seminar's successes, there are potential side effects that should be addressed in future projects, especially those organized within "mainstream" institutions. First, there is the danger of appropriation. While attempting to foster more accurate and respectful representations of Aboriginal people, we ran the risk of undermining the hiring of Aboriginal journalists by creating a new pool of non-Aboriginal "experts." However responsible and concerned these new journalists might be, they could end up with the salaries and the credit, perpetuating the use of Aboriginal journalists for unpaid expertise.

Given the nature of their job, journalists excel at becoming overnight experts. Holding a one-day seminar could play into the problem of the instant authority. The sudden rush of information could bring a "high" and a sense of great new knowledge. We tried to address this challenge by emphasizing that journalism training is not about learning answers but about learning where to go to ask questions, and by stressing the need to visit communities and learn first-hand instead of relying on non-Aboriginal "experts."

A third flaw is that students sometimes "freeze," overwhelmed by the magnitude of the issues. Indeed, some said they were reluctant to access any information, because they realized that all information is inadequate and incomplete. Part of the answer to this dilemma lies within the tradition of journalism education. Too often, we perpetuate the myth that a story can be *told,* that a single brief news item gives all the important information to the news consumer. We deal too little with the importance of the cumulative and the complex, oversimplifying both our mythically monolithic public and our messages. There is the danger of tokenizing and marginalizing the deep issues. We risk pretending that improved coverage of First Nations guarantees improvement of all news coverage. Certainly, such a program can provide a model to broaden the community of coverage, but we must take care that the model is clear. Students said the seminar was interesting and useful but addressed only one of many minority communities. I agreed, and added a series of seminars on other issues and communities.

The final difficulty we encountered was a certain amount of resistance. It always came from a small number of students, but it came predictably each year. Our challenge was twofold: we had to deal with our own frustration at encountering resistance, and we needed to find appropriate ways to respond. Each year, a few students asked, Why do we need this? Why so much attention to First Nations? Why learn something we know instinctively? In a seminar evaluation, one student wrote, "Journalists are already doing fine. I'm not a racist." One of the most effective ways to address this challenge emerged from the seminar and the post-seminar projects that inevitably developed from it. Some of the students who were most strongly convinced that journalism is "fine" discovered the racism in their own mistaken assumptions – for example, when they went to a First Nation to cover a story and discovered how "ordinary" the community looked, with none of the exotic qualities they had anticipated. While covering stories in communities they had come to know better than many professional journalists did, they also sometimes learned how inaccurate the mainstream media could be.

It is at once fortunate and unfortunate that even the students who learned for the wrong reasons did learn. During the years of this seminar, their coverage of Aboriginal issues vastly improved. After graduation, many students went on to produce important coverage for major media organizations. Some went on to collaborate with First Nations communities on training and journalism projects. In general, the students stopped being afraid to go into First Nations communities or agencies to research stories first-hand. They learned the names of Aboriginal leaders, organizations, and nations, the dates of powwows and symposia, and some of the local, regional, and national issues.

Most of the students learned that they needed to do better than their predecessors. Not all of them cared about the reasons. Nevertheless, I'm enough of an idealist to think that sometimes understanding creeps in where it is least welcome or expected. Occasionally, over the years, I have seen it happen. The real test is time – and journalism. Not long after the first of our seminars, I encountered one of the student television production teams at a Native Justice symposium. Because the guests included the Ontario premier, the news media were there in force. There was a sacred opening ceremony, and although it was explained that this ceremony could not be recorded, the cameras started rolling. Gently, one of the students turned to the network cameraperson near him and explained that the ceremony was a spiritual, not a media, event. The camera was turned off. That, I think, is progress – and good journalism.

I hope that in the future, similar programs will bring more depth and more attention to coverage of northern and Aboriginal people. At Western Washington University, I worked with Pete Steffens, who developed an outreach program to Native American communities in Northwest Washington with the help of state and university funding and grants from the Washington Newspaper Publishers' Association. From the 1970s until his retirement in 1999, Steffens worked on collaborative projects with First Nations journalists, educators, and community leaders in the region and on efforts to recruit Native American and other "minority" students and faculty.

The continuing need for such programs was brought home as I was finishing this book. In late August 1998, the Makah Nation (at Neah Bay in Washington, the westernmost point in the continental United States) had its annual Makah Days celebration. Because of a recent court decision upholding the tribe's right to an annual whale hunt, the Makah had attracted international media attention. There were reporters and broadcast crews from more than fifty newspapers and television and radio stations. Amidst rumours of possible disruptions, the community was already inundated with members of the National Guard, the police, anti-hunting activists, and an array of hecklers and observers. Ironically, "the only real protests during yesterday's opening of Makah Days were directed by tribal leaders to an intrusive news media," wrote *Seattle Times* staff reporter Christine Clarridge. At the welcoming ceremony, members of the Makah Nation lined the beach to greet guests arriving by canoe. The journalists "were asked repeatedly to step back and to respect the sanctity of the ceremony. Repeatedly, the media crowded in front of tribal dancers, disrupting the ceremony ... 'They're invasive, very invasive,'" said Makah tribal member Mary Hunter. Lisa Diaz, a Native American (Yaqui Indian) who is a reporter with Washington's *Peninsula Daily News,* also covered the event. She said her colleagues should take responsibility for their ignorance. "If they're covering Native events, I think they should brush up on the culture so they don't insult or offend people" (Clarridge 1998, A1, A8).

Other Initiatives
In the mid-1990s John Miller, head of the Ryerson Polytechnical University Journalism School, undertook a study of diversity in journalism education and then hired Dan David, a Mohawk journalist from Kanehsatake, to serve as the university's first professor of diversity. One of the distinguished alumni of the Program in Journalism for Native People, with a strong career in both print and broadcast journalism, David had often been told by mainstream media that because he is Mohawk he is "too biased" to cover Aboriginal issues. While his appointment at Ryerson was an important step toward progress, it was a halting one. The university's commitment and funding were tentative and incomplete: the position was not designed to be either full time or long term.

In journalism generally, as at Ryerson, hiring practices are improving at a very slow rate. A handful of newspapers and radio and television stations have hired Aboriginal and other minority reporters, but most of them – including Dan David – are part-time or freelance and are subject to the "last-hired, first-fired" syndrome. They are rendered relatively powerless in the structures of their institutions, and are often dismissed, turned over, or "downsized" before they have been able to have much impact.

In 1995 Don Curry of the Canadian Centre for Social Justice organized a project to examine and promote diversity in Canadian journalism schools (Curry 1995). The centre developed a monograph with resource materials and guidelines, which was made available free of charge to journalism schools, journalism educators, journalists, and news organizations. This was followed by the Nation of Immigrants Project, whose goal was to develop diversity training resources and facilitate projects to improve representation of diverse people in news media. I was one of a number of media people, organizational representatives, and educators appointed to an advisory committee. The centre has developed publications and undertaken community-based dialogues and studies. It founded the Aboriginal Youth Network (AYN), an on-line news service designed primarily as a discussion forum and information centre for indigenous youth, but this has recently disappeared from the Internet, perhaps for lack of funding.

In another initiative, besides collaborating with Bud White Eye to create the First Nations Intensive Seminar at the University of Western Ontario, I was sometimes able to help arrange internships for students who expressed a strong interest in the North. Some went North for a month and returned to careers in the South. Others stayed a year or two and left. Yet some of the former interns have become long-term northern journalists (Todd Phillips, for example, who for several years edited *Nunatsiaq News* in Iqaluit, and Greg Coleman, who continues to write for Inuit organizations and Nunavut publications).

It is clear that Aboriginal communications can be neither understood nor improved without addressing the context in which they emerge and operate. It makes no sense to strengthen literacy programs and weaken print media, or to provide more newspaper or broadcast jobs for Aboriginal journalists, in either mainstream or Aboriginal media, while closing the programs that educate and train them. As first peoples take control of their own communications media, they are able to develop culturally appropriate programs that integrate aspects of social, education, and political life – areas defined and administered by government and other agencies as separate entities.

Increasingly, first peoples are creating new media outlets and training grounds for journalists to run them. At least in their formative stages, such efforts have for several decades received support from a federal government whose policies acknowledged the importance of communications for effecting positive social change. The next chapter places northern Aboriginal communications in historical context and considers how Canada has developed the most extensive array of Aboriginal communication services in the world.

3
The Evolution of Communications in the North

Northern journalism is grounded in a history shared with Outside journalism. The following pages sketch the evolution of North American journalism. This material should help to clarify which aspects of the evolution of northern journalism are attributable to the patterns seen in the field as a whole, and which are particularly or uniquely northern. For example, although it is strongly identified with what some have called the "idea of North," the frontier spirit that even today infuses the northern journalistic mystique derives at least partly from characteristics that at various times were associated with the more general journalistic enterprise.

Journalism has had a violent history. Early newspaper editors and publishers were often jailed for their behaviour in what were sometimes mildly called "disputes." Mobs wrecked print shops, smashing equipment and burning newspapers. If people disliked a newspaper, they shut it down, one way or another. Along with this history of violence is a long history of symbiotic relations between journalism and government. At least five of the "fathers" of Canadian Confederation were journalists (Fetherling 1990, 40). In the 1860s editors of newspapers in Toronto, Brantford (Ontario), and Montreal held Cabinet posts. Although today's news media tend to separate themselves more sharply from the political arena, the tradition continues. It is especially evident in the North, where a handful of people hold public positions and often move back and forth between journalism and government.

Newspapers arrived relatively late in Canada, following their emergence in Europe and the United States. Most were founded by printers. Often, they began as newsletters, a trend that continues in the North today, where community newsletters often evolve into newspapers. The publishers of northern newspapers and magazines such as *Nunatsiaq News* in Iqaluit, *Up Here* in Yellowknife, and the *Yukon News* in Whitehorse often operate out of much larger printing businesses that issue other newspapers and magazines and provide an array of printing and publishing services.

Early English-language "news books" emerged in London, England, in the 1620s (Pete Steffens, personal communication, 1998). The first newspaper in North America, *Publick Occurrences Both Foreign and Domestick,* began publishing in Boston in 1690. Canada's first newspaperman, Bartholomew Green, came from Boston, having apprenticed on his printer father's *Boston News-Letter* before starting his own *Boston Gazette.* He settled in Halifax, and in 1751 opened a printing office, from which he planned to publish a newspaper. In jeopardy when Green died before the first issue of the paper was published, the project was revived by John Bushell, who began publishing the *Halifax Gazette* in March 1752. There was an "explosion of pro- and anti-British newspapers" from the 1750s to the 1770s, leading up to the American Revolution in 1776. This was followed in the 1780s and '90s by the rapid and widespread growth of political party presses. In the 1820s the first African American newspapers emerged in North America, and the decades that followed marked the rise of the popular press (Steffens, personal communication, 1998). Into this new, popular-press-dominated scene came a technological breakthrough that would permanently change the nature and dissemination of news.

With the invention of the telegraph in 1844, distance became less of an impediment to journalism. The first American wire service, Associated Press, began operating in 1848. It was not until 1917 that Canadian Press (CP) was established, and it was six more years before CP's eastern and western wire services were merged into a nationwide service. Until that time, Canada's national railway clung tenaciously to its monopoly over dissemination of the news, which meant that as the United States expanded and developed its wire service, information in Canada continued to be distributed through an unnecessarily cumbersome railway-based system. (Canada did use the wires, but in a different way. Information was sent by wire from station to station on the Great North Western Telegraph system, an affiliate of the Grand Trunk Railway. When the news arrived, it was translated from Morse code, transferred to paper, and carried by runner to each newspaper office.)

In 1858 the first transatlantic cable was laid. The result of this communication revolution was that newspapers no longer had to send their own reporters overseas except to major events. Some people thought this consolidation of reportage would take the bias out of reporting by making standard information available to everyone. Instead of making reporting less biased, however, telegraphy merely standardized information and narrowed it by furnishing only one version of the truth. With greater distances to cover, scarcer resources, and dependency on the Outside for news, the North suffered even more than other regions from this narrowing of information sources.

In the early 1850s the first newspaper in western Canada emerged in Victoria, BC. In 1859 William Buckingham and William Coldwell founded the *Nor'-Wester,* the first newspaper published in the Northwest, in the area that is now southern Manitoba. The paper was first published in the Red River Settlement, in a village near present-day Winnipeg, and later spread to several of the surrounding communities. It was distributed by Red River cart in summer and dogsled in winter. In 1868 it was sold to Dr. (later Sir) John Schultz, a non-practising physician and practising merchant who planned to use it as a forum to promote agricultural settlement of the Northwest and challenge the Hudson's Bay Company's continuing control of much of the region. In 1870, during the Red River Rebellion, Louis Riel and his Métis militia seized Fort Garry, imprisoned Schultz and other newspapermen, took over the printing establishment, and began publishing the *New Nation.*

The strong political stands taken by many publishers in their newspapers in the nineteenth century made them vulnerable to sometimes violent opposition. This was particularly true in the West. As one media historian has noted, "Journalism, always a rough trade in the 19th century, was nowhere rougher than in the West" (Fetherling 1990, 48). Riel's treatment of Schultz and the *Nor'Wester* during the Red River Rebellion was but one example. In 1872 John A. Kenny and W.F. Luxton started the *Manitoba Free Press* and mobs wrecked the offices of the *Manitoban,* the *Nor'-Wester,* and *Le Métis.* "In 1886, when John W. Dafoe was in his first tour of duty as a reporter at the *Free Press,* the paper he would end up editing for forty-three years, he was threatened by a dog-fight promoter. Dafoe sought protection from the chief of police, who simply advised him to carry a revolver. Which he did" (Fetherling 1990, 48).

During the 1880s newspapers emerged throughout the West, along with the new towns that accompanied the building of the Canadian Pacific Railway. When development came to the North, newspapers followed there as well. As we will see later, the Klondike gold rush brought new cities and newspapers to Yukon. The link between transportation and communication was underscored by the publication of the *Medicine Hat News* out of an aging Canadian Pacific Railway boxcar. (That tradition continued in the 1990s, when for several years Miles Morrisseau and Shelley Bressette published *Nativebeat* newspaper from a trailer at Kettle Point, Ontario.)

Once radio became available, newspapers were quick to adopt the new medium. Early radio broadcasts were closely tied to newspapers and wire services, setting the stage for today's media monopolies and common ownership of print and broadcast media. Among those participating in the Winnipeg General Strike of 1919 were Canadian Pacific telegraphers. When its owners found the city's *Free Press* newspaper cut off from access to the wire service, they responded by installing a radio transmitter atop the newspaper building and starting radio broadcasts from *Free Press* headquarters. In the 1920s and '30s the *Calgary Herald* installed a full-fledged broadcasting station on top of its newspaper headquarters, and a host of commercial radio stations also began to operate across the country. Radio continued to develop from the 1940s to the present. As we look from the contemporary era of communications toward the future, we can expect this trend of print-broadcast linkages to continue. Eventually things will come full circle, with new technologies dissolving the boundaries between print and broadcast media.

"Alternative" Media

It is a longstanding tradition among northern indigenous communities, continued in today's public meetings and informal gatherings, that feasts, potlatches, and public events of all kinds are important – often central – communications media. Thus in a fundamental way, Aboriginal communities are well disposed toward what might be characterized as "alternative" media. However, I believe that we need to review the terminology here. With respect to remote communities, we should perhaps reverse the usual designations of "mainstream" and "alternative" media. In communities where daily or weekly newspapers arrive days or weeks late, bulletin boards, fax, phone, and trail radio, or "moccasin telegraph" – also used to refer to word-of-mouth information sharing, sometimes called gossip – are far more reliable news sources. In many northern communities, news media get their start as underground or above-ground "alternative" media. In northern Ontario, for example, the Wawatay Native Communications Society began its broadcast programming as a trail radio rental service to trappers out on the land. The small, high-frequency transmitters formed an emergency communications system that remained based in, and responsive to, the communities.

In northern communities bulletin boards are primary, not supplementary, information sources. I refer here not to computer "bulletin boards" but to the old-fashioned kind that can still be seen on the walls of many northern buildings. Especially in small communities, long-distance news is posted at band offices, post offices, general stores, schools, and other public places. This kind of public posting of information and other local, small-scale modes of information sharing harken back to the days when European and North American communities had their news delivered on street corners by town criers.

The various Aboriginal cultural institutes are communication and educational centres that often assist in disseminating news. The Dene Cultural Institute in Hay River, founded in 1987, affiliated with the Native Communications Society of the NWT and the Dene Nation, produces literature and educational and cultural programming. Avataq Cultural Institute has served Nunavik Inuit from its Inukjuak headquarters since 1981. It sponsors conferences, educational programs, literature, archaeology, and a program to collect and reinstate Inuktitut place names. It also works with youth and elders and is a potential base for electoral education forums. The Inuit Cultural Institute, founded in 1974 and based in Rankin Inlet, provides similar programming, with emphasis on language; it has produced dictionaries and oral histories and sponsors an annual elders' conference.

The term "alternative media" must be used with care. Especially where northern and Aboriginal communications are concerned, it is important to emphasize that "alternative" does not mean "marginal," "unprofessional," or "inferior." Time after time, we see examples of innovative survival strategies that evolve into so-called mainstream communications. Pirate stations go "legit," bulletin boards become newsletters, newsletters become newspapers or magazines, local newspapers or magazines become regional, national, or even international. "Alternative" media merit full attention and credibility.

The Development of the Provincial and Territorial North

The Federal Presence in the North

The provincial North has often been ignored in studies of the North as well as of the provinces' southern regions. As one observer notes, "The land between the Yukon and the Northwest Territories and the populated south, the Canadian provincial north, is a truly forgotten area. It has little or no place in the public consciousness. It has not been, until recently, very important to governments or bureaucracies either at the federal or the provincial level. Moreover there has never been any general agreement on the territorial extent of the provincial north" (Weller 1983, 480). Because of shared history, the provincial North has more in common with the territorial North than with the southern region of the provinces. One shared characteristic is a strong, continuing federal presence in both the provincial and territorial North. Indeed, because of the history of the region, the federal government is often far more visible than are the provincial governments to the residents of the provincial North.

Federal interest in the North in general was piqued by defence concerns during the Second World War. Between 1940 and 1950, "federal policy in the north shifted dramatically ... from the somewhat laissez-faire attitude of the 1930s to one of active intervention ... All this came about with the support of a southern electorate who were excited by the vision of a new northern frontier, yet who were also apprehensive of any major American military presence which might diminish Canada's sovereign rights or control. But by 1950, the fear of a nuclear war overrode all other concerns" (Grant 1988, xvi). Thus, while the Second World War began to stimulate joint Canadian-American interest in the North, the Cold War guaranteed the region's continued centrality to strategic planning. The most visible sign of collaboration between Washington and Ottawa is the necklace of northern defence sites – the former DEW Line (Distant Early Warning system) which, in recent years, has been updated and renamed the North Warning System.

In addition to military concerns, the development of northern resources has also involved a strong federal presence. When the provinces of Saskatchewan and Alberta were created in 1905, Ottawa kept control of their natural resources, even though all other provinces except Manitoba had been granted jurisdiction over their own resources. Such a policy has had serious implications for the provincial North.

Economic development in the North was often related to resource extraction. Indian and Métis traditional economies were not incorporated into the new economy, and their communities suffered a "startling lack of ... basic services [and] high degree of [government] paternalism" (Weller 1983, 491). The development of northern company towns brought in a new population of non-Aboriginal peoples with their own agendas, interests, and concerns. Their impact is felt most keenly in political boundary disputes, some of which represent efforts of Aboriginal people to retain influence or voice in regions in which gerrymandering has suddenly rendered them a minority.

Communications in the Provincial North
The following sketches provide an overview of communication in the northern regions of the provinces, focusing on the availability of Aboriginal media and the impact of non-Aboriginal media on Aboriginal people and communities. I gathered the information with the help of a team of northern and southern researchers as part of the project undertaken for the Royal Commission on Electoral Reform and Party Financing (Alia 1991a). While the picture has been changing since 1990, especially with the expansion of Internet access and the advent of TVNC, patterns of media usage and representation remain essentially the same, as do the conclusions one can draw from them.

Northern British Columbia
British Columbia has no specific ministry for northern development or Indian affairs, nor does it have a coordinating agency or framework for policies affecting these areas. The Ministry of Industry and Small Business Development alone represents the interests of northern British Columbia at the Interprovincial Conference of Ministers Responsible for Northern Development.

One of the researchers, Kelley Korbin, found British Columbia by far the hardest northern region on which to get information. She remarks that "there are many northern aboriginal communities, with few effective links. They do not seem to have any comprehensive communications structures" (Korbin

1990). While noting that most Aboriginal communities in northern British Columbia have broad access to radio stations, CBC radio and television, the *Vancouver Sun* and the *Province,* and local weekly or daily newspapers, she speculates that inundation with mainstream media that give "the illusion of providing comprehensive coverage" of First Nations issues might actually inhibit development of First Nations news projects. Other observers attribute the lack of development to scarcity of funding. The lack of an effective information network among British Columbia's northern Aboriginal communities must be considered in the context of factors such as diversity of communities, interests, problems, and geography. The researchers consulted representatives of Aboriginal friendship centres in northern British Columbia to get a more accurate picture.

In Fort Nelson no one subscribed to Native publications, but some publications were occasionally brought into the friendship centre. Community members had broad access to mainstream broadcast media – CBC Northern Service, BCTV, CITV Edmonton – as well as an array of print media, including the *Fort Nelson News,* the *Vancouver Sun,* and the *Province. Native Network News* is an important and highly praised print resource. No one expressed concern about a lack of Native media coverage.

Terrace is a production centre for Northern Native Broadcasting Terrace (NNBT). There are no local Aboriginal newspapers, but the friendship centre subscribes to Aboriginal newspapers from across Canada. There are two community newspapers, the *Standard* and the *Review.*

The Prince Rupert friendship centre subscribes to *Kahtou,* the Sechelt Nation's newspaper, and the community has two local newspapers, the *Daily News* and *Prince Rupert This Week,* which an informant said provided "much better coverage of native issues" than other non-Native papers. Mainstream television and radio are abundant, and the community receives programming from NNBT. In general, informants were "quite positive about Native media access."

Although the population of Chetwynd is 50 percent Aboriginal, informants there said that they had no control over, or input into, local media. The friendship centre subscribes to Aboriginal newspapers, but we were told that people in the community "generally feel very left out" as far as coverage of Native issues is concerned. Korbin found this the only friendship centre where concern was expressed about poor coverage of Aboriginal issues. Like other centres, the Chetwynd friendship centre had very limited knowledge about other northern Native communities or politicians in the province. In general, informants across northern British Columbia said that their communities had adequate media access, but they expressed a lack of connection with other Aboriginal communities in the region.

Northern Alberta, Saskatchewan, and Manitoba

Aboriginal people in these three provinces are deeply affected by the ambiguities of federal administration. The federal Department of Northern Affairs, which was established in 1947, has de facto, but not precisely defined, jurisdiction over some Indian and Métis people. In 1953 the Northern Affairs Branch was created within the Department of Natural Resources, supplanting the Department of Northern Affairs.

In Saskatchewan the 1970s brought in a Task Force on Northern Affairs, which evolved into the Department of Northern Saskatchewan. The administration of northern Alberta, on the other hand, is focused primarily on economic development, with the Northern Alberta Development Council at its centre. In Manitoba the Northern Affairs Act established the Office of the Commissioner of Northern Affairs in 1966. The act provided for a commissioner in Winnipeg, a director in Thompson, and one coordinator to cover both Lac du Bonnet and The Pas. Company towns have come to dominate the scene in northern Manitoba, all but Flin Flon founded after 1945. Thompson, the newcomer, was founded in 1960. It has since become northern Manitoba's largest community and has changed the face of northern Manitoba politics with a large influx of non-Native people, many of them from outside the province.

Some people in the study said that the lack of clearly defined or elaborated Aboriginal rights has caused major problems for people throughout this region. In Saskatchewan the ambiguity has been especially problematic for Aboriginal education. An informant pointed out that Saskatchewan First Nations people's access to postsecondary education "is not recognized as a treaty right," and there are ceilings limiting the number of Aboriginal people who are entitled to postsecondary education. A poorly articulated policy on postsecondary education is coupled with limitations placed on earlier levels of education. Funding cutbacks have hurt primary education on the reserves, and one informant called such underfunding "one of the major impediments to self-sufficiency."

The province's 60,000 Métis, represented by the Métis Society of Saskatchewan, have no access to even the poorly defined treaty rights, and are as disadvantaged as the members of First Nations when it comes to access to communications. If underfunding of education is a major impediment to self-sufficiency, the underfunding of Aboriginal communications is an equally crucial impediment. The two go hand in hand. To develop Métis and First Nations journalists requires education; once journalists are educated, they need access to jobs in media outlets. One of the bright spots is Saskatchewan Indian Federated College, which provides both general postsecondary education and education in print and broadcast journalism. The problem is what happens after the journalists graduate.

Those interviewed in these three provinces said that scant funding is the primary obstacle that prevents Aboriginal broadcasters from adequately serving Aboriginal communities. An editor, for example, expressed the need to "hire reporters to track candidates and issues and [provide] an adequate broadcast distribution system." This informant noted that while the radio program *Native Perspectives* is broadcast (with sound only) on television, "one program three hours per day is not enough to cover Native issues" (Hardie 1990).

Although one community member believed that any conscientious journalist can cover any issue, others said that Aboriginal journalists are better equipped to cover First Nations issues because they bring an insider's perspective: "The dominant culture tends to impose its perspective on Native issues, with little regard for the possibility that Native people might weigh issues differently." TVNC has improved the picture, however, by broadcasting more programming produced by and for Aboriginal people.

Some informants commented that Aboriginal media, especially publications, do not have the credibility they deserve and are not regarded as viable places to advertise. To help to remedy this situation, "efforts to form Native advertising agencies and National Native newspapers should be encouraged and financially supported." People called for the reinstatement of funding for Native newspapers, most of which are not yet self-sufficient.

Observers saw "a critical need to keep communication lines in the Native community open while the publications grow." As in so many indigenous communities, alternative media play a significant role in keeping communications open. In this region, alternative media include community newsletters and community group notice boards. In Saskatchewan, after the *Saskatchewan Indian* – a major Aboriginal newspaper with nation-wide influence – closed due to government cutbacks, First Nations in the province were left with "no single organ that reaches and unifies the Indian community." Aboriginal people in the northern part of the province have since had to depend on district newsletters, telex, fax, word of mouth, and mail services.

Alberta Attorney General Dick Fowler argued that it is not Aboriginal media but mainstream media – and attitudes of mainstream journalists – that are the "main problem with the access Indians have to the media." He said the problem is not scarce facilities or funding, but neglect and misplaced priorities, and offered an example: In November 1990 a Land Agreement granted Indian people over 100,000 acres. Despite the presence of several mainstream journalists at the signing in the Legislature, "the event and underlying issues got just a 'blurb' on CTV. On the same day, three cows escaped from the Premier's farm, and that non-event received significantly more coverage than the [land agreement]." Some observers agree with Fowler's assessment. Several people mentioned the "mainly negative coverage of Native issues." One Saskatchewan informant noted that Aboriginal people in Saskatchewan have access to major media. The problem is, they "don't get good press. Media tend to stress the tragedies and ignore the triumphs."

The large Métis population of Saskatchewan has its own particular concerns. One Métis person explained, "We are not Indian, not Eskimo; we are a separate people with our own legal and political status and cultural traditions." *New Breed,* the Métis newspaper, survived funding cuts by going monthly and being run "as a lean business," with a circulation of approximately 10,000. Even with the paper, "there is a need for more stories and documentaries that tell the story of the Métis people. This would make Canadians aware of the cultural heritage of the Métis people and distinguish them clearly from Indians."

Aboriginal newspapers are praised for "doing a good job of raising awareness and covering issues given the constraints they are under." One politician predicts an increase in mainstream media coverage as the number of Aboriginal politicians increases. He reports adequate Native representation on school boards and municipal councils and predicts that Aboriginal politics will move from basic administrative issues to larger concerns, such as the maintenance of Aboriginal languages and cultures.

Those interviewed made a number of recommendations: mainstream journalists should use Native sources in their stories more often; development of Aboriginal newspapers should be a priority; Aboriginal news networks should be developed; more Aboriginal news should be provided in Aboriginal languages. Some First Nations communities cannot get broadcast news because they don't have cable service; few stations are available to those who do. Several people mention the need to educate mainstream journalists, challenging stereotypes and journalists' "apprehension about visiting the communities ... [and] unfounded fears for their safety."

Northern Ontario
The Northern Development Branch was established in 1911 within the provincial Department of Lands and Forests. Over the years, responsibilities and ministries have shifted and merged, and today the Ministry of Northern Development and Mines works with Indian and Métis people but shares responsibility with other agencies, notably the Native Community Branch of the Ministry of Culture and Recreation.

In general, Aboriginal communities in northern Ontario are remote and are accessible only by air, which means that "news often doesn't get out." Lack of personnel for news media was cited as the main problem. Many people said that more mainstream television coverage is needed, citing "very poor service," especially in smaller communities, and a predominant "parochial view." Those interviewed called for more depth, and less sensationalism.

As one person put it, northern and Aboriginal news should be "treated as part of the national political agenda." Another person said that national broadcast media should send people to remote areas to learn first-hand what it means to travel by snowmobile or air and cope with cold, fog, delays, and breakdowns.

Northern Ontario political workers, politicians, and news consumers who were interviewed said that journalists need to become more aware of northern issues, particularly those affecting Aboriginal peoples. They said media are generally fair but are "never specific enough" and gave examples such as the sketchy coverage of land claims, which they felt merited deeper explanation and analysis.

As is true elsewhere, "alternative" resources are a rich source of information. In remote communities, people tend to drop by the store or band office daily, to share the news and read whatever bulletins are found on the public bulletin boards that invariably grace the entrances.

As is often the case in northern Aboriginal communities, radio received the highest praise and television the lowest. One Aboriginal community leader praised print and radio but said reporters don't come often enough or on short enough notice. Regional television, it was noted, is entirely absent (Thorbes 1990).

Northern Quebec (Nunavik)
In 1962 the Direction Général du Nouveau Québec was established by the provincial minister of Natural Resources, René Lévesque, to secure a Quebec presence in an area dominated by the federal government. Economic development was the focus. The James Bay and Northern Quebec Agreement of 1975 absorbed most functions of the new agency and in 1977 it was replaced by the Secretariat des Activités gouvernementales en milieu Amérindien et Inuit.

Quebec has never had an Aboriginal member in its National Assembly. One informant said that federal and provincial politics are "foreign to the daily routines and needs of northern native peoples." Adrienne Arsenault, one of the researchers, noted that "many northern communities exist, it seems, without the knowledge of political agencies – except at tax time." She found that an Aboriginal informant "spoke of the Canadian political process ... as if he were describing the government of a foreign land. In many respects, this is the overwhelming response I received during the study: 'Their politics is not our politics'" (Alia 1991a).

Arsenault found herself "both impressed and frustrated" from her discussions with the Aboriginal politicians, political workers, and journalists because of their "almost universal ability to speak several languages when politicians elected to represent Canadians are not wholly bilingual. There is so much to learn ... even with a study of this size, we are nowhere near understanding the complexities of the problems or the routines of the North" (Arsenault 1990).

One informant said the vastness of northern Quebec makes it impossible for mainstream or alternative media to cover that region adequately, and that Cree programming is "not sufficient." Aboriginal politicians and other leaders in the region would like to see more "analytical programming ... We only have information services; we [need] tools to criticize [people] or issues." They repeated a complaint heard in every part of the North – that coverage of northern and Native news is crisis oriented.

A complaint heard in Quebec as well as the western provinces and Yukon is that satellite television has brought predominantly American programming. The only Canadian coverage northern Quebec residents receive is BCTV, TVNC, and CBC-TV. A politician complained that "there is little or hardly any coverage related to issues in Northern Canada or ... Northern Quebec" because most of the programming comes up from CBC Montreal rather than down from the CBC Northern Service.

There is no sense that media access or quality of coverage have improved over the past few years. Moreover, as an informant said, "There's a very serious language barrier in Northern Quebec between the organizations and Native people." It was pointed out that the Oka/Kanehsatake crisis and other such confrontations get the coverage. One person said that it seems as if people must be "on the brink of war before ... [their] concerns are heard." Such concerns include crises in housing, changing demographics, and education – issues that would be "in the forefront of newspapers and media in the south" but do not make news if they originate in the North. Only when "mega projects are constructed and the Cree people [oppose them]" is there media response, an Aboriginal leader said.

Across the North, people saw television as the most deficient medium. A politician said that most northern Quebec people "love to watch television and they can sit for hours in front a television set ... If we can get access to that television set I believe that most people will be up to date on what is happening." The priority for Aboriginal access to television is northern news coverage.

When he was interviewed, Chief Billy Diamond called for "a thorough Northern Education Program in the North concerning ... how issues can be solved by using the media, and how you can tell your story by telling the media," in hopes of improving the skills of Aboriginal people to handle interviews by non-Aboriginal media and to become more media wise in general.

Labrador
Northern administration of Labrador began in unity and ended in multiplicity. Originally the provincial Department of Labrador Affairs, established

in 1966, was responsible for all aspects of the entire region. In 1973 Labrador administration was diversified, and since then each department has had separate jurisdiction in its particular area of responsibility.

In Labrador, Arsenault observed a "tightly knit aboriginal community," which encompassed several smaller communities. She found it easy to locate First Nations leaders and journalists because the communities seemed in touch with each other. Although Innu and Inuit communities and communications are often separate, there has been cooperation among them on social and political issues of mutual concern. Print media are limited. The Nain area receives the *Globe and Mail* "a week late, if at all." The local newspaper was cut in half after government budget cuts. Several people expressed frustration with their communities' alienation from Canadian politics and communications. "Labrador Native people feel left out of mainstream communications."

The message from the provincial North is that the quality and quantity of news coverage must improve. News media must be willing and financially able to cover remote communities and the issues that concern their citizens. There is a widespread call to educate non-Aboriginal and non-northern journalists about these issues. Access to particular media varies greatly, but there is near-universal protest against inadequate television coverage. Several communities have extensive media access although many others do not, but many of the broader linkages are based outside the North (for example, the wide availability of programming from Detroit and Chicago through cable networks). The alienation inherent in remote, northern regions is compounded by problems specific to Aboriginal communities and by a funding climate that indicates less, rather than more, media access in future.

The Territorial North

The Northwest Territories and Nunavut
The pre-Nunavut NWT had a legislature of twenty-four independents who made decisions by consensus – a very unusual system. Nunavut will most likely use a similar system, tailored to the needs and culture of its substantial Inuit majority. Although Yellowknife is nearly 90 percent non-Aboriginal, the Northwest Territories have a large Aboriginal minority, which consists of Dene, Métis, and Inuvialuit (western Inuit). The NWT Territorial Assembly meets in nine official languages – Chipewyan, Cree, Dogrib, English, French, Gwich'in, Inuktitut, North Slavey, and South Slavey. The question period that follows legislative debate differs from southern assemblies and from Yukon's, as it has no time limit. The house has a full committee system but is not divided along party lines.

We were told that the Nunavut weekly newspaper *Nunatsiaq News* is the major media source of published news and information, but people were careful to qualify this statement, calling its coverage of Inuit concerns "limited." A political candidate said that the Keewatin region needs a newspaper of its own: people in this region are caught between the eastern, Iqaluit-based *Nunatsiaq News* and the *Journal* out of Fort Smith in the west.

Radio remains central among media, especially where it is available in Inuktitut. Aboriginal radio was preferred to non-Aboriginal radio and to other media by Aboriginal politicians and many community members, because phone-in shows were of unlimited duration, continuing as long as there were callers. That practice is closely tied to Aboriginal oral traditions, which do not rely on the Euro-Canadian/American broadcasting principle of allocating equal segments of limited programming. The same principle is found in Yukon, where programming sometimes extends far beyond its specified time slot. In Whitehorse during the Oka/Kanehsatake crisis, I observed a television round table in which participants were asked to return after lunch to continue what had been scheduled as a morning show, because people were still phoning in and the discussion had not finished.

Pressured by funding shortages, the *Press Independent,* originally a Dene paper, went from twice monthly to weekly publication in an effort to sell more papers and advertising space and began to work more closely with the Inuvialuit newspaper *Tusaayaksat* to share coverage in communities where both Dene and Inuvialuit lived. For a short time, it looked as though intercultural cooperation and more frequent publication would be positive outcomes of post-cutback northern journalism and that the cooperation would make an important contribution to better relations among the two peoples, but in a matter of months the *Press Independent* had to close its doors, unable to increase its revenues with sufficient quantity and speed.

Lack of travel funds was the most significant problem cited by Inuvialuit Communications Society members and other NWT journalists. They said mainstream media coverage would improve if journalists travelled more (Thorbes 1990). *Press Independent* editor Lee Selleck reiterated the need for increased travel, but said weather and terrain often make travel impossible. In addition to the weather, distance and cutbacks in scheduled airline routes were cited as major problems. Despite these problems, Selleck found more coverage of first peoples' concerns in the North than in the South, a view shared by many others. He expressed the desire to see cross-cultural workshops sponsored by media organizations for Aboriginal and non-Aboriginal journalists. Many people supported this idea of the need for better training of journalists who cover the North. A political candidate said that "the quality and professionalism of journalists is lacking" and called for specific training programs (Smythe 1990).

Recession will hit small business, says Wray

by Cooper Langford

The small business, arts and crafts and tourism sectors of the NWT economy will be hardest hit as the Canadian economy slips into recession, says Economic Development minister Gordon Wray.

But the north will be partially shielded from the latest economic downturn if it is shallow and short-lived, he adds.

"Given the forecasts of a six to nine month recession in Canada, we do not expect to experience a notable spillover," Wray told the legislature last week.

He said a longer recession, like the 1981-82 slump, would have a more dramatic impact. Mineral prices would fall, decreasing the value of one of the territories' main exports.

The NWT is also partially protected because it gets much of its revenue from federal spending, Wray said.

Small businesses could be in for a rough ride too, over the next few months. Rising fuel costs, high interest rates and the implementation of the goods and services tax will be the cause. Still, the volume of sales should remain stable because of government spending and mineral development.

"The most immediate impact is on new investment, as investors put off capital expansion or product improvement because of reduced profit margins caused by higher borrowing rates," Wray said.

He noted that arts and crafts are considered "luxury items" and are therefore unstable during periods of economic instability. Tourism revenues are expected to drop because higher fuel prices have raised the cost of air travel. A weaker economy also discourages consumers from spending money on holidays.

INSIDE

Mildred Hall students goof around as the lunch bell sounds.
photo/J. Holman

Animal rights group claims victory
Fur salon chain will close

by Lee Selleck

Fur salons belonging to Nordstrom Inc. will be closed for good after February 1 next year, the department store chain has announced. Only its Anchorage, Alaska fur wear outlet will stay open.

The 63-store firm, which includes department stores and seven fur salons, is based in Seattle, Washington. Two salons will be closed in Virginia, plus those in Walnut Creek and San Francisco, California; and two in Washington state.

Anti-fur and animal rights activists had nothing to do with the decision, a company spokeswoman claimed. "We're simply seeing a declining demand for these products," said Chris Brldenbaugh.

The company would not release any information on the value of furs sold or a percentage decline in fur sales. Total sales for all departments, however, was $801 million for the latest three month period available.

Seattle animal rights groups were quick to claim a win over the fur trade. "We have got

through to the public that there is no glamor in wearing a coat of corpses," said Mitchell Fox, animal issues director for the Progressive Animal Welfare Society.

The groups picketed Nordstrom stores, Fox noted. "We've been campaigning against Nordstrom for the past half a decade (and) discussing the issues with them for the past year, trying to persuade them to close their fur salons.

Poor sales over the last few years is the cause, says Nordstrom's, but would not release figures to back that up.

"Nordstrom is very approachable. Their reputation is built on responding to their customers," added Fox. "We can't get other department stores to cooperate at the same level."

He echoed Nordstrom's claim that the halt of fur sales was a simple business decision, and "there are a few factors being thrown around to explain it." These included recent warm

winters and a faltering economy as well as the animal rights movement.

"I choose to think the predominant factor driving people away from fur salons is the ethical and moral one" of causing "unmitigated suffering to the animals."

Nordstrom spokeswoman Joanne Langendorfer said picketing of Nordstrom stores was not regular, did not disrupt business and did not influence the decision to close the fur salons.

While sales of other items have increased, fur sales have dropped, Langendorfer said. "We could use the floor space for new or other departments."

Fox said his group does not oppose subsistence hunting by aboriginal people, but asked, "isn't there another alternative?" to making a living from trapping.

People who are against trapping animals for fur should also be "willing to help people whose lives depend on that," Fox said. "We shouldn't place the interest of animals over those of humans — who are also animals, of course."

Dene Nation, Metis Association ...
Regional claims get the green light

by Cooper Langford

Ottawa will negotiate regional land claims with the Dene and Metis, Indian Affairs minister Tom Siddon announced Wednesday. And, Ottawa is cutting off claims funding for the Dene Nation and Metis Association.

In a telephone press conference from Edmonton, Siddon said the final agreement for the western Arctic was "dead," along with other agreements such as the development freeze in the North Slave region.

"I think this will be good news for a large number of Dene and Metis people in the NWT," Siddon said, referring to Sahtu and Delta proposals for a regional claim.

"In an ideal world, I prefer to settle claims on as broad a base as possible (but) I felt I could not turn my back on these people."

Siddon blamed the collapse of the comprehensive claim on a "rejection" of the deal in a disagreement between Ottawa and the other regions over extinguishment of aboriginal rights.

Regional claim negotiations with the Gwich'in and Sahtu tribal councils will be based on the agreement initialled April 9 in Rainbow Valley, he said.

"We have to have a sense of clarity and certainty when these agreements are signed," Siddon said. "To reopen negotiations would negate our fundamental goal."

Dene national chief Bill Erasmus said the new policy for western Arctic claims shows the federal government doesn't want to deal with all the Dene/Metis people in the Mackenzie Valley.

"It's no longer a nation-to-nation agreement. It's an agreement for people of a region," Erasmus said.

"We never rejected the final agreement. We rejected extinguishment. We rejected the March 31 (ratification) deadline. The government is rejecting the agreement."

Metis Association president Gary Bohnet said Siddon's announcement contained "no surprises" but left him with "mixed feelings.

"I don't see many options out there," he said. "It's either regional claims or going through the courts or nothing."

The effective death of a comprehensive claim in the western Arctic opens up many new issues for the Dene Nation and Metis Association.

So far, only the Sahtu and Delta regions have said they want separate claims. The North Slave is considering the option, but has yet to decide what to do. The South Slave and Deh Cho regions oppose the terms of the initialled claim.

Bohnet said separate Metis claims south of the lake are a possibility if Dene in the region stand firm in their opposition to the current status of the claim.

The complicated case of land claims also leaves the question of land ownership up in the air, Erasmus said. He said court decisions cast enough doubt to support Dene/Metis court challenges over title.

Along with Ottawa's new approach to the $500 million, 70,000 square-mile deal, Siddon also announced that as of January 31, the Dene Nation and NWT Metis Association will no longer be funded for claim work.

Erasmus and Bohnet said the cutbacks will mean big changes in their organizations, including layoffs.

Bohnet and Erasmus said they will meet with the Dene and Metis leadership in the coming days to discuss what Ottawa's endorsement of regional claims means for the NWT. They said separate and joint leadership meetings will be held in the near future.

Siddon said he wants to come to Yellowknife within a month to discuss the claim situation with the Dene/Metis.

The *Press Independent* was the later incarnation of *Native Press* and an attempt to broaden the newspaper's perspective and readership to include more non-Native people. Unfortunately, it ceased publication in 1993. In 1996 and 1997, two issues of a new version of *Native Press* were published under new editorial leadership but with no continuing newspaper staff.

Another NWT journalist criticized the poor quality of television journalism. There is "too little background to stories," and "oversimplification" causes journalists to fall into "stereotypical traps." She said NWT media generally provide better coverage of northern and Aboriginal news than do the national media, but called the non-Aboriginal Yellowknife radio station CJCD "out to lunch." Another informant said that CJCD had fought "tooth and nail" against the licensing of CKNM – the First Nations radio station (Thorbes 1990).

Yukon Territory
Yukon is home to about 33,000 people, about 23,000 of them in Whitehorse. This small territory has had a large impact on Canadian politics. It has produced a national party leader, a landmark coalition of Aboriginal people (the Council for Yukon First Nations), a prominent premier, and a number of political breakthroughs. Among Canada's northern citizens, Yukoners are perhaps the least alienated from federal politics. We will look more closely at Yukon communications in the case study in Chapter 5. Although many of the problems and characteristics of the rest of the North are shared, Yukon has a separate identity (as Yukoners remind Outsiders energetically and often) and sometimes seems less like a territory than a province.

Northern Newspapers and Magazines
Print media emerged in the North in the 1800s. Early newspapers, newsletters, and magazines designed for, but rarely by, Aboriginal people were developed primarily by special interest groups, including missionaries. There were five nineteenth-century publications produced by and/or for Aboriginal people. *Pipe of Peace* (1878-9), which was produced in Ojibway and English, was published in Sault Ste Marie, Ontario, by the Shingwauk Home, Canada's first residential school. The Home was founded in 1873 (Miller 1996, 7). It also produced the monthly *Our Forest Children* (1887-90), edited by the Anglican minister Reverend E.F. Wilson. The journal's paternalistic title was compounded by the subtitle *And What We Want to Do with Them*. From 1880 to 1892 the Canadian Indian Research and Aid Society in Ottawa published *The Canadian Indian*. In Kitamaat, British Columbia, *Na-Na-Kwa* (Dawn on the West Coast) was produced between 1893 and 1895. The longest-running journal was *Kamloops Wawa*, a Chinook magazine that was published from 1891 to 1904 by the Reverend J.M.R. Le Jeune (Petrone 1990).

Petrone (1990, 95) calls the period between the First World War and the 1969 government White Paper on Indian policy, "a barren period for native writing in Canada." She attributes this to several factors,[6] including an increase in "white" control as exercised by the Department of Indian Affairs, the rise of assimilationist federal policy, the effects of the Depression, and publishers' preference for Aboriginal narratives "retold by non-natives" (ibid., 95).

Between 1949 and 1955, as mentioned earlier, the BC Squamish leader Andrew Paull, published *The Thunderbird* (1949-55) and *The Totem Speaks* (1953). In the same period, the Native Brotherhood of British Columbia published *Native Voice,* starting in 1946 and continuing into the 1990s.

The late 1950s and 1960s saw a rapid rise in federal services to first peoples, which included the funding of Aboriginal cultural and communications programs and institutions. Along with the development of Native friendship centres came government-funded Aboriginal associations, magazines, and newspapers. It was a time of general political foment that included the rise of the Indian Movement, guided by BC Shuswap leader George Manuel. From 1950 to 1959 Vancouver's Pan-American Indian League published *Indian Time.* The federally administered and funded Indian and Inuit Affairs Program, Ottawa, published *Indian News/Nouvelles Indiennes* from 1954 to 1982. The Federation of Saskatchewan Indians publication *Indian Outlook* lasted only from 1960 to 1963, but two Alberta papers launched in 1968 continue today: *Native People,* published by the Alberta Native Communication Society for Edmonton; and *Kainai News,* an independent First Nations paper founded in Hobbema and now based in Standoff.

The 1970s were a time of indigenous cultural renaissance in North America. Aboriginal journalism thrived in a climate that supported a wide range of creative writing, from poetry and fiction to history and children's literature. *Akwesasne Notes* began publication in 1969 from the Mohawk Nation in Rooseveltown, New York (on the Canadian border), and continues today. Although not a northern publication, its writers, readers, and influence extend worldwide. The British Columbia Indian Homemakers' Association of Vancouver launched the still-published *Indian Voice* in 1969, and the independently published, politically conscious community newsletter *The First Citizen* emerged in Vancouver in 1969 and survived until 1972.

The Saskatchewan Cree-Saulteaux writer Eleanor May Brass was a prolific writer and broadcaster known in the 1970s and '80s for her CBC radio and television broadcasts as well as for her articles for the daily newspaper the *Regina Leader-Post.* The Federation of Saskatchewan Indians started the *Saskatchewan Indian* in 1970, the same year that the federal Department of Indian Affairs began publishing *Tawow* from Ottawa. *Tawow* ceased publication in 1980; the *Saskatchewan Indian* still survives. The influential and widely read *Micmac News* was published in Sydney, Nova Scotia, from 1971 to 1992. The Ye Sa To Communications Society in Whitehorse, Yukon, published its newspaper, the *Yukon Indian News,* from 1974 to 1991 and then intermittently for several years the magazine *Dännzhà'.* *Wawatay News* entered the scene in 1974 as the newspaper of the Wawatay Native Communications Society, based in Sioux Lookout, Ontario. The Ottawa-based

National Association of Friendship Centres published *The Native Perspective* from 1975 to 1978, the year the Union of Ontario Indians began publishing *Ontario Indian.*

The indigenous literary and journalistic renaissance of the 1970s continued into the 1980s with *Sweetgrass* (1984), paving the way for 1990s publications such as *Aboriginal Voices.* The English department of the University of Lethbridge, Alberta, became a welcoming forum for the poetry, fiction, and essays of Aboriginal writers. Ontario poet and playwright Daniel David Moses, Lenore Keeshig-Tobias, and others involved with the Committee to Re-establish the Trickster published the *Magazine to Re-establish the Trickster.* Other periodicals that emerged in the 1980s included *Windspeaker,* the important newspaper put out by the Aboriginal Multi-Media Society of Alberta; *Masenayegun,* published by the Winnipeg Friendship Centre; *New Breed,* a Métis magazine published by Saskatchewan Native Communications; and *The Phoenix,* published by and for Aboriginal and non-Aboriginal people by Toronto-based nationwide Canadian Alliance in Solidarity with Native Peoples (CASNP).

Of all northern media, it is the newspapers and magazines – particularly Aboriginal print media – that have suffered most from the 1990 and subsequent budget cuts. Since print publications have always been scarcer than radio and television programming, some call the present situation a crisis.

Not long before he wielded the axe, for example, the Secretary of State sent magnanimous wishes to one of the publications that would be most deeply affected, *Windspeaker,* on the occasion of the newspaper's sixth anniversary (Weiner 1989, 4). Because of the document's importance, the entire text is included here:

Dear Friends,

I welcome this opportunity to extend my very best wishes on the publication of the Sixth Anniversary issue of Windspeaker.

The Aboriginal peoples of Canada were the First to frame our multicultural identity. The diversity of our languages and cultures has personified what our country is and can become. It is through the preservation of your traditions that you ensure that Canada's heritage can meet its promise for the future.

Media are key elements in the full realization of our potential; they are the instruments through which we transmit our most cherished traditions and philosophy, and at the same time serve our community's cultural and social needs. This relationship between self-expression and cultural identity is one of the cornerstones of a community's survival. In this respect, your community reflects, in a dynamic way, what it means to be Canadian.

I am pleased that my Department, through the Native Citizens' Directorate, has been able to support your publication since its inception. I share in the pride of your management and writers on the resounding success of

Windspeaker and may you continue to serve as a model for others for many more years to come. My most heartfelt congratulations on six years of loyal service to your constituency and my best wishes for your future endeavours!

Sincerely,
Gerry Weiner

He said all the right words. Then the department he represented effectively killed the newspaper. I am happy to report that it has since been resurrected – at least intermittently. In 1997 *Windspeaker* was named one of the top Aboriginal North American newspapers by the Native American Journalists' Association.

Print publications have had to be resourceful in the face of such blows to their operation. *Kahtou,* the monthly newspaper that calls itself "The Voice of B.C. First Nations," for example, has chosen total self-sufficiency. Its masthead proudly asserts that it is published "as a private aboriginal business; Incorporation No. 425946, without assistance of government grant. *Kahtou* news is wholly supported by subscribers and advertising ... *Kahtou* news is politically non-aligned. Published material does not necessarily reflect the views of the publisher or staff. Submissions of written material, photographs and art are vigorously encouraged."

In addition to constituting an important literacy source, as discussed in Chapter 2, northern newspapers and magazines provide an important forum. In political campaigns they have often been the sole source of information on candidates. They print First Nations meeting notices, clan announcements, events coverage, campaign advertisements, columns for political dialogue, candidate forums, opinion pieces, and letters to editors on a scale unknown in the urban South. There are numerous, creative efforts to strengthen and maintain these media. The costs are enormous. Staff overwork and burnout are reported almost universally. Some editors research, write, edit, and sell ads to keep their publications alive, taking severe salary cuts or working on a voluntary basis while funding searches are pending. Their hardships are increased by the high cost of northern living.

The number and range of publications are striking (see the list in Appendix D). While not all of these publications will survive the various funding cuts and continuing difficulties, most are hanging on. Especially in the case of magazines, a number of publications cover all of the Canadian North. Most newspapers include news from across the North, beyond their particular home base, especially where major developments are concerned. It remains to be seen whether Nunavut will catch up with Greenland (the only other region with an Inuit majority home rule government), which today has two national Aboriginal newspapers – *Atuagagdliutit* (a weekly) and *Sermitsiak* (published twice weekly) – and several local weeklies.

KAHTOU
The Voice of B.C. First Nations

VOLUME 5 NUMBER 3   Newstand Price $ 1.00   MARCH 1996

HISTORY ^{IN} _{THE} MAKING

Nisga'a Initial Agreement-in-Principle.

B.C. Citizens are being asked, "Is it a good deal for B.C.?"

OF COURSE IT IS! .... It is a good deal, is the answer by all citizens who want to see justice done. They say, "First Nations people have been abused for over three hundred years." The resolution is visible, Aboriginal Affairs Minister John Cashore had his Team working overtime to honour the principles of the Canadian Constitution but now interest groups of the dominant society is attempting to reverse the situation by calling the Nisga'a Deal a sell out by the NDP Government. The citizens of B.C. should be applauding the February 15, 1996 Agreement-in-Principle initialling by the three parties; Canada, Nisga'a and the Province of British Columbia. It's taken the Nisga'a People almost a century to get the Federal and Provincial governments into the same room to resolve the Aboriginal Rights and Title Question and now they are in the final stages of their long journey home. The Nisga'a People at home ratified the agreement. Now the public will be called to scrutinize the Agreement-in-Principle.

Those few moments with Chief Gosnell; Sim'oogit, sitting in the empty conference room contemplating what happened over the past - since 1793 when

Captain Vancouver first made contact with his people in the Nisga'a Territory to our present day, makes one wonder at the man, in my eyes as I sat with him, I watched him and listened, he spoke softly, with meaning in every word as he explained their progress. His anticipation to get on with the negotiations showed clearly he was in charge. He arrived early. He and his Team of Negotiators had to stick to the plan they started over a hundred years ago. A consensus was in the air, the government cannot delay justice to the Nisga'a People.

If they came to a point of ratification by the three parties, it would be just the beginning for his people. Chief Gosnell knew it wasn't going to be easy from here on in. I could only come to one conclusion - Chief Joe Gosnell is a great man

Frank Calder; 1990 Nisga'a Tribal Council President **emeritus** said, "What we are telling Canada is to recognize us as equals, and that we are the original peoples of this land. Our language, our culture, our title to our land must be explicitly entrenched in the Constitution. Canada's Constitution cannot be complete until this has taken place."

Royal Proclamation of 1763 - A proclamation by King George 3rd, that required the colonial authorities of Britain to aquire land from natives through purchase; and to prohibit the molestation of any native people on their lands by settlers.

The Nisga'a Tribal Council were always prepared to what had to be done to accomplish this enormouis task. They never ever gave up.

The fruits of their labour will result in the official signing ceremony BY ALL THREE PARTIES; CANADA, NISGA'A & BRITISH COLUMBIA AT NEW AIYANSH ON MARCH 25, 1996. △

Feb. 7, 1996 - Nisga'a Chief Joe Gosnell; Sim'oogit, arrives at the Parkhill Place hotel early to meet friends before beginning the first day of this round of negotiations. Pictured here he has a quiet meeting —with Stan Dixon of Kahtou. The two men entered the empty conference room and chatted quietly of the aspirations of the Nisga'a People.

KAHTOU
thought

God does not deduct from man's given span the time he spends fishing.

INSIDE			
K'watamus Speaks	2	The Talking Stick	13
Letters to the Editor	4	Tribal Police	16
First Nations Health	8	Kahtou Calendar	17
Beverley O'Neil	9	Chilliwack Pow-Wow	19
Province Walks	10	Happenings	20

Kahtou is published in Sechelt, British Columbia, by K'watamus Publications. It is wholly supported by advertising and subscribers.

Northern Journalists: Life on the Margins

The development of northern communications long preceded the creation of networks for northern communicators, who – for obvious reasons – seldom encountered each other. When the Native Journalists' Association (NJA) was founded in 1993, its members had every intention of including northern Aboriginal journalists. The election of Abraham Tagalik – Television Northern Canada chair and the director of network programming for the Inuit Broadcasting Corporation in Iqaluit – to the NJA board of directors formalized the new organization's northern connection. However, the reality is that many Aboriginal journalists were unable to attend the founding meeting at Six Nations, in southern Ontario, and the formidable travel costs and distances rendered northern Aboriginal journalists even more removed from NJA's meetings. At the time of this writing, NJA appears to have disbanded, with many of its members absorbed into the US-based Native American Journalists' Association (NAJA), a well-organized and active association but one that remains far removed from northern journalists' home ground. Native Alaskans and northern Canadians have a hard time getting to the important networking, information, and skills sessions featured at the NAJA conferences.

Within the broader community of journalists, all northern journalists – whatever their backgrounds, locations, or cultures – are similarly marginalized with respect to membership and participation in the Canadian Association of Journalists (CAJ). Given the realities of membership and cost, neither organization is likely to change its practice of holding its annual meetings in major urban centres. And, by southern standards, there are no major urban centres in northern Canada.

The 1998 NAJA conference included a much-discussed session on the relationship between Aboriginal publications and First Nations governments, a year after Alaska's *Tundra Times* (nominated for a Pulitzer Prize under the leadership of its founder, Howard Rock) ceased publication. Lael Morgan attributes the demise of *Tundra Times* to a drop in credibility, circulation, and advertising that reflected the paper's focus on "public relations handouts" and its policy of allowing "only positive news about native people" (Morgan 1998, 33-4). Morgan's assumptions should not be read uncritically. He maintains that 80 percent of the content of *Tundra Times* was public relations-based, but this figure is based on a 1989 study and needs to be updated. Moreover, there is no evidence correlating "positive" news with poor circulation. In fact, Morgan's comparison of the *Times*'s "public relations" coverage with the non-Native, Pulitzer-winning studies in the *Anchorage Daily News* of the "native suicide rate and alcohol abuse" hits a sore spot. In private discussions, tribal editors, writers, and publishers have complained that non-Native journalists sometimes win prizes for "mostly negative," inadequately researched portrayals of Native American people, issues, and communities.

Yet there are problems within indigenous media as well. In an article titled "Sometimes Big Brother Is Your Brother," Miles Morrisseau expresses his concern about the "dangerous control Aboriginal organizations have over the [Aboriginal] media" (Morrisseau 1998, 9). He cites two examples: the control by the Union of Ontario Indians, an association of Ontario chiefs, of the Ontario-wide magazine, *Anishnaabek News;* and the Assembly of First Nations' (AFN) sponsorship of a national magazine, *AFN Voices*. Morrisseau comments that both are "the equivalent of the federal government controlling CBC or CNN" (ibid., 9). In making this comparison, he avoids addressing the reality that, in many ways, Ottawa and Washington *do* control at least significant aspects of those media outlets. His concern is certainly valid, but the comparison is misplaced. So is the assumption by many people that simply going "private" will solve the problem of control. Advertisers eliminate the problem of government-run media but bring new concerns about their own efforts to control content and presentation, and sometimes even the journalists themselves.

A group of Native people in Ontario is looking at ways to avoid the dual traps of government funding and advertising. Native News Network of Canada (NNNC) was founded in 1990 by a group of journalists (notably its first president, Bud White Eye) and a handful of volunteers. It grew out of the London, Ontario, Native Writers' Circle, which for a time met regularly at the N'Amerind Friendship Centre. Today, NNNC is incorporated and affiliated with the Native American Journalists' Association and has begun to market print and radio stories. It has a home base at Ohsweken (Six Nations), a donated office at the University of Western Ontario, and a link with Smoke Signals First Nations radio, hosted by Dan Smoke-Asayenes and Mary Lou Smoke-Asayenes Kwe.

From the beginning, the goal was to avoid the agony of dependence on government funding. NNNC has received small grants, individual donations, and modest revenues from bingo and other fundraisers, and from story fees. As subscribers increase, it is hoped that they will sustain the network. The present reality is that the editors and reporters must survive on jobs outside of journalism, or on freelance work for non-Aboriginal news media, and the service is not a full wire service.

In 1997 I was asked to write a statement of principles for NNNC, in consultation with the president and directors, which would reflect its members' priorities and ethical concerns. To prepare, we reviewed hundreds of codes and statements from journalism organizations around the world. In some respects, the NNNC reflects other codes and statements of principles. In other ways, it represents a significant departure from conventional journalistic practice – for example, in seeing the journalist as a citizen and member of the community rather than as a politically pure, neutral bystander. The complete text of the statement of principles is included in Appendix A.

NNNC is one of the media organizations that emerged in the years following the establishment of the Aboriginal Communications Societies (described below) and the early years of Aboriginal broadcasting in the North. If it continues to develop, it may eventually strengthen links between and among the various societies. The following sketch of the evolution of politics and communications in the provincial and territorial North will help to set the stage for viewing current trends and forecasting future developments.

Northern Broadcasting and the Aboriginal Communications Societies

Broadcasting is the best known of the northern communications media. In fact, when people speak of northern communications, they usually refer to television or radio. For one thing, broadcast projects have received the most consistent commitment from government funding sources and have tended to be more durable than print programs. Nevertheless, it's important to remember that what we think of as northern broadcasting was not always in or of the North.

The first northern broadcast services originated in other regions and were provided *to* the North. These "northern" programs were produced by Outsiders and often had little bearing on the everyday lives of northern people. Some of the programming was paternalistic and offensive. Some was merely southern focused and irrelevant. Gradually, services became more relevant to northerners. And northerners became increasingly involved in producing their own programming and less dependent on people and services from Outside.

Northern broadcasting and communications policy continues to be dominated by ironies and contradictions. Canada's leadership role continues, but it is jeopardized by waning government funding and challenged by improvements to services to remote communities and first peoples in other countries. Northern broadcasting has been marked by a volatile funding situation in which services are alternately provided and removed, expanded and cut. Like northern politics, northern broadcasting is an eclectic mix of the global and the local, and everything in between. Northern listeners and viewers can access an array of radio and television ranging from high-budget regional, national, and international programming to low-budget local programming.

Back when Canada's current prime minister, Jean Chrétien, was minister of Indian Affairs, he produced the 1969 White Paper, a policy paper proposing the removal of the special status for Aboriginal people that had been constitutionally entrenched in the Indian Act. Among the unintended consequences was the rapid development of Aboriginal communications. The White Paper served to unite Aboriginal peoples and strengthen their efforts to lobby for provincial and territorial Aboriginal organizations (Valaskakis 1990, 18). As the organizations emerged they began immediately to set up communications branches. In many cases these branches of the regional organizations soon became full-fledged communications societies, and in 1974 the federal government set up a program to support Aboriginal communications.

The formal start of northern broadcasting originated with the emergence of a specialized northern service provided by Canada's national broadcaster, the Canadian Broadcasting Corporation (CBC). CBC Northern Service – designed to serve the special needs of the northern communities from studios in Whitehorse, Yellowknife, and Iqaluit – was created in 1958 and fully launched in 1960. Twenty years later, in 1980, the Thérrien Report, prepared for the CRTC, linked communications to the preservation of Aboriginal languages and cultures (CRTC 1980). The report set the stage for a new era in Aboriginal broadcasting, not only in Canada but throughout the world. As we approach the millennium, Canadian programs and policies on Aboriginal broadcasting continue to establish international precedents and to inspire indigenous projects in many regions and countries.

In 1983 Canada launched its Northern Broadcasting Policy and Northern Native Broadcast Access Program (NNBAP), supported by a commitment from the federal government to fund thirteen northern Aboriginal communications societies with $40.3 million over four years. Some of the societies were already in place and were simply incorporated into the new framework and given additional funding. Most of the societies were located in the North. Their mandate was to serve Aboriginal communities across Canada, with a concentration on service to remote and underserviced areas. Linked after 1986 to an umbrella organization, the National Aboriginal Communications Society (NACS) – originally located in Ottawa – they would become regional umbrella organizations for the creation of radio, television, and print media services to the communities of each society's region. Although radio was the centrepiece of most of the societies, they evolved into comprehensive communications service units, consolidating and coordinating print, radio, and television programming. Over time each of the societies has developed its own priorities and personality.

Within two years of announcing its funding of the Aboriginal communications societies – when most of them had their programming well under way – the government had reneged on its commitment. This was only the first wave of what would become an apparently endless series of funding cutbacks to Aboriginal communications programs by the federal Secretary of State. The cutbacks left in their wake a major upheaval in northern communications.

Map 3.1

Native communications societies of Canada

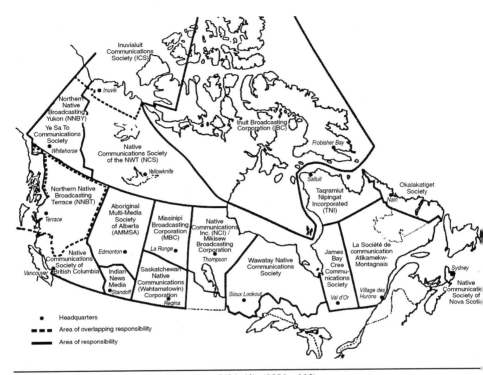

Source: Adapted from Lougheed and Associates 8/86; Alia (1991a, 115).

A year after the first cutbacks, in 1986, the National Aboriginal Communications Society was founded. Later that year, Aboriginal groups were stunned by a second wave of federal funding cutbacks. These cutbacks were all the more devastating – and, to some, simply incomprehensible – because they coincided with the Task Force on Broadcasting Policy's report (the Caplan-Sauvageau Report), which strongly supported Aboriginal broadcasting. But, as earlier discussions of cutbacks to print programs make clear, the NNBAP cutbacks were not an isolated incident of government inconsistency in the framing of Northern communications policy and funding.

In 1990 NACS moved its headquarters from Ottawa north to Lac La Biche, Alberta, to save money (Dahl 1990b). What follows is a discussion of the original societies, with information on closures or suspensions where available. The information was gathered from 1990 to 1997 and updated wherever possible in 1998. Nevertheless, inconsistencies and fluctuations abound in the data obtainable and all figures are of necessity approximate.

Serving northern Alberta (see Map 3.1), the Aboriginal Multi-Media Society of Alberta (AMMSA), based in Edmonton, was incorporated in 1983. In addition to publishing the newspaper *Windspeaker,* which managed to survive the 1990 budget cuts, the society produces a daily three-hour radio program in Cree and English on CFWE-FM. The society has a training facility and a community radio station and produces programming for both television and radio.

The Inuit Broadcasting Corporation (IBC), founded in 1981, covers the Northwest Territories, Nunavut, Labrador, and northern Quebec (called Nunavik by Inuit). The IBC has transmitted its programming over the CBC northern network since 1982 for radio and television broadcasts in English and Inuktitut. In 1991 it launched a TVNC uplink. The IBC has offices in Ottawa and studios in Iqaluit.

The Inuvialuit Communications Society (ICS) was founded in 1976 as Inuit Okangit Inumgun and reorganized in 1984 under its present name. Based in Inuvik, in the Beaufort district of the Northwest Territories, it publishes the newspaper *Tusaayaksat* in English and the Seglit dialect of Inuvialuktun. It also produces two half hours of Inuvialuit- and English-language television programming a week: *Tamapta,* on culture and entertainment; and *Suangaan,* a business and current affairs show. ICS lost its complete annual grant of $106,000 from the federal government in March 1990.

Based in Lake Mistissini, Quebec, and serving the northern part of that province, the James Bay Cree Communications Society has published the quarterly newspaper *Cree Ajemoon* since 1973. Originally under the Cree Regional Authority but now independent of that control, the society started television production in 1990 and also has seven community radio stations, in Chisasibi, Eastmain, Mistassini, Waskaganish, Wemindji, Whapmagoostui, Waswanipi. The Cree Regional Network in Mistassini produces eleven hours of cultural and public affairs programs in Cree each week. These are sent to Montreal through uplink, fed by telephone line to CBC Northern Quebec Services, and rebroadcast to northern Quebec Cree.

The Missinipi Broadcasting Corporation (MBC) reaches forty-two communities in northern Saskatchewan with six full-time and two part-time staff. Based in La Ronge, Saskatchewan, it produces cultural and current affairs radio programs broadcast in Cree and Dene. It has been subject to funding cuts since its founding in 1984.

Serving 23,000 people in twenty-three communities, the Native Communications Society of the NWT (NCS) is based in Yellowknife. It published *Native Press* and the *Press Independent. Native Press* was launched in 1971 by the Indian Brotherhood of the NWT (precursor to NCS) and later replaced by the *Press Independent.* It was revived as a quarterly in 1996 with the earlier name reinstated. The Communications Society was founded in 1976, and now broadcasts twelve hours of programming a day on CKNM radio, which also has seven live hour-long community-access programs on the weekend, broadcast in English, Dogrib, North Slavey, South Slavey, Chipewyan, and Gwich'in.

Native Communications Incorporated (NCI) was founded in 1971 and later took over the Mikisew Broadcasting Corporation, which was established in 1984. Based in Thompson, Manitoba, NCI covers northern Manitoba, serving 80,000 Cree and Oji-Cree people. With its staff of twenty-five to thirty, the society produces over twenty hours of radio as well as one and a half hours of television each week. It broadcasts its programming – music, news, and profiles – in Cree and English on the CBC northern satellite.

Founded in 1985, Northern Native Broadcasting Terrace (NNBT) is based in Terrace, British Columbia, and covers the northern region of that province. It produces community radio programming: fourteen hours a week over the province's CBC network and private radio, and ten hours on local CBC-AM. Programs specialize in public affairs, news, and music, including a program featuring Native musicians. NNBT serves 60,000 status and non-status Indian people in twenty-six communities. A 16 percent budget cut in 1990 halted a satellite distribution project to add twenty more communities and forced NNBT to seek increased advertising.

With its staff of twenty, Northern Native Broadcasting Yukon (NNBY) reaches twelve communities on CHON-FM. Despite having its translators cut in 1990 and being forced to air commercials to stay afloat, CHON-FM broadcasts in English, Southern Tutchone, Northern Tutchone, Gwich'in, Kaska, and Tlingit with twelve hours of programming a day, five days a week. NEDAA is NNBY's television service and also the name of its capstone program, distributed over TVNC. NEDAA-TV produces documentaries as well as a weekly half-hour magazine. NNBY operates a recording studio from its radio facilities.

The Okalakatiget Society, founded in 1982, is based in Nain, Labrador. It publishes *Kinatuinamot Ilengajuk* (To whom it may concern) in English and Inuktitut. Each week its radio network produces fifteen hours of current affairs, news, and cultural programming in English and Inuktitut. These programs are carried on a network of community stations: Nain, Makkovik, Postville, Hopedale, Rigolet, and Happy Valley. Five hours of radio programming per week are broadcast to the Labrador coast over CBC Happy Valley/Goose Bay. The society's staff of twenty serves thirteen reserves and twelve non-status communities.

La Société de communication Atikamekw-Montagnais was founded in 1983 to improve media coverage of negotiations between Le Conseil Atikamekw-Montagnais and the Quebec and federal governments. Its network of community radio stations broadcasts twenty-two and a half hours a week in English, Montagnais, and Atikamekw. A staff of twenty-three work at its production centres in La Tuque and Sept-Îles and its main centre at Village des Hurons. Special programming has included the pope's 1984 visit as well as First Ministers' conferences.

Based in Dorval, Quebec, Taqramiut Nipingat Incorporated (TNI) was founded in the late 1970s, as part of Project Inukshuk (described in detail in Chapter 4). TNI, which broadcasts in Inuktitut, includes both radio and television. Its programming is rebroadcast from Iqaluit to Inuit in northern Quebec and the eastern Arctic.

The Wawatay Native Communications Society, based in Sioux Lookout, Ontario, originally rented trail radios to trappers. These were monitored from community bases as an emergency communications system. Founded in 1974, the society now publishes *Wawatay News,* a monthly newspaper, in English and Ojibway-Cree. Wawatay produces radio and television broadcasts in Cree and Oji-Cree, with two and a half hours a week distributed over TV Ontario transponder and radio programs distributed through twenty-six community radio stations in northern Ontario. There was a staff of fifty-seven before the 1990 cuts; numbers have fluctuated since then.

Not all communications societies are associated with the National Aboriginal Communications Society. The societies listed below function independently of NACS.

Indian News Media, which has been in continuous operation since 1968, is the oldest communications society. Based in Standoff, Alberta, it publishes the weekly *Kainai News.* Its subsidiaries include Eagle Graphics, Bull Horn Video, and a recording studio. Like so many other groups, its funding was cut in 1990.

Saskatchewan Native Communications (Wehtamatowin) Corporation was also founded in 1968. Based in Regina, it publishes *New Breed,* a monthly magazine for Métis, status, and non-status Indians. The society also has facilities for radio and video production.

Makivik Corporation is the economic development arm of the post-James Bay Agreement Inuit government. It is independent of federal and provincial government control and is run by Inuit of Nunavik. The corporation publishes the magazine *Makivik News.*

In Vancouver, the Native Communications Society of British Columbia was founded in 1983. It published *Kahtou,* which is now published in Sechelt by the Sechelt First Nation. On the other side of the country, the Native Communications Society of Nova Scotia published *Micmac News* out of Sydney from 1969 to 1990. Though it was founded earlier, it was officially organized under NACS in 1975. The paper folded after the Secretary of State cut its funding in 1990. *Micmac News* had actually originated in 1932; it disappeared and was revived in the 1960s and was later taken up by the Union of Nova Scotia Indians and published as a monthly, and was again revived under the Native Communications Society (Lougheed 1986).

Tewegan Communications, in Val d'Or, Quebec, was founded in 1984. It was originally attached to the James Bay Cree Communications Society but later challenged this link. With its staff of two, Tewegan produces two fifty-seven-minute Algonquin-language programs a week. It conducts a journalist-training program in Winneway, Quebec.

Based in Whitehorse, Yukon, the Ye Sa To Communications Society, formerly Thay Lun Lin Communications Society, was founded in 1974. It publishes *Dännzhà'* [7] and its summer supplement, *Shakat*. Publication of *Dännzhà'* was suspended in December 1990, but new issues of the magazine continue to appear intermittently.

There are two communications societies in the Northwest Territories not affiliated with NACS: the Inuit Radio Society, in Cambridge Bay, and Nits' Da Ko Radio Society, in Wha Ti (formerly Lac La Martre). The Cambridge Bay society is not currently operating.

All of these communications societies are part of a network of organizations providing constituency-based services to northern indigenous peoples. According to Roth, Canadian broadcasting policy has shifted from a "right-to-receive services" approach, which applied to all of Canada, including its remote regions, to a policy that "legally enshrines the broadcasting rights of three minority constituency groups: women, First Nations peoples, multicultural and multiracial communities ('visible minorities')" (Roth 1996, 73). Each of these groups is granted special status in the current (1991) Broadcasting Act. The act specifies the right of all Canadians to be fairly portrayed and equitably hired in public, private, and community broadcast media (Roth 1996).

As Roth reminds us, "Canada has a longstanding alternative tradition of 'constituency-based services,'" a term first used by Liora Salter (Roth 1996, 73; Salter 1980). These services have continued to grow. As of 1996 the following constituency-based services were available nation-wide: eight "ethnic" radio stations (a term in wide use, despite its misleading implication that "ethnicity" refers only to non-white, non-anglophone, or non-francophone people), four "ethnic" television stations, thirteen northern regional Aboriginal communications societies affiliated with NACS plus several other unaffiliated ones, 117 First Nations community radio stations, fifty-seven non-Aboriginal community radio stations, twenty-six university and college campus-based radio stations, and the dedicated Northern satellite transponder service known as Television Northern Canada (TVNC), which provides Aboriginal- and English-language programming to ninety-four Arctic and sub-Arctic communities (Roth 1996, 9). In addition, the national all-news network of CBC Newsworld and the national faith network, Vision-TV, provide regular time slots for programming produced by the Disability Network group, and closed-captioning service is widely available on all Canadian channels.

Canada's strong tradition of promoting communications for minority constituencies has meant, above all, the creation of the world's most extensive and highly developed collection of Aboriginal radio services. Many pioneering radio projects were developed in the North. These days the northern project best covered in the mainstream southern press is Television Northern Canada (TVNC). As well, there is much excitement about TVNC in the northern press and in Aboriginal newspapers north and south. While the excitement is certainly justified, the attention sometimes obscures the fact that northern radio is still the dominant medium and is likely to continue to be so in the foreseeable future.

Radio journalists like to point out that their medium engages the imagination of the listener and requires more creativity in scene setting and scene painting than any other. Print media have access to photographs and other visual representations to supplement the text; television makes everything explicit. Radio is also the most affordable medium in terms of both production and community access. The next section sketches the history of northern radio in Canada and the other circumpolar nations.

Northern Radio
Radio broadcasting in Canada began in the 1920s and reached the North soon thereafter. One of the early broadcasters, Bill Anderson, says that before 1958 "radio in the North was simply a 'sometimes' thing. There'd be an

J.D. Soper took this photograph of himself and David Wark broadcasting at Cape Dorset in 1928, thirty years before the official arrival of northern radio and the development of IBC and the CBC Northern Service.

occasional programme on shortwave from southern Canada or Russia, or programmes put together by people with amateur sets, but for the most part there was nothing – certainly nothing in the daytime" (McNeil and Wolfe 1982, 112).

Before the advent of CBC Northern Service, non-indigenous northerners organized community volunteer stations. Bush pilots sometimes added "a little programme of news about things they had picked up in their travels" to the information transmitted over their radios. Dawson City, Yukon, was one of the first northern communities to have radio, when it arrived along with a branch of the Royal Canadian Corps of Signals (McNeil and Wolfe 1982, 112).

In the 1940s and 1950s Canada and the United States collaborated on a continuing series of projects aimed at strengthening sovereignty, services, and security in the North. Although there was some pretence of equality in this relationship, it was obviously affected by the inherent power imbalance between the two countries. That pattern continues today, with the American superpower continuing to maintain a strong presence in the "Canadian" North. Whatever the methods and motives, these joint activities established weather stations, signal stations, and air-defence posts across the North. They greatly enhanced the potential for effective communication services to northerners, as well as benefiting Ottawa and Washington and providing barriers against perceived or potential enemies.

Although they were not always acknowledged in the accounts of non-Aboriginals such as Bill Anderson, Aboriginal broadcasters were part of communications development from the start. In the 19 January 1996 edition of his *Nunatsiaq News* column – called, with deceptive simplicity, "My Little Corner of Canada" – John Amagoalik saluted "pioneers like Elijah Menarik and Ann Pudlo from the early days of radio in Canada's North [and] Jonah Kelly who has lived the history of radio in the Arctic" (Amagoalik 1996b, 9). He also mentions the singer-songwriter William Tagoona, who is a long-time broadcaster for CBC Northern Service, and the artist and writer Alootook Ipellie.

Amagoalik argues that such Aboriginal pioneers saw radio as a way to promote indigenous language, culture, cultural literacy, and traditions (1996b, 9). These good intentions were not universally shared by those promoting the development of northern broadcasting. A 1931 advertisement for Burgess batteries, for example, reveals a great deal about southern attitudes toward the North – and northern radio. Headlined "Arctic Nights aren't so lonely now!" the advertisement tells the readers of *CNR Magazine* that "Burgess aids the northward course of civilization" by aiding radio – "the marvel of the age" – in "breaking the centuries-old silence of the Arctic." Below the headline is a photograph of an Inuk boy and girl at Pond Inlet, listening with headphones to a concert via radio. Far from promoting indigenous traditions, then, northern broadcasting is seen as a tool to "civilize" the Aboriginal North. In this context, it is no coincidence that the picture accompanying this message is of Inuit, not non-Aboriginal northerners. The advertisement, for batteries produced in Winnipeg and Niagara Falls, is directed to Outside consumers. It represents the North as an alien locale, removed from the rest of Canada: "In the far north – and *here at home,* Burgess gives longer and better service" (my italics).

Arctic Nights
arent so lonely now!

Photo courtesy Canadian Westinghouse Co., Ltd. and Hudsons Bay Co.

BURGESS aids the northward course of civilization

RADIO . . . the marvel of the age . . . is breaking the centuries-old silence of the Arctic. No trading post or mounted police station is now considered fully equipped without a receiving set.

Burgess Chrome-built Batteries, the better radio batteries with the familiar black and white stripes, are serving Canada's northland just as efficiently as they serve radio listeners in older parts of the Dominion.

This photograph, taken at a post at Pond's Inlet on Baffin Land, shows Eskimos listening in to a concert, through the aid of Burgess Batteries.

Here again Burgess leads. In the Arctic there is no store "just around the corner". The hardy pioneers choose all their supplies and equipment carefully. Because of their superior performance, staying power and all-round dependability Burgess Batteries meet the exacting requirements. In the far north—and here at home, Burgess gives longer and better service.

BURGESS BATTERY COMPANY
Niagara Falls, Ontario

BURGESS DRY CELLS, LIMITED
Winnipeg, Man.

"Arctic Nights aren't so lonely now!"

Such views notwithstanding, northern radio developed quickly. Today, in addition to national, regional, and international programming carried over the outlets of CBC Northern Service, northern radio includes northern, regional, and local programming on CBC and an array of private and public, Aboriginal and non-Aboriginal stations. Some northern radio remains close to its roots in the survival-oriented efforts of amateur operators working in limited broadcast areas. It includes informally run single-community stations, pirate stations, and ham and citizens' band networks. Despite the North's leading role in utilizing the most highly sophisticated new broadcast technologies, and all the futuristic and rapid changes, the North remains the home of intimate broadcasting, informal experimentation, and "trail radio."

Radio has been called the most grassroots of all news media. It is well adapted to oral cultures and nomadic life. Radio – particularly what has been labelled "talk radio" – provides a forum for social and political dialogue, especially in areas where people are often scattered, with some people out on the land and others remaining in the communities. In the historic 1999 election of Nunavut's first territorial government, community radio and the phone-in shows it features were a major campaign issue at Cambridge Bay, which currently has no radio of its own. According to Conway Jocks, the founder and former station manager of CKRK-FM in the Mohawk First Nation of Kahnawake, Quebec, "talk radio forges the communication links in ethnic neighbourhoods, small towns and aboriginal communities from the farthest Arctic coasts to the outskirts of major Canadian cities, sending hundreds of languages through the air" (Jocks 1996, 174). As a former talk-show host, he is especially interested in the connectedness and intimacy this medium brings to people who live in small and/or remote communities. He says that "phone-in shows are lively extended family affairs."

Although southern Canada and most of the United States experience talk radio as an AM phenomenon, Jocks says AM is not a player in the more remote regions. In First Nations communities, "FM, easier and cheaper to build, is king, followed by trail radio, sometimes called 'moccasin telegraph'" (Jocks 1996, 174). Sometimes radio is more than a symbolic link between people. "During the summer crisis of 1990 [at Kanehsatake], CKRK-FM in blockaded Kahnawake was the sole connection with the outside, and as such was an important link between the communities" (Jocks 1996, 180).

For Aboriginal communities, radio is sometimes a medium of survival and is almost always the primary medium of linguistic and cultural continuity: "First Nations stations regularly broadcast in their own language as a matter of course. In those communities where the language is threatened, Native-language programs become the star attraction to their listeners" (Jocks 1996, 180).

Gjoa Haven, Hudson's Bay post with radio mast, early 1940s.

The 1960s were a time of cultural renaissance throughout the circumpolar North, and especially in Greenland and Canada. In Canada, the start of both northern Aboriginal radio and northern Aboriginal-language broadcasting can be traced to 1960, with the airing of the first Aboriginal-language radio program. It was broadcast in Inuktitut by CBC Northern Service via shortwave, rebroadcast to the North out of CBC's studios in Montreal. A year later, Inuit in the eastern Arctic began their own regular radio broadcasts. Although community radio formally arrived in Inuit communities in 1961, radio was in evidence much earlier (see, for example, the early 1940s radio facilities at Gjoa Haven depicted here). In 1967 the "Frontier Package" brought radio into communities in the western Arctic (Valaskakis 1990, 17), and Kenomadiwin Radio was launched in northern Ontario, with its broadcasts originating in a travelling van.

In 1970 the Native Communications Society of Nova Scotia was founded and the Alberta Native Communications Society received funding from the federal government. Both societies operated radio services. A year later, the Northern Pilot Project set up Aboriginal radio experimental projects in

Keewatin (NWT) and northern Ontario, with funding from the federal Department of Communications. Also in 1971, CRTC licences were granted to community radio stations in several Inuit and other First Nations communities. The federal government continued its project of strengthening northern and Aboriginal communications with the creation of the Native Communications Programme (NCP) in 1973, the same year it launched the CBC northern television service. In 1974 the Wawatay Native Communications Society began operating radio and producing print media in northern Ontario. The Inuit Broadcasting Corporation (IBC) was founded in 1981 and officially launched in 1982. Some of its units preceded the official start date. The unit at Salluit, northern Quebec (Nunavik), established in 1978, was the "first native-language radio production facility in the Arctic. It began distribution by mailing copies of its programs to other stations, to be used at their discretion" (Giuliani 1983, 17). When IBC began operating, it provided both radio and television broadcasts and became the first Aboriginal television network. Satellite radio service in the NWT and Yukon also started in 1981.

As Aboriginal broadcasting was emerging in the Canadian North, Greenland was also enjoying its own communications revolution, which featured a Kalaallit (Greenlandic Inuit) cultural renaissance. After an early history dominated by Danes, radio programs by the 1950s were broadcast in both Danish and Greenlandic. Hans Lynge recalls that "the radio broadcasts quickly became as necessary a part of life as food" (quoted in Stenbaek-Lafon 1982, 41). In 1978, a year before the official launch of Greenland Home Rule, Kalaallit-Nunaata Radioa (KNA) became an associate member of the European Broadcasting Union, thus legitimizing Aboriginal Greenlandic radio and television in the eyes of European broadcasters. It established exchange programs with Faroe Islands Radio, Radio Iceland, and CBC Northern Service. "It is a measure of its importance to Greenland's cultural, educational and political life that Kalaallit-Nunaata Radioa was one of the first institutions to come under Home Rule jurisdiction on 1 January 1980" (Stenbaek-Lafon 1982, 45).

Today, KNR has its headquarters in Nuuk (the capital) and regional offices in Qaqortoq and Ilulissat. It broadcasts a daily radio newscast from a station in Copenhagen for Greenlanders living in Denmark. KNR's television service is linked to Danmarks Radio (DR), Danish public radio, which distributes its newscasts throughout Greenland via satellite. Greenland also has a handful of privately owned radio and television stations. KNR hopes eventually to provide most of its programming in Greenlandic. The number of radio programs in Greenlandic increased from 2,454 in 1989 to 2,613 in 1995. In the same period, television programming showed a more striking shift, from 126 Greenlandic-language programs in 1989 to 239 in 1995 (Statistics Greenland 1997, 121).

Elsewhere in the Arctic, Aboriginal broadcasting is slowly emerging. In Bethel, Alaska, KYUK-AM – the first Native American-owned and -operated radio station in the United States – began broadcasting in 1971. Its television service, KYUK-TV, was launched in 1973. The founding of KYUK originated in the conditions of the Alaskan bush. "The region had no electronic media [of its own] and could not reliably receive transmissions from elsewhere" (Smith and Cornette 1998, 29). KYUK radio and television are the only stations broadcasting in the Yup'ik language and the only Inuit (Alaskan Eskimo) television news service in the United States (*Whitehorse Star* 1991, 6). Despite lively productions, enthusiastic audiences, and the continuing need for media outlets in the state, the government of Alaska "has been steadily reducing its commitment to public broadcasting in the state, to both Native and non-Native stations." Rural Native stations "with few other options for raising money feel the squeeze most acutely" (Smith and Cornette 1998, 31).

Not all northern community radio is run by, or for, Aboriginal people. The official launching of CFRT-FM 107.3, the francophone community radio station in Iqaluit, by l'Association francophone d'Iqaluit took place on 18 March 1994. The announcement, carried in *Nunatsiaq News,* was published in French, English, and Inuktitut. Other community radio outlets, such as CKRW-AM in Whitehorse, broadcast exclusively in English and have a target audience of non-Aboriginal and Aboriginal anglophones. For a list of northern community radio, see Appendix C.

It is my hope that the journalism of the future will reflect and respect Canada's many cultures. I am convinced that the cause of inaccurate coverage is less ill-will than misplaced priorities, deadline-induced panic, inadequate research, and lack of education. Despite the proliferation of opinion pieces and features, old stereotypes persist. Despite growing awareness and increasing respect, non-Native journalists persist in presenting Aboriginal people and events as cross-cultural kitsch. While no news story can fully capture an event, accuracy requires that we research the cultural context. Sometimes, it also requires more than one voice. The combined voices of Aboriginal and non-Aboriginal, northern and southern journalists will help to increase accuracy and understanding.

Important changes are occurring. Aboriginal leaders now get news coverage. The North sometimes makes the news for political developments as well as celebrations or disasters. Major developments are sometimes placed on the front page or high in broadcast news lineups. However, overnight change means haste, and, however well intentioned, haste means carelessness. Despite many significant improvements, reporters and editors are still not doing all of their homework.

As we have seen, the development of northern communications has sometimes paralleled and sometimes diverged from the more general development of communication. The close ties between politicians and journalism still prevalent in today's North echo earlier, now rejected, practices in mainstream journalism. Links between print and broadcast media were established early on (and if we extend the meaning of "broadcasting" to oral presentations, are rooted in pre-electronic European and North American troubadour and street-corner news delivery). In northern communities, media that southerners might call "alternative" are often located in the journalistic mainstream. Our research showed that across the North television is considered the most deficient and radio the most successful and widely available of the news media. The success of northern Aboriginal print media varies with funding and literacy levels, and newspapers and magazines come and go with disconcerting frequency.

Although they are not the only Aboriginal communications organizations, and were sometimes predated by others, the thirteen Aboriginal communications societies that were formalized and funded by the federal government have been the linchpins of northern Aboriginal communications. Despite funding cutbacks, the societies continue to produce an array of programming, and most continue to sponsor both print and broadcast media outlets.

With its close connection to survival on the land and its grassroots, people-centred dialogue, radio will probably persist as the strongest of the media. Perhaps broadcasts will soon be accessed as often from computers in homes and community centres as from the more familiar radios. But radio itself will continue to thrive, and the most sophisticated new technologies will not readily supplant the ease or convenience of carrying one's portable radio on the land. The following chapter looks at the ways in which technologies are and are not altering the production and distribution of news in the North. Technology alone cannot guarantee progress.

4
Technology and the Circumpolar Village: Networking, Broadcasting, and Accessing the Future

> We now find ourselves in the middle of the age of communication ... the millennium is upon us and it seems at times we're more isolated than ever before. TV and computers are taking us further and further away from human contact. Yet, we yearn for human interaction ...
>
> Seventy-five years ago, we were all we had except for Saturday night radio. A hundred and fifty years ago, we were all we had. We must have been a hell of a lot more fascinating. We had to have been great storytellers. We certainly had a lot more time for each other ... No TV to keep us amused, or e-mail love to find a relationship. Yet, the amount of information we have at our finger tips is astounding. Access such as we have never had before ...
>
> I wonder about our existence in the future and what communication skills will be required to survive ... Can we live off our creativity and our ability to communicate?
>
> Gary Farmer, "Time in a Computer Chip"

Farmer's words of caution and inspiration infuse every aspect of *Aboriginal Voices,* the publication he founded and one that, despite his reservations, has a thriving Web page (see Appendix E). His concerns are heard widely in Aboriginal communities around the globe. But few people advocate avoiding the Internet or ignoring its potential power, especially in northern and remote communities. Instead, the trend is toward using that power to communicate the messages and languages of the senders clearly and carefully from community to community and from Aboriginal communities to the Outside. By the time this book is published, I suspect there will be as many new Web pages, e-mail addresses, and Web sites as are included in Appendix E.

While Gary Farmer struggles to find the proper balance between human and electronic contact from his informationally advantaged, urban home-base in Toronto, the founders of Nunavut are embracing new telecommunications technologies without hesitation. In 1996 the Nunavut Implementation Commission released a report about the role it hoped

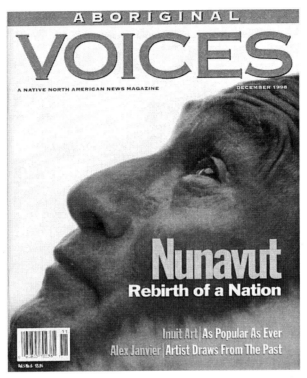

One of the most interesting publications, recently arrived
on the scene, is *Aboriginal Voices,* created and published by
the multi-talented, apparently endlessly energetic actor
and journalist, Gary Farmer.

telecommunications would play in the new territory. "The road to Nunavut
is along the information highway," they wrote (Bell 1996a, 16-7). In late
1999 Telesat Canada will launch the first in its new Nimiq satellite series,
featuring a technology capable of bringing televisions signals into every
Canadian home and paving the way for the proposed Canada-wide Aboriginal television network. The Nimiq satellites will be companions to the Anik
series, which continues with Telesat's announcement that it will launch the
sixth generation of Anik satellites in 2000. The digital telecommunications
network will create jobs for Nunavut citizens (a technician for each community as well as regional technologists and systems engineers), develop
and link libraries and databases, and establish a sophisticated videoconferencing system that will amount to an arm of government.

The unique conditions of northern life are ideally suited to such experimentation. While teleconferences cannot replace direct human contact, they
can certainly replace a good deal of the very difficult travel that stalls government processes and absorbs northern budgets. In Nunavut, futuristic

communications systems will help maintain the Inuit way of governing, with power broadly distributed and structures decentralized. The widely scattered, remote communities will be able to stay in touch without the dangers and delays experienced in the past. The system will allow members of the Legislative Assembly to attend meetings in their home communities without having to leave Iqaluit, or to attend caucus meetings in Iqaluit without having to leave their home communities.

Given sufficient funding and facilities, Nunavut's citizens will have greater access to each other and to government. And its well-developed videoconferencing system will reduce the enormous travel budget (in 1992-3, politicians in the government of the NWT spent $70 million on travel, about half of which was for Nunavut). As we have observed, northern travel not only absorbs funds but requires enormous expenditures of time because of the frequent delays caused by vagaries of weather and aging aircraft.

It is perhaps not surprising that the people of Nunavut are so comfortable travelling the information highway. They have long been well disposed to new technologies, having learned that new technologies could link with old ways and support an array of Inuit-run cultural literacy and communications projects. Indeed, they were among the first Canadians (and the first Aboriginal Canadians) to take television and radio into their own hands and to adapt television to their own needs.

As we have seen, representation on film has been replaced by a world in which film and television are partners. Before that could happen, broadcast programming and technology had to develop and reach a certain level of maturity. The following pages introduce some of the major milestones, challenges, and dilemmas facing northern Aboriginal people as they ease, and sometimes leap, into the technological future. After first considering the development of satellite television delivery and Aboriginal broadcasting, starting in the late 1960s, we look at the next stage – Television Northern Canada (TVNC) – which I and many others consider the most important achievement in Aboriginal communications in the world. TVNC is viewed in its international context, and a sketch is provided of kindred and sometimes connected projects such as Sámi broadcasting in Norway and Kalaallit broadcasting in Greenland.

The chapter also describes radio and telecommunications policy and addresses the impact of advertising on previously ad-free Aboriginal radio. It looks at radio and television as extensions of pre-broadcasting communications in "the circumpolar village," and considers two examples of the misuse of technology in promoting Aboriginal communications.

The Development of Northern Television
While most major northern television developments began in the early 1970s, there were important breakthroughs in the 1950s and '60s. CBC

Northern Service, also known as CBC North, was established, as we have seen, in 1958. The service was originally from a group of ten former military and community radio stations, plus a shortwave service based in Montreal. CBC Northern Service operates from the following regional headquarters: CBC Yukon in Whitehorse; CBC Mackenzie in Yellowknife; CBC Eastern Arctic (Nunavut) in Iqaluit; CBC Western Arctic in Inuvik; CBC Kivalliq in Rankin Inlet; CBC Kuujjuaq Bureau in Kuujjuaq; and CBC Northern Service Quebec in Montreal.

After getting its Northern Service radio broadcasts fully under way in 1960, the CBC Northern Service proceeded to develop its television service. As in the case of radio, early northern television was produced primarily by and for non-Aboriginal people. The "Frontier Package," composed of four-hour packages of television programs as well as radio, was carried to seventeen communities starting in 1967. Its main claim to northernness was its availability in one northern region. The programs were taped from CBC's southern service and rebroadcast in the North. It eventually extended to the eastern Arctic, starting in Frobisher Bay in 1972, but the Frontier Package continued to be a relay service bringing programming by and about southern Canadians to the North.

The 1970s were a time of rapid change in society and in communications. During this decade, CBC's objective was to provide radio and television transmitters for every community with a population of 500 or more. Additional coverage was furnished by the territorial governments and a number of other agencies and organizations, which provided relay transmitters for most of the smaller communities, so that CBC broadcasts now reached almost all of the Canadian North.

The arrival of satellite-transmitted television marked an international breakthrough: Canada became the first country to develop a domestic telecommunications satellite system. In 1969 the Telesat Canada Bill established the Anik satellite system, which made it possible to distribute radio and television signals live. Telesat sent the first satellite-transmitted broadcast to Canadians over the Hermes Anik A satellite in 1972, and in 1973 CBC used the satellite to transmit the first live television newscast to the North (Television Northern Canada 1987, 15). In 1975 the Nunatsiakmiut Community Television Society began broadcasting over the satellite from Frobisher Bay (now Iqaluit – the name was changed in 1987) with support from the National Film Board. CBC's stations in Whitehorse, Yellowknife, Inuvik, and Iqaluit were able to serve a network of transmitters within the region surrounding each of the host-station communities.

In response to extensive lobbying by Inuit organizations in the late 1970s and early 1980s, the federal Department of Communications developed the Anik B trial-access program – a series of interactive audio and video experiments. In 1976 the satellite carried an experimental interactive audio project across northern Quebec. Titled Naaklavik I, the project linked eight radio stations. It was run by the Aboriginal communications society Taqramiut Nipingat Incorporated (TNI), which at the time was affiliated with the land claims lobby group the Northern Quebec Inuit Association (Roth and Valaskakis 1989, 225).

In 1978 the Anik B satellite carried the launch of the programs initiated by Project Inukshuk, named for the human-form stone sculptures that Inuit use to mark important places on the land. The federally funded project heralded the start of Inuit-produced television broadcasts. It was sponsored and organized by Inuit Tapirisat of Canada (ITC), with video production facilities in Frobisher Bay and Baker Lake. The Inukshuk project had several goals: "to train Inuit film and video producers, to establish Inuit production centres in the North, and to conduct interactive audio/video experiments utilizing the 12/14 GHz capability of the satellite to link six Arctic settlements" (Roth and Valaskakis 1989, 225). When Inukshuk first went to air in 1980, it sent sixteen and a half hours a week of television programming and teleconferencing to the six communities. A parallel project, Naaklavik II, was organized for northern Quebec, and was run by TNI. Based in Salluit, it served five communities.

From the start, it was known that these two projects were short-term and would receive only seed money. There were strong lobbying efforts by ITC and TNI to establish a permanent Inuit broadcasting service. In 1979 CBC opened a new northern service production centre in Rankin Inlet to serve the Keewatin region. Montreal remained the base for satellite-delivered radio service to the James Bay region. In 1980 the CRTC struck a committee to consider proposals to develop satellite television services for northern and remote communities. The nine-member committee, headed by Réal Thérrien, included John Amagoalik, who would become the first Aboriginal person to help set national communications policy in Canada. The committee emphasized the role of broadcasting in preserving and maintaining Aboriginal languages and cultures (CRTC 1986b, 515). The committee identified "a new broadcasting universe" and wrote, "Our first unanimous conclusion is that immediate action must be taken to meet the needs of the many Canadians who believe that, as regards broadcasting, they are being treated as second-class citizens ... We cannot stress too strongly the immediacy of the problem: alternative television programming must be provided from Canadian satellites with no further delay" (CRTC 1980, 1).

In recognition of the CRTC's goal to ensure the distribution of more alternative programming to underserved areas, in 1981 Ottawa provided broadcast funding to both TNI and ITC. TNI used the funds to develop Inuktitut programming for northern Quebec, while ITC developed the Inuit Broadcasting Corporation (IBC), which produced radio and television, sharing a channel with CBC Northern Service on the Anik B satellite. Also in 1981, the CRTC licensed Canadian Satellite Communications Incorporated (CANCOM), a private satellite distribution service, with the stipulation that it make a significant commitment to providing Aboriginal programming. There were now two television distributors serving the North, CBC Northern Service and CANCOM (Roth 1996). In 1982 the Nunatsiakmiut Film Society, which was based in Frobisher Bay where it helped develop Inuit film and television, merged with IBC. Among the founders of the new amalgam was Joanasie Salamonie, one of the leaders who in 1971 had helped to establish the Inuit Tapirisat of Canada (ITC).[8]

Following the birth of the Northern Native Broadcast Access Program (NNBAP), there were complaints from the North that Inuit and other northerners had received short shrift from both satellite services, which gave priority to national and regional English network programming and often relegated IBC programming to late-night time slots or pre-empted it entirely (IBC 1985, 22). Ottawa's response was to strike a task force on broadcasting policy, which issued what became known as the Caplan-Sauvageau Report. It recommended CBC-produced Aboriginal-language broadcasts and a separate satellite system for the distribution of Aboriginal language programming (Canada 1986, 520-2).

The Aboriginal leadership criticized the report for using weak and ambiguous language, and in 1987 organized a meeting of all the northern Aboriginal communications societies to discuss the development of a dedicated satellite television channel (IBC 1985; TVNC 1987). They sought support from the federal government, the governments of Yukon and the Northwest Territories, and CBC Northern Service, which continued to share satellite space with the Aboriginal broadcast outlets. The communications societies issued a proposal for a non-profit corporation that would distribute, and eventually produce, programming by and for Aboriginal northerners. This proposal was to be realized with the creation of Television Northern Canada.

TVNC Enters – and Alters – the Picture

> At exactly 8:30 p.m., an Inuktitut voice signals the start of the world's largest aboriginal television network. Elder Akeeshoo Joamie of Iqaluit asks Jesus to guide TVNC to success. An English translation rolls slowly across the screen ...
>
> The vision of TVNC became a reality with a montage of Inuit, Dene, Métis, Gwich'in, Kaska, Tuchone, Tlingit and non-aboriginal faces beamed to 22,000 households from Northern Labrador to the Yukon-Alaska border ...

> TVNC is a non-profit consortium which aims to use television for social change.
>
> Lorraine Thomas, "Communicating across the Arctic"

When Television Northern Canada (TVNC) – a $10 million, federally funded dedicated satellite transponder service – began broadcasting via the Anik satellite system, it became the primary First Nations broadcasting distribution service in the North. TVNC now delivers programming in indigenous languages and English, sponsored by the governments of Yukon, NWT, and Nunavut, and by Arctic College and Yukon College, to over ninety-four communities from the Alaska-Yukon border to the Labrador coast, an area of 4.3 million square kilometres. (See Appendix F for a list of current TVNC broadcast sites.)

TVNC was incorporated 18 June 1990 as a non-profit corporation and licensed by the CRTC on 28 October 1991 to serve the Canadian North by "broadcasting cultural, social, political and educational programming to Canada's Native people," as its promotional literature says. The new network was heralded in both the northern and southern press. The *Ottawa Citizen* splashed the news, with three photographs, across most of a page, with the headline "Canada's Third National Network? TV Northern Canada is television by the North, about the North – and for the North" (Atherton 1991). The *Globe and Mail* gave the story more modest play in its National

Satellite dish at Pangnirtung, Nunavut. Satellite dishes like this one bring an array of international programming, and TVNC, to northern communities.

News section with the rather quiet headline "North Channels Its Resources." The reporter was more enthusiastic than the headline writers: "The network is the realization of a dream of many northerners to have a northern-produced alternative to the largely southern TV programming now coming into their homes" (Platiel 1992, A5). Three days after the *Globe and Mail* published the story by Native affairs reporter Rudy Platiel, the *Winnipeg Free Press* ran an almost identical story credited to Canadian Press, with a Toronto dateline. The *Winnipeg Free Press* gave it a more enthusiastic headline: "Nation's First Northern TV Network Launched Today" (Canadian Press 1992, C29) but buried it near the bottom of the major stories on one of its arts pages. The northern presses gave the story more prominence, usually on the front page. "TVNC Hits the Air," said the Yellowknife-based weekly *News/North* (Saunders 1991).

TVNC was funded by the federal Department of Communications and is distributed via the Anik E1 satellite, with television uplink facilities in Iqaluit, Yellowknife, and Whitehorse. Its membership includes the Inuit Broadcasting Corporation; Inuvialuit Communications Society; Northern Native Broadcasting Yukon; Okalakatiget Society; Taqramiut Nipingat Incorporated; Native Communications Society of the NWT; Government of the Northwest Territories; Yukon College; and the National Aboriginal Communications Society. There are also associate members: CBC Northern Service; Kativik School Board; Labrador Community College; Northern Native Broadcasting Terrace; Wawatay Native Communications Society; and Telesat Canada.

TVNC serves approximately 100,000 people, roughly equally divided between Aboriginal and non-Aboriginal ancestry. The region's Aboriginal languages served by TVNC programming are Inuktitut, Inuvialuktun, Chipewyan, Dogrib, North and South Slavey, Cree, Gwich'in, Han, Kaska, Tagish, Northern and Southern Tutchone, and Tlingit. The vision of TVNC founders included a fully pan-Arctic and Canada-wide network that promises to greatly enhance the opportunities for north-south communication. In 1998 TVNC petitioned the CRTC to become a national Aboriginal television service, and in 1999 received permission to become the Aboriginal Peoples Television Network (APTN). The new service will be part of all the basic cable packages.

In a recently published decision renewing CANCOM's licence for its national satellite relay distribution undertaking (SRDU), the CRTC reaffirmed its dedication to serving remote communities: "The Commission notes the concerns expressed in interventions regarding the reception quality of SRDU signals, particularly in Canada's High Arctic. The commission expects the licensee to ensure, as resources permit, that its signals are available for reception in all communities in Canada" (CRTC 1998, 2). The CRTC also underscored CANCOM's commitment to continue funding four northern

Aboriginal radio network services at $250,000 annually; $85,000 for Wawatay's transmission facilities at Moose Factory, Ontario; and $150,000 to TVNC for satellite uplink facilities at Whitehorse, Yukon. CANCOM also agreed to continue to provide marketing assistance, and "to provide TVNC with five free hours per week of video uplink time for the delivery of southern based Aboriginal programming" (CRTC 1998, 3).

Given the scarcity of journalism education for northern Aboriginal people, especially after the failure of the Arctic College program noted in Chapter 2, IBC and TVNC have both become involved in training new journalists and offering programs to upgrade the skills of working journalists. As we noted in the previous chapter, since 1996, IBC has conducted training sessions at its New Media Centre in Iqaluit. In 1998 TVNC started a new service to help find appropriate programs for prospective journalism students as well as working professionals who want to improve their skills. As of 1998, TVNC has a Web page featuring internships and training programs for filmmakers. At the time of writing, the latest listing included the following programs, grants, and awards: the Canada Council for the Arts' Project Grants to Production Organizations for Media Arts Development; the Canadian Film and Television Production Association's National Training Programme as well as their International Intern Programme for Canadian Youth; a CTV Fellowship to attend the Banff Television Festival; the Manitoba Indian Cultural Education Centre's Aboriginal Broadcast Training Initiative; the National Film Board of Canada's Aboriginal Filmmaking Program; Ross Charles Awards to Aboriginal people specializing in telecommunications and broadcasting; and the Women's Technical Internship from WTN (Women's Television Network) Foundation.

TVNC Programming

TVNC airs a broad spectrum of programming. In the early days of TVNC Lorraine Thomas summarized a typical Wednesday evening of TVNC fare: an English-language CBC Northern Service current affairs program from Yellowknife is followed by an Inuktitut production by IBC in Iqaluit, aimed at Inuit teens in the eastern Arctic; then, a distance learning course from Arctic College, a teen show produced in English by the NWT government's Culture and Communications Department, a show about traditions and current issues produced in Inuvialuktun by the Inuvialuit Communications Society for Inuvialuit in the western Arctic. "After a visit to the Inuvik region, TVNC swings over to Yukon leaders discussing current issues, produced by Northern Native Broadcast [sic] Yukon. An international documentary about aboriginal peoples ... [then] an Inuktitut program ... by CBC North [Northern Service]. National aboriginal issues are then covered ... and the broadcast evening wraps up with the Government of the NWT's Question Period" (Thomas 1992, 20).

In 1995 TVNC, which was continuing to develop its programming, launched northern Canada's first daily newscast. *Nunatsiaq News* topped its front page with the story in Inuktitut syllabics, followed by the energetic English version headlined "TVNC Leaps into Daily Newscast": "It's only two minutes a day and it's produced by volunteers in Yellowknife, but it's northern Canada's first daily newscast and Television Northern Canada is hoping it will grow into something much bigger" (Bell 1995, 1, 2). The newscast originates in Yellowknife in the studios of the Native Communications Society of the NWT. Gerry Giberson, TVNC's director of operations, said the early effort is "more like a headline news service ... than a full-fledged news report" and features a pan-Arctic review that points viewers to stories they can follow in more depth in other media. Giberson said "We're the only region in Canada, perhaps in North America that does not receive a daily regional television newscast. What we're trying to do is fill that gap" (Bell 1995, 1, 2).

One of the TVNC's first major stars was the children's superhero Super Shamou, an Inuk in cape and leotards played by Peter Tapatai. Super Shamou was created by Barney Pattunguyak and Peter Tapatai for IBC and was aired by IBC on the CBC Northern Service Network (Melanie Legault, personal communication, 18 November 1998). With humour, energy, and intelligence, the character addresses all of the most serious issues confronting northern children and adults. A Super Shamou comic book addresses everything from solvent abuse to community cooperation. The premier (and only) issue, which was published in both English-Inuktitut and French-Inuktitut versions, contains the story of the origin of the superhero, born a "mild-mannered Inuk" named Peter Tapatai and transformed by spells and charms into the hero who will "right wrongs and combat evil" and is told, "Peter, you have been chosen. The people of the Arctic must have peace and justice." *Super Shamou* gave birth to another popular TVNC-broadcast, IBC-produced children's program, *The Takuginai Family,* which teaches "respect for elders, traditional Inuit culture, and the Inuktitut language" (David 1998, 37). *Takuginai* means "look here" in Inuktitut (Burns 1992).

Still another Inuit children's show premiered in October 1998. Produced by the Kativik School Board for KSB-TV in Nunavik (Inuit northern Quebec) and broadcast over TVNC, *Allai* airs twice a week during the school year and features a puppet family who explore a range of issues on Inuktitut language, Inuit culture, and Nunavik geography (George 1998, 33).

Programs Produced by TVNC Members

The Government of the Northwest Territories (GNWT) produces seven hours of original programming each week for TVNC. *GNWT Presents* includes a variety of programming. *Live and Well* is an interactive discussion program. It broadcasts live with phone-in lines encouraging viewers to participate in discussing themes related to health and well being.

Super Shamou, front cover, Inuktitut version.

"The Origin of *Super Shamou.*"

Crew of Inuit Broadcasting Corporation filming *Takuginai* in Iqaluit, NWT.

The Inuit Broadcasting Corporation produces five hours of original Inuktitut programming weekly. *Kippinguijautiit* (Things to pass time by) is a half-hour entertainment show with what IBC calls "funny and interesting stories on traditional and contemporary Inuit ways of life." It includes music, sports, and special events coverage. A 1992 audience survey named it the most popular Inuktitut-language program. *Qanuq Isumavit?* (What do you think?), IBC's only live production, runs two and a half hours and invites the audience to discuss current issues and events in detail, via phone-in links. *Qaggiq* (Drum dance gathering) is a half-hour journal of news and current affairs. *Takuginai* (Look here) is a half-hour program targeted at five to seven year olds but watched by people of all ages. Its young hosts are joined by Johnny the lemming and other locally made puppets. *Qaujisaut* (To see, to find out) is a half-hour program directed to Inuit youth "facing hard choices – caught between two cultures." *Qimaivvik* (Pass on knowledge) is a half-hour cultural program.

Two half-hour programs in the Inuvialuktun language are produced by the Inuvialuit Communications Society (ICS). *Tamapta* is a cultural and information program. *Suangaan* covers current events in the Beaufort region.

The Native Communications Society of the NWT (NCS) produces two half-hour programs a week called *Dene Weekly Perspective,* broadcast in four Dene languages – Dogrib, Chipewyan, North Slavey, and South Slavey.

Northern Native Broadcasting Yukon (NNBY) produces two programs for TVNC, one in English and one in Gwich'in. *NEDAA* (Your eye) is NNBY's

Crew of Northern Native Broadcasting Yukon filming for their weekly program, *NEDAA*, outside Whitehorse, Yukon, 1997.

flagship program, an award-winning hour-long magazine show. *Haa Shagoon* is a Gwich'in cultural program.

Each week the Okalakatiget Society produces a half-hour program: *Labradorimiut* (People of Labrador) is a magazine with current affairs, information, and entertainment. The program alternates between English and Inuktitut.

Taqramiut Nipingat Incorporated (TNI) produces four original programs totalling two hours a week: *Nunavimiut, Ungavamiut, Taqramiut,* and *TNI Presents.*

Although it does not produce its own programming, Yukon College presents a variety of educational programming acquired from other sources. In 1997-8 the featured program *Dotto's Data Cafe* dealt with the Internet.

Programs Produced by Associate Members
CBC Northern Service produces two half-hour daily news programs. *Igalaaq* (Window) is a daily news program in Inuktitut, hosted by Rassi Nashalik from Yellowknife. CBC *Northbeat* is a half-hour program in English, hosted by Paul Andrew and Patricia Russell. It features news, profiles, and northern documentaries. Documentaries shown in Inuktitut on *Igalaaq* are repeated on *Northbeat* with English subtitles later the same night. CBC Northern Service also has a Real Audio service at its Web site, from which to download these programs.

Four hours of educational programming are provided by the Kativik School Board. *KSB Presents* offers a broad spectrum of programs, including work by other producers and original Inuktitut programs on business, economics, and history. *Education in Nunavik,* a monthly magazine included in the *KSB Presents* time slot, covers Kativik School Board activities.

Wawatay Native Communications Society produces a half-hour program in the Cree language. *Wawatay Presents* is a magazine that includes a range of issues, cultural affairs, documentaries, and entertainment.

The Pan-Arctic Vision
The intention of TVNC's founders was not only to have southern distribution, but to develop a broadcasting service that would eventually reach the entire circumpolar North. That objective, and the very existence of TVNC as a disseminating agent of Aboriginal languages, strongly suggests the need to modify Nelson Graburn's cultural-genocide vision formulated in the early 1980s. Like many Aboriginal and non-Aboriginal people, Graburn had argued that "television in the Arctic not only reinforces the use of English as a first language, but also it has become an instrument for slow assimilation and hence for cultural ethnocide" (1982, 7). In the 1970s the Anik satellite system had brought high-quality telephone service to the 25,000 Inuit living in fifty-seven communities and transmitted sixteen hours a day of English-language television programming over CBC (Valaskakis 1982, 20). Yet even in the early 1980s, when Graburn was writing, Kalaallit-Nunaata Radioa was producing regular Greenlandic television and radio programming, Taqramiut Nipingat was broadcasting Inuktitut radio in northern Quebec, and TVNC was already a gleam in the eyes of the pioneers on the Inukshuk project, who had been watching the evolution of satellite technology since 1970 (Graburn 1982, 16; Valaskakis 1982, 19).

Like Graburn, Valaskakis expressed concern about the relationship of television to the cultural marginalization of northern Aboriginal people. However, she foresaw more Native-language programming than ethnocide in Canada's northern future, and the rich programming outlined above seems to support her optimism.

Clearly the prominence of indigenous-language programming is key to allaying concerns about cultural marginalization of Aboriginal peoples. Canada is not the only northern nation where Aboriginal-language broadcasts are a priority. There are parallel developments throughout the circumpolar North. Nordic nations are cooperatively producing two Sámi language courses, *Davvin,* for people whose first language is not Sámi, and *Samas,* for primary Sámi speakers. A variety of media are in use, with textbooks linked to broadcasts on the national radio networks of Norway, Sweden, and Finland.

Sámi broadcasting is evolving slowly. As of 1994 there were only four to seven hours a year of Sámi-language programming in Sweden, and Norway had established a permanent Sámi television department that was producing ten to fifteen hours a year. Finland had no production units of its own, but was broadcasting four to six hours a year of programs from the Swedish and Norwegian networks (Minority Rights Group 1994, 162). Radio was more highly developed. Finland was the first country to establish a radio channel entirely in Sámi control (ibid., 163). The station produces all-day Sámi programming in northern Enare and Skolt Sámi dialects as well as Finnish, with about five hours a day of Sámi-language programming. Sámi Radio in Norway produces three broadcasts a day from Karasjok in the northern Sámi dialect and a small program from Trondheim in the southern Sámi dialect. Sweden produced a half-hour weekly national Swedish-language program on Sámi issues, three and a half hours a week of national programming in the Northern dialect, and a half-hour weekly program in the southern dialect. To broaden the scope and availability of Sámi programming, Sámi Radio departments in all three countries organized a cooperative news team that oversees transmission of news and public affairs programming throughout the region (ibid., 163).

In Alaska, the radio/telecommunications future is evolving differently, but with technologies that will eventually be closely tied to those in the rest of the North. In the Yup'ik village of Toksook Bay, in western Alaska (400 miles from the Russian border), the new Alaska Wireless company has installed boxes that bring in satellite-beamed transmissions and provide Internet access about "three times faster than the current standard at American corporations and 10 times faster than in most American homes" without the need for telephones, modems, or Internet user fees (Fine 1998, C1). Like Canada's Anik satellites, which have brought both telephone and TVNC services, the satellite link has the potential to bring, and transmit, not only the Internet but also indigenous programming to and from Alaska.

Success, Failure ... Recovery?

It would seem that the impressive roster of programs assembled within the first few years of TVNC's history would inspire increased support. Instead, in 1997, the Canadian government announced a 30 percent funding cut to TVNC to be spread over the 1997 and 1998 seasons. In response, the TVNC board of directors decided to work to turn TVNC from a northern to a national Aboriginal television network. The new network, formed in 1999, the Aboriginal Peoples Television Network, replaces TVNC (Miller 1998, 26-9). It will have an Aboriginal CEO and twenty-one Aboriginal board members from different regions. APTN is licensed to broadcast 120 hours of programming a week in English, French, and up to fifteen Aboriginal languages.

**Aboriginal Peoples
Television Network
(APTN)**

Brochure advocating the transformation of TVNC into
the Aboriginal Peoples Television Network (APTN), June
1998. The licence was granted 22 February 1999.

The TVNC cuts can be seen as the next step in a long line of withdrawals
of government support from Aboriginal media. Since 1990 cuts have reflected the government's policy of increasingly encouraging the privatiza-
tion of news media (for example, by allowing commercials on public radio
and by diminishing or cancelling the funding of print media). The implication is that media institutions are meant to be profit making or at least
self-sustaining. The reality is that many are forced into volunteerism – yet
no one would suggest that Toronto's City-TV should switch to volunteer
labour if it could not afford to continue broadcasting. There is an underlying double standard that assumes that although no self-respecting "mainstream" journalist would consider such an option, Aboriginal journalists
should be willing to work for free to keep their media alive (literally at all
cost). Canada has long supported the notion of allowing its citizens' many
voices to be heard. These days the trend is toward corporate "wisdom" (not
unlike that heard in the United States), which dictates the "new" funding
policy: if you can't turn a profit, you don't deserve a voice.

The reactions to the 1990 round of funding cuts were many, and strong. A non-Native journalist wrote, "What a botched job! The way in which Secretary of State Gerry Weiner slashed funding for native newspapers and broadcasters is a classic case of political arbitrariness ... It's a tale of failure to justify action by policy ... a tale of shameless abandonment of what capable government administrations are supposed to do ... There are ways of achieving federal savings without imperilling the existence of native media that have made a substantial contribution to education, civic consciousness and skills training in the last 20 years" (White 1990, A4).

Phil Fontaine, then head of the Assembly of Manitoba Chiefs, attributed the cuts in part to ignorance, but said "they also rise out of a deliberate strategy to silence those who have been vocal. This government doesn't appreciate dissent, in fact it won't tolerate it ... The cause of aboriginal people is seen simply as an irritant" (Russell 1990, 12).

The early 1990s saw repeated federal cuts to the Northern Native Broadcast Access Program and the Aboriginal language programs. The axe continues to fall. A 1996 headline in *Nunatsiaq News* reads, "IBC Gets Nasty Surprise in Latest Budget." The story, which was not covered in the southern media, identifies a 14.7 percent budget cut "that will strip $250,000 from IBC's incoming revenue in 1996-97, nearly twice the shortfall that IBC officials had been expecting ... Added to that is question after question about whether IBC will even survive in the future" (Bell 1996b, 14). IBC executive director Debbie Brisebois said the uncertainty is "really wearing people down, year after year." She said Inuit broadcasters were led to believe the cuts would be smaller. The duplicity and the unexpected loss "means another blow to the morale of IBC's underpaid and overworked staff" (ibid., 14).

Cuts to television broadcasting have been echoed in underfunding of radio. Given severe cutbacks, broken commitments, and insecurity about the future, northern community radio has had to struggle against the temptation to rely on whatever funding happens to come its way. Like the print media (although with more consistent success), community radio has come to depend on low wages, minimal staffing, volunteer personnel to supplement paid staff (where it exists at all), and other forms of assistance from within the community. Along with the formally CRTC-approved stations, "pirate" and "trail" or "moccasin telegraph" stations continue to thrive.

New CRTC policy, which was set in September 1990, offset some of the losses from the 1990 cutbacks and fostered greater independence, by permitting Native radio stations to earn advertising revenues. Stations without competitors were allowed almost unrestricted advertising, up to 250 minutes of sales spots per day (Langford 1990). However, not everyone considers the advent of advertising a positive development.

I was in Whitehorse, tuned in to CHON-FM, the radio station of Northern Native Broadcasting Yukon (NNBY) the day it shifted from a no-advertising policy to a broadcast day filled with ads. The effect was jarring, to say the least. At the time many people expressed concern about the intrusiveness of advertising in the broadcast day, but most NNBY staff members expressed relief that the station would survive the funding cuts and continue to serve its listeners (Alia 1991a). In a letter to me dated 6 December 1995, Helen Fallding, who was working at CHON-FM at the time it adopted the ads, reflected on the situation:

> I have lots of concerns about the move to commercial aboriginal radio. I have no idea how it's all playing itself out at this point at CHON-FM, but while I was there, there was more and more white business "expertise" at the management and advertising sales level, aimed at increasing the station's commercial viability. The people hired had no clue about aboriginal culture or values and didn't seem interested in learning anything. The result [included] some terrible decisions. One top administrator saw the station as essentially a country-and-western station whose target audience should be C & W listeners, not aboriginal people. An ad salesperson designed ads for a strip show at a local tavern, which were aired. Perhaps these were growing pains and the board has taken back control.

The jury is still out as to the continuing extent of the "growing pains." In purely economic terms, CHON-FM is a stunning success. In 1998 the Yukon-wide service kept its seventeen community stations occupied with programming supported by $250,000 in advertising revenues (Curley 1993).

There have been other responses to cutbacks. One precedent-setting move came in Saskatchewan. When the CBC Saskatoon station was forced to shut down, employees obtained a grant from the Saskatchewan government and in December 1990 formed a corporation from which to manage a restructured employee-run station.

The Circumpolar Village: Strengths and Weaknesses

> Inuit are nomads ... There is nothing that frustrates Inuit
> more than being made to remain in one spot ... It is no wonder
> that Inuit treasure the Internet, for if they cannot bodily leave
> their communities, at least their minds can wander at will ...
> [They] rejoice in the ability to compare opinions abroad, as they
> did when traveling at will.
>   For the hamlet is the new iglu, and the Internet is the new Land.
>
>   Rachel Qitsualik

The North's "small town" qualities, which were discussed in the introduction to this book, persist in the computer age. In fact, in many ways the Internet and satellite technology have picked up where town meetings left off. In some cases, they have *become* the town meetings. Satellites carry community-to-community meetings, enabling people to convene in weather that would prohibit travel and to bridge distances beyond the capabilities of budgets. The Internet carries interpersonal, intergroup, inter-regional, and international dialogue. It helps bring Aboriginal people and Aboriginal media to each other, and to non-Aboriginal people. It helps to "mainstream" marginalized media – a mixed blessing because "alternative" and "minority" media have in the past both lost and gained from privacy and smallness.

Most of the negative effects of technology are due not to the technology itself, but to the ways people use it. Often, there is such a romance with the possibilities, we fail to consider the relationship between the machinery and the actual human needs and uses for its services. In the following sections I discuss two examples of what I consider shameful failures – failures all the more disappointing because each project should have had considerable success. The people in charge failed to consider the fact that the finest media productions and the availability of state-of-the-art technology are valuable only if they are distributed to people who can use them. In both cases, the agency in question lost funds, good will, and the opportunity to reach a global audience with the very works it was designed to promote.

Wasting Opportunities

Throughout the North, Aboriginal filmmakers and broadcasters are taking control of their own productions, and the presence of Outside filmmakers is diminishing. When Outsiders do come North, they are supervised, advised, and sometimes monitored by official and unofficial territorial, regional, or community authorities. More indigenous actors are being hired than in the past, and not always as extras. The Aboriginal broadcasters are tackling an increasing number of extended documentary projects: series, made-for-TV movies, and documentary films to be shown on their own networks and marketed elsewhere as well.

In 1998 the National Film Board sent out an Internet advertisement for its Aboriginal Directors Series. It was a wonderful way to promote Canadian Aboriginal filmmakers worldwide. However, would-be purchasers from outside Canada were then told the films could be purchased only from the New York distributor (at prices several hundred percent higher than those in Canada), or, in many cases, could not be purchased, rented, or shown outside Canada at all. To an extent, this is symptomatic of the NFB's poorly coordinated promotion and distribution programs in general. However, the effect on Aboriginal filmmakers is particularly problematic, given the NFB's special commitment to their work.

In the late 1990s I found myself in an ironic situation. As the first recipient of Western Washington University's Professorship in Canadian Culture (a position whose endowment came partly from the Canadian government), I was charged with the task of bringing Canadian culture to a wider audience in the United States. Because one of Canada's major cultural contributions is its wealth of films – particularly documentaries – and the National Film Board itself, it should come as no surprise that one of the first things I planned was a program of NFB films. Imagine my dismay upon learning there was no way to show them! Some could be purchased at wildly inflated prices from the American distributor (in 1998, a film costing Cdn$29.95 cost US$400.00). Some could not be shown at all. In a surreal conversation with an NFB official, I argued to no avail. It made no difference that I am both a Canadian and an American citizen, that I had come to Washington State directly from Canada for the sole purpose of teaching and demonstrating Canada's cultural riches. I was told that even the videos I had purchased for use in my Canadian university classes could not legally be shown to students in the United States. The situation never was resolved, and the people in Washington never did have access to most of the films I'd hoped to show. How silly it seems, to endow a culture chair and keep the culture locked away in private closets! It's time for someone to think more clearly, and for the various departments and programs to learn how to communicate more effectively with each other.

The second example involves CBC Northern Service recordings. Since the 1970s the CBC Northern Service has been creating a miniature recording industry of its own, an enterprise that has fed its programming day and encouraged a number of northern Aboriginal musicians. For several reasons, the project's only success has been its production – and airplay – of a number of fine recordings, using (in most cases) the finest technology, equipment, and personnel available.

At the same time that Greenland has sent a stunning array of recordings across its own country and to Denmark, Nunavut, and other parts of the world via well-developed public and private outlets, most of Canada's northern artists have remained narrowly distributed and little known. Only the occasional northern artist reaches a wider audience. It takes the Nashville machine or another American marketing outlet to push a Susan Aglukark or a Jerry Alfred beyond the Nunavut or the Yukon border.

CBC Northern Service launched its recording operation in 1973 with a two-record 45 rpm set of the Inuit singer Charlie Panigoniak. Two years later another two-record set was released, featuring the Sugluk Group from Sugluk (now Salluit) in northern Quebec. More funds were allocated in the late 1970s, and about 120 records were produced. Thanks largely to non-CBC recordings, some of the artists are quite well known today – for example, songwriter/singer and CBC broadcaster William Tagoona and singer/songwriter and prominent filmmaker Alanis Obomsawin. In the early 1980s the production unit was moved from Montreal to Ottawa and the recordings were released as twelve-inch stereo LPs (Linttell 1988, 292-3).

Unfortunately, CBC never made a major commitment to marketing or promoting the recordings. As with many other fine projects the corporation undertakes, this was apparently intended primarily to produce materials to air on CBC radio – an admirable but inadequate objective. In 1988 the communication officer for CBC Northern Service, Perry Linttell, described the more recent recordings as "commercially available," but such a designation requires a large imaginative stretch – they never have been easy to obtain.

The follow-up of marketing in the 1990s has been poor to nil, and the whole recording program remains one of CBC's best-kept secrets. I have had a hard time obtaining so-called "current" recordings, even from CBC. On a couple of occasions I was able to purchase albums in the lobby of the CBC studio in Whitehorse. Usually, when I ask about them in one of the northern broadcast outlets (in Whitehorse, Yellowknife, and Iqaluit) or in the national distribution office in Toronto, the response is a blank look.

CBC's shortsightedness about its recording artists is a shame – a major loss to the artists and to Canada's knowledge of its own artists, not to mention their promotion to the rest of the world. There has never been a consistent policy or consistent funding or promotion effort. Few people know the recordings even exist. With CBC's marketing office at its new Toronto headquarters, there is a perfect opportunity to re-issue the old albums on CD or cassette and to release some of the many other recordings done in-house and given limited air-play. The CBC recording program remains one of the weakest links in the Canadian communications picture, and one that is especially damaging to northern artists for whom access is so costly and difficult.

As broadcast and electronic media expand, more information and culture are brought to more people, with less and less control from Ottawa. Questions of distribution and broadcast rights will still have to be negotiated nationally and internationally, but the opportunities for wider distribution will continue to increase and will eventually push some of the boundaries and bureaucratic tangles aside. Aboriginal northerners are learning to use the Internet to facilitate this process.

The North on the Net
When I began the research for this book in early 1990, the Internet was the province of a few "techies." Today, it is rapidly becoming the primary medium of expression for the voices of many individuals and groups. Of the earlier communication media, only radio continues to relay grassroots

information frequently, freely, and rapidly throughout the North. In terms of North-South communication, the Internet is far more effective than radio. Thus, what may have begun as carefree local expressions are becoming increasingly carefully chosen and constructed messages. The same concerns Aboriginal journalists are expressing about who controls their newspapers, in discussions between editors and Aboriginal councils and politicians, affect Internet communications, which are often linked directly to the newspapers and therefore are subject to the same struggles for power, expression, and control. The one unarguable truth is that these sites are expanding and increasing and are likely to continue to do so in the foreseeable future.

By 1998 all fifty-eight of the communities in the Northwest Territories (including the portion that in 1999 became the Territory of Nunavut) were connected to the World Wide Web. The connections were the result of a two-year project undertaken by Ardicom, a consortium of predominantly Aboriginal-owned northern businesses (Zellen 1998, 50). Using cable services provided by the Arctic Co-op and NorthwesTel's telephone network, Ardicom's two-way, high-speed digital communications network will gradually expand to support a range of information services, including videoconferencing, telemedicine, distance education, and the Internet (Wilkin 1997, 10).

There is a variety of opinion among Aboriginal journalists and leaders on the benefits and dangers of the Internet. Several observers contrast the new medium with television, which has been viewed as the most assimilationist of the media. James Hrnyshyn, a copy editor for Northern News Services in Yellowknife, thinks the Internet is a less inherently assimilationist medium than television, because it strengthens the virtual community. At the same time, he acknowledges that communicators on the Net lose some of their cultural distinctness because of the worldwide connection. The Net paradoxically both dilutes and strengthens the culture of origin (Zellen 1998, 51-2).

Jim Bell, editor of *Nunatsiaq News,* also draws a contrast between television and the Net. In his view, the Internet provides an antidote to the cultural demolition that has occurred in non-Aboriginal television. Another observer contrasts the new technology's culture-preserving potential with the negative effects of television described in the famous speech of Inuit leader Rosemarie Kuptana: "We might liken the onslaught of southern television and the absence of native television to the neutron bomb ... Neutron bomb television ... destroys the soul of a people but leaves the shell of a people walking around" (Brisebois 1983, 107).

One way of countering this soul-destroying onslaught is through the preservation and dissemination of Aboriginal culture. Jim Bell sees great potential for Aboriginal communities in CD-ROM, digital video discs, and other multimedia technologies, which can provide storage for important audio and visual material (Zellen 1998, 52). These technologies offer an effective way to store and transmit oral histories, materials from community and regional archives, music, and visual art. Bell thinks the Internet offers a way of "fighting back" – a chance for Aboriginal people to "send the information the other way" (Zellen 1998, 52).

Fred Lepine, a Métis writer, musician, and philosopher from Hay River, NWT, loves the Internet but is less optimistic about its capacity for preserving cultural integrity. He sees the same lure of the "outside world" that worried Inuit leaders who held out against the proliferation of non-northern, non-indigenous television in the Canadian North (Zellen 1998, 52).

To avoid being overwhelmed by the lure of the Outside, northern and Aboriginal groups must be able to put their own information on the Net. The Northwest Territories Community Access Program (CAP) was established to aid communities in developing their own Web sites and to teach uses of the Internet to people in the territories' communities.

There are now many rich sources on the Internet for and about northern indigenous peoples. Appendix E provides a list of such Internet resources current to February 1999. For a Canada-wide overview of information on first peoples, Miles Morrisseau recommends *The First Perspective On-Line*, which he calls "the best on-line publication for ... news, information and current events in Native Canada ... Unlike most publication sites, it doesn't just ... try to suck you into buying the hard copy. It actually provides the best of the newspaper online" (Morrisseau 1997, 53). The beautiful, information-packed arts and culture magazine, *Aboriginal Voices*, has a Web page and an e-mail address (abvoices@inforamp.net). Aboriginal entrepreneurs are represented by *Native Cyber Trade*, with pages on arts and crafts, nations, Indian gaming, and resources (links). *Spirit of Aboriginal Enterprise* is a site created by First Nations Communications (FNC). It includes an on-line magazine, profiles of Aboriginal entrepreneurs, and an FNC page with movies – such as a tour of the Canadian Museum of Civilization – that can be downloaded in Quicktime format (Morrisseau 1997, 53).

The usefulness of the Net for northern peoples is not, of course, limited to Canada. In the Sámi world, 1996 marked the turning-point in the information explosion. Before 1996 there were Sámi Web sites in Finland and Sweden, and "a few pages on university servers in Norway" (Forsgren 1998, 34). In 1996 Sámi youth organizations created a Web site offering daily updates of the Fourth World Indigenous Youth Conference, an experimental beginning that spurred other projects. In 1997 the journal *Samefolket* (The Sámi people) and the North Sámi *Min Aigit* (Our time) created Web sites. While most communication is likely to continue to be in Swedish, Norwegian, and Finnish, the North Sámi are also able to use and promote their own language, with fonts developed by Apple. Apple also developed an Inuktitut program for use by Canadian Inuit in and around Nunavut and Nunavik, and Dene fonts are now available for downloading for Windows and Macintosh in Dogrib, Chipewyan, North Slavey, and South Slavey.

In a recent development in the United States, the American Indian Radio on Satellite network distribution system (AIROS) began a twenty-four-hour-a-day distribution system, using the Internet and public radio. Run by Native American Public Telecommunications, it has partial funding from the Corporation for Public Broadcasting and headquarters in Lincoln, Nebraska, with a Web site and e-mail address (see Appendix E). It also has a video distribution service, VMV, with an archive of Native American videos and public television programs available to tribal communities.

Phone, Fax, Frustration: Companions to the Networked North

It is clear from the rapid development of northern Web sites and distance education programs in Nunavut, NWT, Yukon, and elsewhere that northerners are often more familiar with high-tech communications than are southerners. Sophisticated computers have been commonplace in eastern Arctic adult education and other centres for years. Satellite dishes sit on ancient rocks in tiny settlements whose inhabitants still spend much of their lives on the land. The Inuit Circumpolar Conference 1989 General Assembly in Sisimiut, Greenland, presented a demonstration by representatives of the Inuit Cultural Institute of the program that translates English into Inuktitut syllabics.

In addition to these technologies, fax machines are a key communication tool in the North. Phone lines are the most reliable and least fallible means of reaching other communities and Outside, and they are used extensively. As Cairns has noted, "I think there is a fax machine in all but two communities in the western Arctic" (1990, 9). Northerners' enthusiasm for the fax machine mirrors their acceptance of other technologies. Notes Leona Meyer, "It's amazing ... It has just sort of mushroomed and the smallest community has a fax machine to the point where some people seldom use the mails ... any more. You sort of wonder how you existed without it" (1990, 25). Northerners use fax and e-mail as alternatives to costly air freight and slow postal service and are looking into other uses for the fax machine. Says Cairns, "I hope that new legislation would allow faxed documents to be accepted as if they were originals" (1990, 493-4). Others such as Lyle Walsh see possibilities for the fax machine on election day: "I am not a salesman for a fax machine, but you ... look at the way you run elections and it is sort of 1932 technology" (1990). But every technology has its limitations, and facsimile is no exception. Some northern communities have only a single telephone, which means adding fax to already overused facilities. And like computer modems, fax machines can not be installed where there are only radio phones.

There is a huge gap between potential and actual availability of new technologies. In 1999 the CRTC is expected to provide for subsidies to improve telephone services in northern and remote regions. This will help bring the North more fully into the new communications universe. In 1997 Taqramiut Nipingat Inc., Nunavik's Inuit broadcasting service, tried to become an Internet service provider, with disastrous financial results. As of March 1999 only seven of Nunavik's fifteen communities had access to the Internet, and this was limited to public access sites maintained by freenet provider Nunavik.Net in six communities and a site at Kiluutaq School in Umiujaq (Appendix E). Calling for strong CRTC support, Jim Bell said, "Canada's thinly populated North is turning into a telecommunications slum ... [with] a few centres of relative privilege: Iqaluit, Yellowknife, and Whitehorse, for example" (Bell 1999, 9).

In summing up, it is well to bear in mind Gary Farmer's cautionary words about the limits to technology. The particular conditions in which northern communications are placed make every technological breakthrough a welcome event. Thoughtful northerners are aware of the pitfalls in assuming that technology will replace human-to-human contact. Even in the Utopian vision of technology that the Nunavut founders have in mind, caution will have to be exercised.

Interactive computers provide a new medium for print, and are swiftly evolving into media that transmit visual and auditory material as well. Interactive radio carries voices across great and small distances. Interactive television goes a step further, allowing body language and facial expressions to be carried. Soon, virtual media will produce facsimiles of "real" experience, including tactile experience. None of these can replace the joys and stresses of communicating in person. But news media haven't been face-to-face since the days when troubadours and town criers roamed the streets. Their closest descendants are probably the storytellers who still inhabit longhouses, tents, and snowhouses, friendship centres, and public libraries. And, as Rachel Qitsualik has said, Aboriginal people continue both the nomadic and the communications traditions in today's communities, using today's technologies.

Leaving the new "iglu" and the new Internet "land" of Nunavut and heading west, the next chapter looks at the communications experiences of Yukoners, to see what can be learned from looking more deeply at communications in one northern region.

5
Communications in Yukon

Most studies of the Canadian North have focused on the Northwest Territories and Nunavut. Yukon has received scant attention in the literature. This may be due to its relatively small territory and even smaller population, of 32,635 (Yukon 1998), or to what one person interviewed called its "greater similarity to the rest of Canada – it's the only northern region that could become a province in the foreseeable future, because it has the most fully developed form of responsible government." This Yukon case study provides a detailed view of northern communications and northern communicators, including a community-by-community survey of what is produced, in what manner, and by whom. The research was conducted over three fall-winter periods: the first year, 1990-1, was taken up with a study of northern communications and political activity for the Royal Commission on Electoral Reform and Party Financing (RCERPF); the second and third years constituted independent research. During that time, I learned that there are some Yukon-specific details, but most of the patterns seen here are observable throughout the North. The research was supervised from my home base in Whitehorse and involved a team of researchers in and from different Yukon communities and from other northern locations, and graduate students based in London, Ontario.

The experience of working in Yukon brought home an old lesson about research methodology: no matter how well we do our homework long-distance, nothing can replace first-hand experience. I have known this for many years. Nevertheless, I had to relearn the lesson in Yukon. In the back of my mind was the assumption that I could figure out how all of northern Canada experienced communications, campaigns, and elections by extrapolating from previous research in the eastern Arctic.

Until 1990, all of my northern research had been conducted in communities in the eastern Arctic, where there are neither trees nor roads – except within communities – and community-to-community travel is limited to air, snowmobile, all-terrain vehicle (ATV), sled, small water-craft, or supply ship. I had a respectable understanding of the time and expense involved in conducting northern travel and communications in a region dominated by fly-in access. The error was in assuming that access in Yukon would be much greater and travel much less costly because all of the communities except Old Crow have roads connecting them with other parts of the territory.

In the process of living and travelling through the Yukon winter, I learned how wrong my initial assumptions had been. Except in summer, the costs are as high, and the scheduling as complex, as in the Northwest Territories and Nunavut. Bus routes link many of the communities, and there are meticulously scheduled buses – at least on paper. In reality, even when they run on time, the buses don't always have room for passengers: the holiday-season van between Whitehorse and Atlin, British Columbia, had room for only one passenger when I took it; others had to wait at least two days to travel. Moreover, in winter the roads are often dangerous or impossible to negotiate, especially for the uninitiated. And "winter" in Yukon corresponds roughly to mid-fall through late spring in the South, encompassing most campaign and election periods. I discovered that technological developments such as fax, satellite transmission, and the Internet were as important here as in the eastern Arctic. However, they were slower to develop in Yukon and western NWT than in Nunavut, and at the time of the study were only beginning to be used.

The primary work for the study was done in Whitehorse – where most of the territory's government, private, and communications institutions are based – with frequent and extended travel to most Yukon communities. In four months during 1990-1, I was able to visit most Yukon communities; but even after the budget and time period were extended, I was not able to visit them all. The follow-up research focused on the same communities covered in the RCERPF study.

In the course of my research I experienced all the factors complicating journalistic coverage of campaigns and elections in the North, including politicians' schedules (which were linked to the Legislative Assembly schedule); uncertain weather; poor highway conditions; (un)availability of vehicles; limited bus and airline schedules; and lack of accommodations. Not all communities have overnight facilities. Billeting and room sharing are common across the North but require planning as well as knowledge of people in the communities.

These lessons were important not just for my understanding of communications in Yukon, but for the accurate assessment (and reassessment) of northern communications in general. The close observation of one region for an extended period of time afforded crucial insights into the day-to-day workings of journalists, communication organizations, and the public throughout the North. In addition, I was able to observe how journalists in one region – the westernmost northern region in Canada – reported on

Map 5.1

Yukon Territory, with communities visited

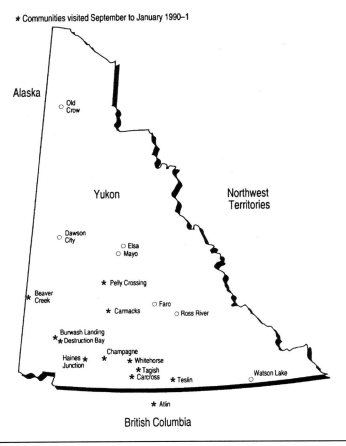

★ Communities visited September to January 1990–1

Alaska

○ Old Crow

Yukon

Northwest Territories

○ Dawson City
○ Elsa
○ Mayo

★ Pelly Crossing

Beaver Creek ★

○ Faro
★ Carmacks
○ Ross River

Burwash Landing
★ ★ Destruction Bay

Champagne
Haines ★ ★ ★ Whitehorse
Junction
★ Tagish
★ Carcross
★ Teslin

Watson Lake ○

★ Atlin

British Columbia

Source: Alia (1991a).

other northern regions, and how journalists elsewhere in the North and South covered Yukon.

I was also able to compare the reportage with first-hand observation of people and events in Yukon. In this light, the most striking observation was the staggering absence of any coverage of Yukon at all. In the North, a region that was already grossly underserved and under-reported, Yukon received less attention than any other area. In fact, despite my years of focus on northern issues, Yukon had been nearly invisible and continues to be so at the end of the 1990s despite the expansion of satellite and Internet access in and to the territory. This case study, then, not only provides an opportunity to train a close-up lens on northern communications in small northern communities, it also adds to an appallingly scarce literature on Canada's smallest and least-known northern territory.

Early History: First Nations, Journalism, and Gold
Before trade and commerce entered Yukon around 1840, it was populated by Indians and Inuvialuit. Today, Inuvialuit live only in the western Northwest Territories, some of them just over the Yukon border. The ethnic makeup of Yukon is about 60 percent British (origin), 23 percent Aboriginal, 15 percent French, and 2 percent Asian and African (Yukon 1998). The Yukon Indian Advancement Association was founded in the late 1960s, and included non-Native supporters. It was replaced in 1970 by the Yukon Native Brotherhood, which focused on comprehensive land claims. The Yukon Association of Non-Status Indians went its own way. In 1980 Yukon Indians reorganized into the Council for Yukon Indians, now the Council for Yukon First Nations, Canada's first coordinated organization of status and non-status Indians.

The 1896 Klondike gold rush led to the creation of Yukon Territory and a communications explosion. Many Yukon newspapers got their start during this period. Dawson City in particular was a thriving communications centre with many newspapers. At the height of the gold rush, Dawson City had three dailies. By 1909 only the *Dawson Daily News* survived. It folded in 1951 when the Yukon territorial capital was moved to Whitehorse. Today Dawson has only one slim weekly, the *Klondike Sun,* printed in Whitehorse at the offices of the *Yukon News.*

The first Whitehorse newspaper, the *Yukon Midnight Sun,* began publishing in 1898. Next came the *Klondike Nugget,* the *Klondike Miner,* and finally the *Whitehorse Star,* which continues today. The *Star* was founded by Percy Fremlin "Doc" Scharschmidt, a West Indian immigrant who was educated in England and at the University of Toronto, where in 1887 he graduated with a medical degree. He later moved West and left his medical practice, first for mining and then for journalism. In 1897 he was special correspondent in Skagway, Alaska, for the *Victoria Daily Colonist.* He started the *Bennett Sun* at Bennett, British Columbia, moving the newspaper to Whitehorse when the White Pass railway was completed in 1900, linking Skagway with Yukon and facilitating access for newspapers and people. Maintaining both astronomical accuracy and journalistic expediency, he changed the name from the *Sun* to the *Star* (*Whitehorse Star* 1990a). One of the *Whitehorse Star*'s best-known writers was June Franklin, who in 1965 was named best columnist in Canada by the Canadian Women's Press Club (*Whitehorse Star* 1990a, 9).

The Evolution of Yukon Political Life
Yukon government resembles the governments of the provinces more closely than those of the Northwest Territories and Nunavut. Parliamentary

Headquarters of the *Whitehorse Star.*

government got its start in Yukon in 1909, with the first all-elected (all-male) Territorial Council (Legislative Assembly). Women were not allowed to vote or run for office until 1919. Although there were no women on council until Jean Gordon was elected in 1967, Yukoner Martha Black became just the second woman to be elected to the House of Commons in Ottawa when in 1935 she won the seat formerly held by her ailing husband. Black was therefore in a position to know when in 1938 she commented that "no election campaign in Yukon is ever mild." She recalled "flagrant corruption" with "numbers of foreigners ... railroaded through a fake form of naturalization and allowed to vote" (Black 1986, 86, 790).

Political parties arrived in the Yukon Legislative Assembly in 1978 – in contrast to today's Northwest Territories assembly, which still has no political parties – marking a turning point from federal to strong territorial government. Yukon tolerates a good deal of diversity of political style, affiliation, non-affiliation, and party crossovers, and election results tend to be close. The redistribution of electoral boundaries in 1978 created at least three Aboriginal-majority districts, which resulted in the first electoral victories of Aboriginal candidates in Yukon. The Old Crow district was redrawn to "ensure that the voting power of the citizens of the community ... was not diluted by the potential influx of workers on Beaufort Sea and Dempster Highway projects" (Michael 1987, 15).

Michael says Yukon Aboriginal people were "largely forgotten" in early territorial politics (ibid., 16). Indeed the first Aboriginal candidates did not run until the 1974 general election. After the initial victories in 1978, the number of Aboriginal MLAs had increased to a total of five by 1991. Despite these gains, not everyone is satisfied with the relationship between First Nations candidates, political parties, and the news media.

Yukon Communications

In the constellation of Yukon communications, radio is dominant. Its long history began in the early 1900s with the creation of the Yukon Telegraph. Its Dawson City-Whitehorse line was "the last wilderness undertaking of its kind in North America, costing several millions of dollars, but serving the nation for almost half a century" (Lawrence [1965] 1990, 40). From the Second World War onward, the military took an increasing interest in promoting and maintaining northern communications for strategic purposes. In March 1949 the *Whitehorse Star* reported that the Royal Canadian Corps of Signals had erected two new antennas near Edmonton as part of the Northwest Territories and Yukon Radio system, which was being "modernized" with teletype equipment designed to coordinate with the radar network then in progress. "The projected system of signals will enable as many as 12 messages to be carried concurrently over limited lines. Army officials described this as a vital factor in a defence system trying to cope with enemy aircraft coming from numerous directions at once" (Whyard 1997, 14).

Again, we must stress the inseparability of communications and transportation in the North. New forms of communication often originate with transportation. For example, Yukon's UHF mobile radio communications network – 600 mobile units and 26 repeaters to extend the mobile broadcast – originated with highway maintenance and the RCMP. Supported by Renewable Resources Yukon, it was launched in 1988. CRTS community radio and television, also in Yukon, had its start as a lifesaving device. In the days when its television broadcasts were solely for survival on the land, it used to be called Timberline TV. Today it is another source of news coverage.

Today, the two central radio outlets in Yukon are CHON-FM, the Northern Native Broadcasting Yukon (NNBY) station that reaches virtually all communities, and CBC, which combines southern and northern programming. Calling itself "the beat of a different drummer," CHON-FM opens and closes its program day with traditional drumming. It provides weekly reports called in from most Yukon communities and occasional on-site remote broadcasts from communities with particularly newsworthy issues, people, or events.

In contrast to more northern programming on radio, CBC-TV's broadcast day is southern-based, with short bursts of CBC's *Focus North* (news and features), programming by NNBY's television outlet, NEDAA-TV, and additional programming developed or sponsored by Television Northern Canada (TVNC). Prior to TVNC, television programs arrived via satellite from British Columbia or originated in Chicago and Detroit – cities whose news and time zones are obviously out of kilter with Yukon and the experiences and concerns of Yukon people.

Whitehorse has two newspapers – the Whitehorse-focused *Whitehorse Star* and the *Yukon News,* which is more broadly distributed in the communities and whose coverage is more territory-wide. Coverage of Aboriginal issues in both papers varies. In the early 1970s the Yukon Native Brotherhood (YNB), the Yukon Association of Non-Status Indians (YANSI), and various individuals began to work to improve First Nations communications. The first publications had been small-scale newsletters such as the *Skookum Jim Newsletter* and *The Firestarter,* published between 1968 and 1971. In 1972 YNB and YANSI incorporated the Thay Lun Lin Communications Society. In 1973 the communications society received $10,000 from the Department of Secretary of State to begin publishing the *Yukon Indian News.* They were awarded $13,780 for 1974-5, enabling them to continue its monthly publication. In 1975 they held a conference to increase First Nations involvement in communications, and a new name was adopted for the communications society – Ye Sa To. The Tlingit name, which means "Voice of all the People," reflected the increasing involvement of Tlingit people from the community of Teslin. In 1976 the *Yukon Indian News* went biweekly, and representatives of Ye Sa To met with CBC to improve links between reporters for the paper and for the CBC program *Yukon Native Voice.* Also that year, the society held its first general assembly, with journalistic skills workshops and organizational meetings. At that time it was decided to revise the structure of the organization to provide for two members from each of the thirteen Yukon First Nations.

Ye Sa To's projects continued to include both independent efforts and collaboration with CBC. In 1978 the society aired its first film production on CBC-TV, a twenty-minute film profiling a well-known Dawson couple, Joe and Annie Henry, produced under CBC's newly created Northern Producers Film Assessment Program. At the same time, Ye Sa To began a community radio project with the help of a $23,500 grant from the Department of Indian and Inuit Affairs. In the early 1980s Northern Native Broadcasting Yukon (NNBY) came on the scene, and Ye Sa To decided to transfer the community radio program to NNBY, a move that helped to strengthen the new radio service. In 1985 NNBY opened its radio station, CHON-FM, with a ceremony that included drumming and songs by elders George Dawson, Kitty Smith, and Annie Ned.

Recalling the process leading up to this event, NNBY chair Ken Kane mentions a vital source of help: "Back in 1980, after about five years of trying to get telecommunications happening, I saw Francis Fox, then minister of communications, giving a press conference. He was basically saying, 'if native people want to use the ANIK D satellite technology, then send me an application.' I almost fell out of my chair because this was like an answer to all the problems I was up against; and it was a chance for instant communications" (Ye Sa To 1988).

NNBY and its television service, NEDAA-TV, also played a central role in the creation of TVNC. Ken Kane and George Henry (then NNBY executive producer) were key players, along with Ross Harvey, assistant deputy minister for culture and communications for the Northwest Territories and Rosemarie Kuptana, then president of IBC.

In 1988 Ye Sa To implemented an idea long under discussion, transforming the *Yukon Indian News* (later *Dan Sha News*) into monthly public affairs magazine *Dännzhà'* and incorporating some of the format of *Shakat,* the newspaper's summer edition. As mentioned earlier, *Dännzhà',* Yukon's first Native magazine, has struggled to stay alive, undergoing intermittent suspensions and revivals, and remaining Yukon's only First Nations publication, except for the newsletters that surface and disappear according to the time, energy, and funds available in each community. Some of the newsletters are excellent, but the intermittent nature of their production makes them unreliable. They are generally produced by volunteer labour, by people who are already fully employed and are often outrageously overworked.

Dännzhà', a public affairs magazine.

Like these newsletters, *Dännzhà'* has laboured to find stable funding. The chief problem is that, as Doris Bill, then editor of *Dännzhà'*, told researchers, in 1990 the Ye Sa To Communications Society was the most poorly funded of all of Canada's Aboriginal communications societies. Frustrated by the constant struggle, she said, "All I want to be is a journalist, and I keep having to be a lobbyist." It is no surprise that this multitalented journalist left *Dännzhà'* for work as a broadcaster for CBC Whitehorse despite the consistently high praise given to the magazine. During her tenure as editor, Bill not only edited the magazine, wrote much of its material, and sold advertising, she also posed for the cover photograph for an issue on family violence. In another community, the editor of the monthly newsletter was working at least two full-time jobs in addition to hunting and trapping. Under these conditions, political coverage, especially during campaigns and elections when extended availability is required, is one of the major casualties of the Aboriginal print media deficit.

The absence of Aboriginal print media is apparent when one visits Yukon communities. Local issues are often covered in community newsletters but newspapers are scarce. The following community profiles provide a sketch of print and broadcast media outlets and media access across Yukon. The extent of each profile reflects the amount of information available.

Profiles of Selected Yukon Communities

Across Yukon, and despite strong differences and the usual array of animosities, people expressed a surprising sense of community, which cut across diverse cultural and geographical lines.

Beaver Creek

Beaver Creek has a population of 140 Aboriginal and non-Aboriginal people. The community, accessed via the Alaska Highway, is a Yukon-Alaska border town and customs point and is the westernmost community in Canada. In summer, the bus from Anchorage, Alaska, to Whitehorse makes an obligatory overnight stop, giving the local hostelries a boost and the travellers a rest. In winter, the hotels are closed and the bus goes straight through to Whitehorse.

Beaver Creek receives newspapers from British Columbia and Alaska but none from Yukon. Community information is posted in public places. As is usual in the small communities, news is often passed along by storekeepers. Because of its pivotal tourist location, the community maintains a small museum and a tourist centre.

Burwash Landing

The small community of Burwash Landing, with a population of eighty-four, is reached via the Alaska Highway. Most of the residents are members of the Kluane Tribal Council. In 1990-1 Council Director Florence Sparvier had just revived the community newsletter after it had been out of print for at least a year. She told us the newsletter was an essential community resource because Burwash "people are too far out and can't get information." She said it was difficult to keep the newsletter going because although "lots of people are eager to work on it, no-one has the experience." Sparvier said that keeping the newsletter alive is a high priority because many community members "don't trust Indian Affairs" and want to maintain their own information source. She would like to see communications training available so that more community members could contribute to the newsletter.

In terms of broadcasting, she said people in Burwash Landing rely on CHON-FM, the NNBY radio station in Whitehorse. They read the *Alberta Indian News* and other publications that are made available on a drop-in basis in the Tribal Council office. However, radio remains the medium of choice.

Carcross
Carcross, a community on the Klondike Highway, has a population of 342 Aboriginal and non-Aboriginal people. Special programs on Visitor Radio CKYN-Yukon Gold are broadcast from the community's visitor reception centre during the summer tourist season. For the rest of the year, residents rely like most Yukoners on CHON-FM, CBC-Radio, and satellite-transmitted television.

Carmacks
The 488 residents of Carmacks are a mix of Aboriginal and non-Aboriginal people. The community is home to the Little Salmon/Carmacks First Nation, whose members speak the Northern Tutchone language. Once a riverboat-fuelling station and a stop on the Overland Trail between Whitehorse and Dawson City, it sits on the Little Salmon River and the road to Faro, and is accessed by the Klondike Highway.

Notice boards outside the general store and other public places are an important medium of public communication. Yukon College, based in Whitehorse, maintains a small learning centre and an instructor/director in the community. Another instructor visits Carmacks every two weeks to offer adult literacy programs.

Dawson City
One of the largest communities in Yukon, Dawson City, on the Klondike Highway, has 1,999 Aboriginal and non-Aboriginal residents. This figure is a mere fraction of its population during the gold rush heydays, when the settlement boasted 30,000 citizens. According to *Yukon News* publisher Doug

Bell, Dawson is in the process of changing again and is expanding more rapidly than any other Yukon community.

Following a customary pattern of publications in small communities, the *Klondike Sun* was founded around 1970 as a mimeographed newsletter. Now the local newspaper, it is put together in Dawson with all-volunteer labour and is printed at the offices of the *Yukon News* in Whitehorse. Doug Bell said that the Dawson paper had some negative impact on his company's primary publication but was published as a public service. As he put it when interviewed, "It cuts into our readership, but they *needed* it."

In summer, Dawson City is Yukon's major tourist centre, with companies of entertainers performing gold-rush-style revues, and several thriving hostelries providing accommodation. The rest of the year Dawson City is just another Yukon town.

Old Crow

Old Crow, the northernmost community in Yukon, is reachable only by air – both scheduled and charter flights originating in Whitehorse and Dawson City – or by slow overland travel. The town's isolation is especially dangerous in the hot, dry, summer fire season. In the summer of 1990 the entire community was airlifted to Inuvik when forest fires came too close to homes.

People have access to an array of satellite television, CBC-Radio and CHON-FM, and Yukon newspapers. The community is widely regarded as pivotal at election time. Calling radio ham operators "the real innovators," *Yukon News* publisher Doug Bell recalled the drama of the previous territorial election, when Old Crow was "the giant-killer. We had all the votes in. It was tied 7-7 between the PC and NDP. We couldn't get Old Crow on the phone. I was still [Yukon] Commissioner. We got the Old Crow vote from a ham radio operator in Alaska" (Bell 1990). The ham operator was said to have picked up the results from a plane flying over, and radioed them to the Whitehorse airport. Old Crow's near-100 percent voter turnout in federal and territorial elections is related to electoral redistribution that made this a Gwich'in majority electoral district – most of the community's 275 people are members of the Vuntut Gwitch'in First Nation. As Bell says, "There's a mystique about Old Crow. It's famous. People Outside know about it." Old Crow is also famous for its musicians and especially for a unique style of fiddling.

Old Crow regularly produces important Yukon politicians and communicators. The elder Edith Josie is well known for her years of service as the community's columnist and the spokesperson who carries news of Old Crow to the rest of Yukon and the Outside via her famous column, "Here Are the News."

Pelly Crossing

North of Carmacks on the Klondike Highway, Pelly Crossing has a population of 285. Most residents are members of the Selkirk First Nation and speakers of the Northern Tutchone language. Yukon College maintains a small building and an instructor/director in the community. A travelling literacy instructor visits approximately every two weeks to supplement the college's program. An innovative wood shop and adult carpentry program based in the school provide both training and much-needed construction and repair. Instead of making standard (and often useless) wood-shop items, the students learn on the job, building new homes and repairing others. They maintain a list of homes in need of repair, setting priorities according to the state of disrepair and the family's need.

At the time of my visit, Jerry Alfred was serving as the editor of the *Pelly Button* (the community newsletter, whose content was usually more serious than its name) in addition to his full-time job in land claims. His high-energy career and many talents did not stop there. He modestly told me he also had an active life as a musician. I had no idea how active until the announcement in 1996 that he and his group, the Medicine Beat, had won a Juno Award from the Canadian music industry for the song "Etsin Shon, Grandfather Song."[9] Today, he is in such international demand that he must take great care to leave time to return to the Yukon communities he continues to call home. He was the first Yukoner ever to win a Juno, an event loudly proclaimed on the front page of the *Whitehorse Star* and more quietly noted on the back pages of some southern newspapers. For Alfred, the Juno was more than an award; it was a celebration of the continuity between his father's generation and his own: "My father set me on that trail ... He told me how the music was dying out, and he was really sad. I took that interest to carry on. He said, 'If you could do that, you are not only doing a big favour for me, but as well, a big favour for the whole culture of Northern Tutchone'" (Tobin 1996, 1). The Juno has helped to publicize Alfred's music and Northern Tutchone language and culture, worldwide.

Apart from Jerry Alfred's considerable talents, it is no surprise that a powerful cultural statement would come from this community. Especially considering its tiny population, Pelly Crossing has a highly advanced information network. In addition their newsletter, which is delivered each month to every mailbox in the community, many people read the *Yukon News* and, more rarely, the *Whitehorse Star*. Everyone listens to CHON-FM, and Ella Harper, the band office receptionist, phones in a weekly radio newscast featuring news from Pelly Crossing. Among the television stations received here are CBC, CBS (US), BCTV, and ITV.

The local MLA sends information to each home and also posts it in the band office, a beautiful new building with a couple of attractive hotel rooms for visitors. Other information is posted on bulletin boards located at the school, store, band office, and the Yukon College facility, a small house with space for small-scale seminars, meetings, reflection, and discussion. Apart from the weekly radio feed, news *from* the community is scarce in the rest of the territory – even the Yukon newspapers don't take regular news from Pelly. I was told that a Whitehorse reporter had been sent there the previous summer to do a story on a local horseback-touring program, but that some community members found the published story inaccurate and patronizing.

Teslin

Most of Teslin's 482 residents are members of the Teslin First Nation, descendants of Tlingit people who moved inland from the Alaska and British Columbia coast to trade with other Aboriginal peoples. The community, in southern Yukon near the British Columbia border, is reached via the Alaska Highway.

David Keenan, who was then Teslin chief and is now an MLA, told us that radio dominates the media here, as in other Yukon communities, and that Aboriginal television provides good coverage within the limits of a much shorter broadcast day than radio is able to provide: "NEDAA [TV] and CHON-FM do a good job – interviews with chiefs, discussions of the issues. CBC Northern Service makes local news available – morning, evening. Land claims is the main thing and it's getting covered." Although northern issues in general are reported, communications within the community are less consistent. Says Keenan, "Community newsletters are time-consuming. They fizzle. They go off with great zeal and fizzle ... Teslin had a newsletter, but it's not functioning now."

Keenan wants more in-depth coverage of issues and more public affairs programming that goes beyond the "basic information on radio." From his perspective, the major problem is the "print gap. We used to get *Shakat* and *Dännzhà'* every two months but their budget was slashed. We get the *Yukon News* and once in a while the *Alberta Indian News*. But the media's not versatile." .

Keenan points to the important interrelationship of communications and politics, noting that "most Native people don't even bother with electoral politics. There's frustration with communications, land claims. We need to fill people in – *our people*." Keenan emphasized his community's independence and a strong preference for non-intervention by Outsiders in community affairs. The Teslin First Nation holds a general assembly and four general meetings each year, which are open to the entire community. Teslin is unique, the only community in Yukon with an appointed chief, following a 1987 decision by the community to return to the traditional system of leadership selection.

Whitehorse

All roads lead to Whitehorse, the Yukon capital. Direct flights connect the city with Alaskan communities and with Vancouver. In summer, the White Pass and Yukon Railway is an alternative route from Whitehorse to Skagway, Alaska, although travellers must go a short way by bus to complete the connection. The Whitehorse population of 23,474 is a broad mix of non-Aboriginal and Aboriginal people, including permanent and temporary residents from all Yukon First Nations, and the Whitehorse-based Kwanlin Dun First Nation. The number of temporary residents is typical of a government town. Whitehorse is home to the Aboriginal and territorial governments – the Council for Yukon First Nations and the Yukon Legislative Assembly and offices of the Government of the Yukon – as well as to the court and other public institutions, and is the major source of permanent and temporary wage employment.

Whitehorse has the richest cultural life of any northern city I know. In terms of both locally generated and visiting production, the music, art, theatre, and writing found in Whitehorse are in a league with Canada's major cities. For the privilege of residing in a beautiful setting with a substantial community of colleagues, artists have their work greatly complicated by northern conditions. One winter, the costumes for a January theatre production arrived from Vancouver about an hour before opening night, after numerous delays.

Whitehorse has two newspapers, the *Whitehorse Star* and the *Yukon News*, and three radio stations – CBC (public), CKRW (private), and CHON-FM (First Nations). Except for scant CBC Northern Service programming and the slowly expanding programming produced or carried by TVNC, Whitehorse television is imported from the rest of Canada and the United States. Yukon's only French-language paper, *L'Aurore Boréale: La voix française de la dernière frontière* was unable to publish for part of 1992 after Ottawa cut $80,000 from the five-year development budget of the sponsoring organization, L'Association Franco-Yukonnaise (Buckley 1992, 1).

Budgetary realities also affect the coverage of the more mainstream media. Jim Butler, editor of the *Whitehorse Star,* expressed some dissatisfaction with his newspaper's ability to cover campaigns, elections, and political developments: "We're a Whitehorse paper and only cover the bigger ridings outside Whitehorse. [During campaign periods] we do phone interviews with 99 per cent of the candidates. I wish I could put somebody on the road. The only thing stopping me is money – hotels at $90 a night, food and gas – the worst, and salary ... We're a newspaper, but we're also a small business" (Butler 1990).

Political coverage is not just thin, it is sometimes inaccurate. Yukon Premier Tony Penikett recalled that his landmark win, which ended Progressive Conservative domination and brought in a New Democratic government was originally reported as an NDP *loss* on CBC television. A Whitehorse resident recalled hearing another media goof. On air, a radio reporter told a *winning* politician, "You, sir, have lost your seat." The politician did not discover the mistake until after the broadcast.

Despite the shortcomings, there is some cause for optimism. Doug Bell observed that northerners often get information before other Canadians, because of satellite and alternative media connections. The "moccasin telegraph" works well in northern communities, and as we have seen, northerners are especially adept at using the Internet.

Atlin, British Columbia

Access to Atlin, a community of 400 residents located in British Columbia, just across the Yukon border, is via a gravel road off the Alaska Highway. Atlin is included in the Yukon study because of its unique status. A small community on a huge lake, it is the most northwesterly town in British Columbia. Its residents maintain strong physical, political, social, and psychological ties to Yukon. The community is a mix of Aboriginal and non-Aboriginal people and includes many artists who settled in the community because of its beauty. The Aboriginal people are members of the Taku River Tlingit First Nation. According to Allison Mitcham, Taku River band members are less pressured to assimilate than "in most other places" (1989, 142-3).

Atlin is unincorporated and therefore has no government of its own. Its identity is split between British Columbia and Yukon. Federal funding arrives in Atlin via Yukon, not its home province. The only highway access to the community is through Yukon. Most residents said that they feel part of Yukon. Some expressed frustration about feeling in limbo. As one person put it, "B.C. won't let us join the Yukon. We tried. B.C. won't let us go. But we get all our services from the Yukon." The layered telephone system exemplifies Atlin's complicated double status: "We pay both BC and Yukon phone companies. It comes in on one bill, but there are two sets of wires! All our doctors and lawyers are in Whitehorse. And most people move when their kids get high school age. Most of them go to Whitehorse."

Public information is posted on bulletin boards and walls of the Atlin Inn, which is open year round (although I was the only Outsider in residence in December, when the inn's primary activity took place in the café and bar). Information notices are also posted at both general stores, the town offices, the museum, and public library. When I visited, I found a wide variety of posted notices ranging from a school bus meeting to social events and classes run by Northern Lights College, a partly distance-education, partly on-site institution with facilities scattered across northern British Columbia.

The education process is highly developed and quite complicated to administer. Because there are no facilities here (and presumably because it is cheaper than building a high school), the provincial government gives Atlin families subsidies to send adolescents to public schools in southern British Columbia or Whitehorse, or to private schools. The high school in Whitehorse maintains a dormitory for students from Atlin and those from remote Yukon communities that do not have their own high schools.

Government agent Fred Jenkins said media coverage of Atlin ranges from poor to nonexistent. "The Whitehorse papers don't cover Atlin except if there's controversy." People tend to share newspapers around – the *Vancouver Sun* when it is available, the *Edmonton Journal,* to which several people subscribe and then share with others.

I was told that Atlin's Aboriginal residents have little interest in politics outside their own community, and rarely participate in community-wide political activities. Elections information is "never on the media. It comes through this [the BC-run government] office." Indeed, the counter in this small office had news releases that were not available anywhere else, which meant that townspeople had to go into the government office to read them.

The Taku River First Nation has its own newsletter. Weather permitting, the mail comes three times a week on the van that also carries travellers when there is room (the mail has first priority). Like the ground traffic, all flights go through Yukon, with the Whitehorse airport as home base. In addition to scheduled flights, there are helicopter and fixed-wing charters, also based in Yukon. Going anywhere is costly. One person said "It costs more to travel in our own province than to go to Ottawa and back, or Hawaii."

Despite many difficulties and inconsistent communication and transportation access among these Yukon communities, the fact that there is road access from one community to the next (with the exception of Old Crow) makes a difference, in some instances and in some seasons. It means that at least in passable weather travel is more affordable for more people, though it is difficult much of the time for many. But increased access may actually have its disadvantages in terms of the development of communications. For example, people in the travel-deprived eastern Arctic, who rely almost exclusively on air access among communities, are more widely computer literate and have developed the most sophisticated broadcast programming in the North.

While Nunavut remains the northern broadcast mecca because of the great advances made in Inuit radio and television, the total communications picture is stronger in Yukon. Ronald Robbins, who has served as director of the Communications Branch of the Yukon government and as a Yukon government representative on the board of directors of TVNC, considers the Yukon communications network better than "anywhere North of 50, except northern Alberta." As evidence, he points to a communications mix that includes air, highway, road, and waterway access; telephone and fax; and television, radio, and print media. He says that such a range means that the tiny community of Burwash Landing, for example, is better equipped in terms of communications than Port Severn, Ontario.

This fits the pattern observed in my own research, in which the smallest and most remote communities are often the ones with the best communications infrastructure – in the context of the broader pattern of a highly developed northern communications system. The history of northern broadcasting clarifies one reason for the generally advanced state of northern communications: the North's extreme need makes it an ideal place to experiment. When northerners' communication needs have not been met by private or community initiatives, the Canadian government has traditionally intervened. The tradition of intervention has carried over from the federal to the territorial and provincial governments. When Ottawa cut CBC funding, and the corporation said it would no longer be able to serve communities with fewer than 500 inhabitants, the Yukon government stepped in. One informant told the researchers, "It's YTG [the Yukon Territorial Government] not CBC that gets CBC into the communities – provides the funding and technology – 16 TV stations, three FM radio stations at Pelly Crossing, Stewart Crossing and Old Crow." By comparison, the Government of the Northwest Territories supports only twenty-four television rebroadcasts.

Sometimes the various governments give higher priority to communications access than to the law. One person interviewed recalled that "in 1976, they put a [satellite] dish at Teslin [Yukon]. It wasn't legal at the time, but YTG did it." This kind of unofficial involvement of government, private citizens, and communities in "illegal" communications activities such as satellite dishes and pirate radio stations is attributable to the North's continuing frontier status. In a system always struggling to catch up, there is often a significant time lag between a project's need-based beginning and its legitimation. As in the past, benevolent "outlaws" – sometimes even in the government – continue to forge links that provide northern people with comfort, connections, and survival.

Having surveyed communications in Yukon – the westernmost Canadian territory – let us move east, turning our attention to the Northwest Territories, which shares its western border with Yukon, and to the new territory of Nunavut, which borders the NWT on the east. The next chapter describes a two-year case study of print media coverage of the North in three newspapers: the Native Communications Society-sponsored *Native Press*, published in Yellowknife, NWT; the independently published *Nunatsiaq News*, based in Iqaluit, Nunavut Territory; and the national Toronto-based *Globe and Mail*. The study brings together themes and issues raised in earlier section of the book, concerning representation of northerners – particularly first peoples – by Aboriginal and non-Aboriginal journalists in the North and Outside.

6
Print Media Coverage Up Here and Outside
Brian Higgins and Valerie Alia

Canada has been described as a country with "two solitudes," a reference to the cultural chasm between its two "founding nations," the English and the French. Now, a "third solitude," the Aboriginal community, is increasingly regaining its voice and its sovereignty, especially in the Canadian North.

Northern political and social issues have a profound effect upon all Canadians. Long-standing land claims are being settled. Maps are being redrawn, new territories created. Hunting and fishing rights, land ownership, resource rights, and significant cash payments are being negotiated at an unprecedented pace. These fundamental changes are creating an intriguing and challenging era for northern and southern Canadians alike. It will result in a new concept of our relationship to each other and, as Native self-government is born, a new concept of nationhood itself.

In the course of redefining these relationships, the media must examine the role they play in northern Canada and must evaluate their effectiveness in the process of information exchange. There is no question that traditional disparities continue to complicate that process. News about the North remains locked into two separate media spheres – the first produced in the North by northerners and the second produced in the South by southerners. The continuing discrepancy between public access to northern information *in* the North and *outside* the North remains an irony in a world supposedly crisscrossed by the information highway.

In large part, the discrepancy is due to attitudes of southern media managers who trust their own staff more than they do northern journalists. Many northern journalists say that their work had been rejected by "major" media, even when they were uniquely available for breaking stories such as the Yellowknife mine explosion and the signing of the Nunavut agreement. For example, in a 1992 interview, a respected northern journalist said that he was considered "too biased" to cover the Giant mine explosion for a national newspaper, although he had contacted them several times. "They'd rather get their information over the phone or from reporters parachuted in for a few days, than from a working journalist who lives here, knows the people, understands the issues and can provide a long-term view."

Such complaints are common. It is rare for a northern journalist to have credibility in the national or global media. Despite the emerging multichannel universe, twenty-four-hour availability of the all-news channel CBC Newsworld, and the CTV-based channel, material produced by CBC Northern Service and the Aboriginal broadcasting companies in Yukon, the Northwest Territories, and Nunavut seldom finds its way to southern audiences.

In the Outside media, northern- and Aboriginal-produced northern news is marginalized at least twice – as *northern* news and as *Aboriginal* news. In other words, it is marginalized first by region and then by culture. Vast geographical expanses, multiplicity of ethnic groups, and unequal population distribution pose special challenges to the dissemination of news.

This chapter examines the representation of northern indigenous people in three northern and southern newspapers over a period in 1991-2. The three papers chosen for study were the *Globe and Mail*, a southern, Toronto-based, non-Aboriginal daily, with no Aboriginal editors or reporters; the *Press Independent,* then an Aboriginal-controlled weekly published in Yellowknife, with a non-Aboriginal editor and both Aboriginal and non-Aboriginal reporters, covering the western Arctic (the region that now remains in the Northwest Territories); and *Nunatsiaq News,* a non-Aboriginal-controlled weekly based in Iqaluit, with non-Aboriginal editors, primarily non-Aboriginal reporters, and Aboriginal (Inuit) translators, covering the eastern Arctic – what is now Nunavut.

The early 1990s, when the analysis of these newspapers was conducted, was a time of forward leaps and backward manoeuvres, with contradictory funding practices that encouraged quantum improvements to broadcasting and discouraged similar shifts in print. Indeed, one of the three newspapers examined, the *Press Independent,* succumbed soon after the study was completed. Meanwhile, the *Globe and Mail* has continued to undergo periodic transformations, usually resulting in thinner background material and less in-depth coverage in general, including that of the North. Of the three, only *Nunatsiaq News* has improved the scope and quality of its coverage. It is no coincidence that it is published in Nunavut. The exhilaration that has accompanied the early stages of Nunavut's official emergence has certainly affected its newspaper, now available online as well as in newsprint.

Overview and Methodology

Content analysis, on its own, is not an accurate or a reliable method for understanding the contents of a publication. Yet despite its limitations I considered it the most appropriate technique for the study, with the important qualification that I made significant adaptations and modifications, particularly in adding qualitative elements to what is usually considered a quantitative methodology. While others have developed kindred methodologies (e.g., Ericson, Baranek, and Chan 1991), the project utilized techniques that I developed over the past twenty years.

All editions of the *Nunatsiaq News,* the *Press Independent,* and the *Globe and Mail* were analysed by a team of researchers throughout the months of September 1991 and September 1992. An individual researcher was assigned

Nunatsiaq News, the bilingual weekly newspaper of the Eastern Arctic, publishes in English and Inuktitut from its offices in Iqaluit.

to each publication in each year. Each researcher read all editions of the publication in the assigned time period, collected data on each paper's coverage of northern Native issues, recorded this data in a report, and compiled an individual analysis of his or her results. Brian Higgins then amalgamated the primary data and the researchers' individual analyses, which he and I re-examined and reassessed. He then wrote the first draft of this chapter, which I subsequently revised and expanded.

The researchers collected their data and performed their analyses using the following variables:

1   the total number of published items in which "the North" is mentioned
2   the total number of published items in which northern Aboriginal people are mentioned
3   the occupations or "area of activity" of newsmakers who were mentioned
4   the name of each writer, where available
5   the ethnicity of each reporter, where available
6   the accuracy, relevance, and "tone" of headlines accompanying the stories
7   the content, relevance, and tone of photographs
8   the relevance and tone of cutlines accompanying the photographs
9   the overall tone of each published item
10 the specific topics discussed in each published item.

The subjective nature of some of these questions permitted a useful latitude for interpretation by each researcher. It also resulted in some inevitable inconsistencies in the recorded data. For the purposes of this chapter, inconsistently recorded data were re-examined where possible, using the original publications. In some categories, incompatible data have been included in this chapter, but have not been used in the overall analysis.

It is impossible to precisely quantify what are essentially qualitative observations and categories – the "tone" of a story, for example. For this reason, the numerical analysis in this chapter is intended only as a supplement to the qualitative observations: the numbers in such a study cannot stand on their own. This presentation differs radically from conventional approaches to content analysis, in which the data are reported as objective and solitary figures. We have deliberately included not only reassessment of the same data by different researchers but extensive discussions of the researchers' perspectives, biases, and assumptions, and of the limitations inherent in collecting and analyzing data of this kind. It is our hope that readers will use this information in a fluid and creative way, as a starting point for critical observation and media analyses of their own.

The aim was to set a time frame at random and observe what coverage occurred. In a sense, the Giant mine disaster near Yellowknife in September

1992 skewed the coverage by eclipsing all other stories and exaggerating the attention southern media paid to northern events. However, this "skewed" coverage reveals an important pattern observed throughout my research from 1985 to the present (for example, Alia 1989a, 1990, 1991a, 1991b, 1991e, and ongoing work not yet published): every crisis involving northern and/or northern Aboriginal people brings the North temporarily closer to non-northerners. This pattern is not just the result of specific attitudes toward the North, but of the persistent bias throughout "mainstream" news media that favours the newsworthiness of crises. The time frame for this study was identified and the research begun long before the explosion at Giant mine resulted in the deaths of nine men. While it could be argued that another time period would reveal more "typical" coverage of the North, it is our conviction that our analysis does reveal typical coverage. Northern and indigenous people receive coverage in "mainstream" media *primarily* in times of crisis, a point borne out by the study, which encompasses coverage before, during, and after the explosion.

Finally, each of the three newspapers chosen for analysis represents a different sample region: the eastern Arctic (the *Nunatsiaq News*), the western Arctic (the *Press Independent),* and southern Canada (the *Globe and Mail*). The three sample areas provided useful contrast between northern and southern cultures, as well as significant differences between the eastern and western regions of northern Canada, which may not be readily apparent to many southern Canadians.

Nunatsiaq News

The *Nunatsiaq News* is published weekly in Iqaluit, the largest community in the eastern Arctic (now Nunavut). Iqaluit, located on Baffin Island, is a predominantly Inuit community; at the time of the study its population was about 3,600. In 1993 Jim Bell, a *Nunatsiaq News* editor, estimated that 30 to 40 percent of the Iqaluit population was Qallunaat (non-Inuit) – the largest single concentration of non-Aboriginal people in Nunavut, whose population is about 85 percent Inuit. The proportions are changing somewhat. With the evolution of Nunavut, an increasing number of Qallunaat are leaving. It is likely that this change will continue, because the overwhelming majority of jobs advertised these days require, or strongly prefer, fluency in Inuktitut. Nevertheless, Iqaluit will probably continue to have more Qallunaat than any other Nunavut community.

Nunatsiaq News describes itself as "the only commercial aboriginal weekly in Canada" and is a bilingual publication, with stories in English and Inuktitut, the language of the eastern Arctic Inuit. The newspaper is owned by Nortext Multimedia, which also published *Arctic Circle* magazine. Nortext is based in Iqaluit and in Nepean, Ontario.

Iqaluit readers have same-day access to several southern papers, including the *Montreal Gazette*, *La Presse*, the *Ottawa Sun*, the *Ottawa Citizen*, and the *Globe and Mail*. According to its editors, Jim Bell and Todd Phillips (who left the post in 1997), *Nunatsiaq News* offers an "alternative" to these southern papers. It also serves many communities outside Iqaluit, where Aboriginal people form a greater majority of the population.

In Nunavut, as in all regions of the North, cultural conflicts between Aboriginal people and non-Natives are a significant issue. Jim Bell reports that Aboriginal/non-Aboriginal relations in the eastern Arctic are "not as amicable as they appear on the surface." For the most part, says Bell, Inuit in Nunavut maintain an outward display of harmony with their Qallunaat neighbours. He says "unity of the group" is a traditional Inuit value, stemming from historical necessities of survival, and he thinks that the failure of some Qallunaat to acknowledge this adds to the underlying tensions in Iqaluit.

The *Press Independent*

The *Press Independent*, formerly called the *Native Press*, ceased publication in March 1993. It was restructured and revived as *Native Press* three years later, technically as a quarterly but actually published less often. Both papers were published in Yellowknife and owned by the Native Communications Society of the NWT, a Dene-Métis organization that originally received federal funding for the publications. At first, *Native Press* was published every other week and focused almost exclusively on Dene and Métis news and information. At the time of the study, the *Press Independent* was a weekly paper catering to the Native community, with a readership of about 5,600 people.

There are significant differences between Yellowknife in the West and Iqaluit in the East. The Northwest Territories has experienced greater exposure to southern culture, economic development, and resource extraction, and has a much larger non-Aboriginal population and greater diversity of indigenous groups.

In early 1992, when cuts were announced by the secretary of state, the Native Communications Society and editor Lee Selleck attempted to maintain the *Press Independent* by publishing weekly instead of every two weeks and by expanding its target audience to include the entire Yellowknife community of 15,000 people. After the closure of the *Press Independent*, a new weekly paper, the *Northern Star*, emerged, published by local businesswoman Vi Beck. It survived for less than a year and ceased publication 10 January 1994. However, Yellowknife still had two established papers, *News/North* and the *Yellowknifer*, both published by Yellowknife-based Northern News Services. After the *Press Independent* folded, Lee Selleck continued to live in

Yellowknife, writing a weekly column for the *Yellowknifer* and a book about the Giant mine tragedy of September 1992.

The *Globe and Mail*

Published in Toronto and owned by Thomson Newspapers, the *Globe and Mail* describes itself as "Canada's national newspaper" and is printed simultaneously in several locations in southern Canada. Its daily readership of about 330,000 is located mainly in Toronto and, to a lesser degree, in other urban centres across southern Canada. It covers the North with a single northern affairs reporter stationed in its Edmonton bureau, but freelance writers occasionally contribute features on various topics related to the North.

The View from Here

Tables 6.1 and 6.2 show the number of times the North or Aboriginal people were mentioned in the papers. Expressed as a percentage of total editorial material published in each paper, the North and its people were the dominant features of northern media, but were virtually non-existent in the south. For example, the fifty-seven stories about "the North" in the *Press Independent* in September 1991 represent about 40 percent of that paper's content. In the same period, the eight stories in the *Globe and Mail* constitute approximately 0.15 percent of its news section. Furthermore, one researcher noted that it "took a bit of stretching" to include any *Globe and Mail* items at all, because all of the stories "dealt with southern concerns" (Chase 1991-2). The definition of what constitutes a "northern" or an Aboriginal story is open to interpretation. The fact that cultural boundaries are constantly shifting in the North raises important questions about what constitutes a purely "northern" issue, and what is the nature of "authentic" Aboriginal culture. Noted one researcher, "I factored out all stories dealing with generic everyday life: those articles or editorials, movie reviews and sports stories that one could find anywhere on the American continents. What was left were those articles that concerned matters indigenous to the people in the region" (McLaren 1993). Those criteria are as good as any for sorting the news in the northern media. When applied to southern media,

Table 6.1

Published items in which "the North" is mentioned, 1991-2

	Press Independent	*Nunatsiaq News*	*Globe and Mail*
1991	57	24*	8
1992	63	68	12
Total	120	92	20

* Stringent criteria used by one researcher resulted in low figure.

Table 6.2

Published items in which northern Aboriginal people are mentioned, 1991-2

	Press Independent	Nunatsiaq News	Globe and Mail
1991	58	9*	7
1992	65	37	2
Total	123	46	9

* Stringent criteria used by one researcher resulted in low figure.

however, northern issues and Aboriginal people vanish from the sample. As noted above, even a more lenient definition fails to identify significant northern coverage by southern media.

The newsmakers most frequently mentioned in northern media were politicians and civil servants (see Table 6.3). In all three media groups, the status of political power and structure of social hierarchies, both northern or southern, are featured and frequently reinforced. In the northern media, this agenda is evolving to include traditional indigenous power structures, by focusing on chiefs and elders as well. The *Globe and Mail*'s frequent mention of union leaders and police is a statistical artefact of their focus on a single northern news story in 1992 – the bomb explosion at Giant mine and

Table 6.3

Occupations or area of activity of Northern newsmakers, 1991-2

Occupation	Press Independent		Nunatsiaq News		Globe and Mail	
	%	Number	%	Number	%	Number
Politics	26	32	44	41	16	3
Elder/chief	22	27	18	16	11	2
Union/labour	10	12	8	7	26	5
Police	6	7	1	1	26	5
Business	10	12	9	8	11	2
Education/ Social services	7	9	9	8	5	1
Hunter/fisher	6	7	6	6	5	1
Judge/lawyer	4	5	1	1	0	0
Criminal	3	4	0	0	0	0
Artist	0	0	3	3	0	0
Student	3	4	0	0	0	0
Religion	2	3	0	0	0	0
Environment	1	1	0	0	0	0
Doctor/nurse	0	0	1	1	0	0
Total	100	123	100	92	100	19

the resultant death of nine miners. Repercussions of the explosion were felt in all three media, as evidenced by the relatively frequent mention of union leaders in all papers and of police in the *Press Independent.*

It is interesting to note that the percentage of stories mentioning business leaders is almost the same in all three papers. The print media are essentially a creation of southern culture. By exporting the mechanisms of mass media to the North, the South appears to be exporting its cultural values and media agenda as well.

Non-Aboriginal reporters contributed significantly more frequently than Aboriginal reporters in both northern regions (see Tables 6.4 and 6.5). This imbalance is probably even greater than the data suggest, since unattributed articles were probably largely the work of non-Native staff reporters. Therefore, media participation, in newspapers at least, is still predominantly a southern, non-Aboriginal cultural activity. This reflects a prevalent trend in the North, where southerners have tended to dominate technical and managerial jobs. The imbalance became even greater in the *Press Independent* in 1992. Non-Native contributions increased more than five-fold and Aboriginal contributions decreased slightly following the paper's repositioning from

Table 6.4

Contributors to *Nunatsiaq News*, 1991-2

Name	Ethnicity	Number of contributions		Total
		1991	1992	
Amagoalik, John	Aboriginal	0	4	4
Bell, Jim	Non-native	1	10	11
Bergman-Illnik, Karen	Non-native	2	0	2
Coleman, Greg	Non-native	0	10	10
Devine, Marina	Non-native	0	17	17
Duncan, Kerrie	Non-native	1	0	1
Itorcheak, Adla	Aboriginal	0	1	1
Jacoopsie, Peter	Aboriginal	0	1	1
MacDonald, Lucy	Aboriginal	1	0	1
Pearson, Bryan	Non-native	0	1	1
Ridell, Bill	Non-native	0	1	1
Sackett, Sydney	Aboriginal	0	1	1
Williamson, Peter	Aboriginal	1	1	2
Zellen, Barry	Non-native	0	1	1
Aboriginal		2	8	10
Non-native		4	40	44
Unattributed		18	24	42
Total		24	72	96

Note: Data include editorial staff as well as freelancers and correspondents.
   "Unattributed" articles were short, unsigned news items.

Table 6.5

Contributors to *Press Independent*, 1991-2

Name	Ethnicity	Number of contributions		Total
		1991	1992	
Bergman-Illnik, Karen	Non-native	1	0	1
Blondin, George	Aboriginal	1	3	4
Conrad, Valerie	Aboriginal	1	0	1
Devine, Marina	Non-native	0	16	16
Derken, Gina	Non-native	1	0	1
Dreger, Shannon	Unknown	0	1	1
Gougeon, Richard	Non-native	9	5	14
Holman, John	Aboriginal	18	14	32
Jerome, Sarah	Aboriginal	1	0	1
Johnson, Doug	Non-native	2	0	2
Jumbo, Brenda	Aboriginal	1	0	1
Kulchyski, Peter	Non-native	0	1	1
Lafferty, Bill	Aboriginal	0	1	1
Lajoie, Karen	Non-native	0	33	33
Laroque, Marie-Helene	Unknown	1	0	1
McPlatter, Clyde	Unknown	0	1	1
Nadli, Lorna	Aboriginal	1	0	1
Norn, Nancy	Unknown	0	1	1
Raemer, Zoe	Non-native	0	3	3
Selleck, Lee	Non-native	1	20	21
Urquhart, Doug	Non-native	1	0	1
Washie, Johnny	Aboriginal	2	3	5
Unattributed	n/a	16	0	16
Aboriginal		25	21	46
Non-native		15	78	93
Unattributed/unknown		17	3	20
Total		57	102	159

Note: Data include editorial staff as well as freelancers and correspondents.
Clyde McPlatter is a pseudonym used by several writers.

a Dene/Métis newspaper to a cross-cultural publication aimed at serving the entire Yellowknife community.

However, there is evidence to suggest that increased southern cultural influence, such as that in Yellowknife, actually increases Aboriginal participation in the media. In the Yellowknife area, Aboriginal reporters contributed 32 percent of all news items, compared to only 11 percent in Nunavut (see Table 6.6). Because southern influence is more recent in the eastern Arctic, this imbalance suggests that there is a "learning curve" to Aboriginal participation in newspapers. Newly established media in the North tend to be dominated by non-Aboriginals, but this imbalance tends

Table 6.6

Ethnicity of contributors as a percentage of total contributions, in *Nunatsiaq News* and *Press Independent*, 1991-2

Ethnicity	Nunatsiaq News			Press Independent		
	1991	1992	Total	1991	1992	Total
Non-native						
Percentage	17	56	46	26	76	59
Number	4	40	44	15	78	93
Aboriginal						
Percentage	8	11	10	44	21	29
Number	2	8	10	25	21	46
Unknown						
Percentage	75	33	44	30	3	12
Number	18	24	42	17	3	20
Total						
Percentage	100	100	100	100	100	100
Number	24	72	96	57	102	159

Note: Ethnicity verified for both papers by Jim Bell, editor of *Nunatsiaq News*.

to decrease with time. In addition to southern culture, other factors may include increased English-literacy rates among Aboriginal groups in the Western NWT as opposed to Nunavut, as well as increased Aboriginal representation in government.

In both regions, the majority of reporting was performed by staff writers, which contributed significantly to the non-Native domination of media contributions. It is interesting to note that in the *Nunatsiaq News* the numbers of Aboriginal and non-Aboriginal contributors were equal (eleven of each), although the number of articles these contributors wrote were not. Still, the high number of Aboriginal contributors suggests that the Inuit ethnic majority in Iqaluit is reflected in the ratio of writers, even though staff writers contribute a greater volume of material.

Accuracy, Relevance, and "Tone" of Headlines

Analysis of headlines is essential to the understanding of a newspaper's treatment of a story. The reader sees the headline first – it is intended to catch the eye and draw the reader into the story. For this reason, it is at least as important as the story itself. If it is accurate as well as catchy, it correctly represents the story. If it is inaccurate, it can do immeasurable damage, by distorting the story and confusing and misinforming the reader.

The nature of newspaper makeup requires consideration of each separate element of a story. Many readers are unaware that the reporter whose name they see in the byline, as the author of the story, is seldom the same person who writes the headline. The editor who edits the story is seldom responsible for writing the headline. The same is true of the captions, called cutlines, that accompany photographs and other illustrations. The reader must process the information without knowing how it was produced. Typically, the news story is absorbed by the reader as a piece of news, rather than as a collaboration among separate members of the news staff. A responsible and useful analysis must make the complexity of the process more transparent.

As part of the analysis of the three newspapers, headlines were examined to determine whether they represented or misrepresented the story. Researchers were asked to evaluate headlines in terms of "tone," accuracy, and relevance to each news story. In general, researchers reported, with only a few exceptions, that most headlines were accurate and relevant. They did cite occasional headlines they believed to be inadequate, but these evaluations are arguably subjective, were not frequent, and were not confined to any one publication. Table 6.7 illustrates the use of three "tones" in headlines.

Interpretation of data on headline tone requires definition and examples of the terms positive, negative, and neutral. A "positive" headline, which is often used with community events, personality profiles, and human interest stories, suggests that readers will tend to approve of the people, events, and opinions in the story. Some examples of positive headlines include "Paradise at Caribou Flats" (*Press Independent*), "Progress Made on RCMP Contract" (*Nunatsiaq News*), and "Where to Find Canada's Heart" (*Globe and Mail*). By contrast, a negative headline alerts readers to the existence of undesirable, regrettable events or situations, often invoking elements of tragedy, conflict, or inadequacy. Examples from the three papers are: "UNV Calls Social Services Investigation 'Totally Inadequate'" (*Nunatsiaq News*), "Lung Cancer Rate High among Inuit Women" (*Press Independent*), and "The Internal Exiles of Canada" (*Globe and Mail*). Finally, a neutral headline does not indicate a strong position or lead readers to form an opinion or a reaction before they have read the article. Often "dry," simple, factual, or "objective," neutral headlines are sometimes vague or lack detail, as the following examples indicate: "Housing in Iqaluit" (*Nunatsiaq News*), "Lottery for Bison Tags Soon" (*Press Independent*), "Natives Value Justice Differently" (*Globe and Mail*). No particular tone is preferable to another, except perhaps when a headline was deemed "neutral" because it was too vague or, hypothetically, when it is deemed "negative" because it is derogatory. In all other situations, each headline tone has a specific function. The frequency and context of its use reflects the editorial focus of a publication, not its quality.

In all of the regions surveyed in 1992, the use of negative headlines increased significantly compared to the previous year (see Table 6.7). This was a result of the bombing deaths in Yellowknife's Giant mine, which was a major news story throughout Canada. The tone of headlines in the *Globe and Mail* changed most dramatically (67 percent negative headlines, up from

Table 6.7

Tone of headlines, 1991-2

	1991		1992		2-year average	
	%	Number of items	%	Number of items	%	Number of items
Nunatsiaq News						
Positive	38	9	36	24	37	16.5
Negative	12	3	26	18	19	10.5
Neutral	50	12	38	26	44	19
Total	100	24	100	68	100	46
Press Independent						
Positive	27	15	21	13	24	14
Negative	19	11	34	22	26	16.5
Neutral	54	31	45	29	50	30
Total	100	57	100	64	100	60.5
Globe and Mail						
Positive	25	2	8	1	16.5	1.5
Negative	25	2	67	8	46	5
Neutral	50	4	25	3	37.5	3.5
Total	100	8	100	12	100	10

25 percent in 1991) as a result of focusing exclusively on the mine disaster through late September 1992. The *Globe and Mail* had virtually no coverage of northern Aboriginal people during this time. It seems an unavoidable fact of the Canadian news industry that extraordinary tragedy is the single criterion that brings southern media coverage to northern issues.

As is common to the majority of weekly community newspapers throughout North America, the *Nunatsiaq News* and the *Press Independent* published mainly positive and neutral headlines. As chroniclers of weekly life in each community, these papers reported the priorities, preferences, and, frequently, the unexceptional events occurring within each community. It is interesting to note that in 1991 the *Globe and Mail* also showed a similar trend, publishing mainly "soft" features about the North. However, the specific topics reported in the *Globe and Mail* had little in common with those in the northern media.

The content and tone of headlines also reveals different value systems in northern and southern Canada. In 1991 the *Press Independent* ran a positive headline that read "Inuvialuit Get a Bowhead." Meanwhile, the *Globe and Mail* used a more negative headline to refer to whaling: "James Bay Plan: A Whale for the Killing?"

Table 6.8

Tone of photographs and illustrations, 1991-2, in percentage

	Nunatsiaq News			Press Independent			Globe and Mail		
	1991	1992	Total	1991	1992	Total	1991	1992	Total
Positive	50	29	33	65	49	52	0	0	0
Negative	0	0	0	0	3	2	20	50	36
Neutral	50	67	67	35	48	46	80	50	64

Note: Due to rounding, not all columns total 100 percent.

Just as headlines jump out at readers and draw them into the story, photographs both illustrate the story and attract readers' attention to the text. Photographs and the cutlines that describe them can enhance understanding of a story or they can distort it. The analysis of the tone of photographs and cutlines of the three papers revealed patterns similar to those of the headlines (Table 6.8). The northern media most often used positive and neutral items. As one researcher noted in her analysis of the *Press Independent*, "The photographs are overwhelmingly positive, many of them featuring children, school kids playing, etc. and therefore lack any real journalistic approach. On the other hand, there is a real community feel through the use of these photographs, of the kind one finds in very small community papers, indicating a close and tight knit community" (Prystay 1992-3).

The production of "negative" photographs often requires that a photojournalist be on the scene of a breaking news story. Limited staff and resources at small community newspapers often make this impractical. Furthermore, many events reported in the northern media take place in remote communities, where it may not be possible to send a photographer.

All of the media used negative cutlines more frequently than negative photographs – particularly the *Nunatsiaq News* in 1992, when no negative photos were published, but 16 percent of all cutlines were negative, and the *Globe and Mail* in 1992, in which 50 percent of photos and 83 percent of

Table 6.9

Tone of cutlines accompanying photographs, 1991-2, in percentage

	Nunatsiaq News		Press Independent		Globe and Mail		
	1991	1992	1991	1992	1991	1992	Total
Positive	–	21	–	66	0	0	0
Negative	–	16	–	5	25	83	60
Neutral	–	63	–	29	75	17	40
Total		100		100	100	100	100

Note: Data not recorded for *Nunatsiaq News* and *Press Independent* for 1991.

cutlines were negative (Table 6.9). This suggests that editorial staff in both northern and southern media increased the news-value of neutral photographs by adding a negative "spin" to the cutline. The *Globe and Mail* did not publish any in-situ photographs related to northern Aboriginal issues in September 1991. The photographs that were published included images of the Aboriginal cast of a play in a Toronto theatre and protesters in New York City who were denouncing the James Bay II hydro-electric project. The photographs published in 1992 were related exclusively to the mine explosion in Yellowknife and were mostly negative in tone.

Of the illustrations published by the *Globe and Mail* in 1991, all were thematic illustrations of maps, compasses, northern landscapes, and Aboriginal people rendered in silhouette. These images suggest the existence of a shadowy people who inhabit a barren, unexplored landscape. No such images appeared in the northern media. In contrast, a two-page photographic feature in the *Press Independent* chronicled the annual process of a Dene family "going out on the land," setting up a campsite on their traditional hunting grounds, followed by a successful caribou hunt. Thus, it is clear that northern and southern media present their readers with, quite literally, very different pictures of the North.

Table 6.10

Overall tone of news stories, 1991-2

	1991		1992		2-year average	
	%	Number of items	%	Number of items	%	Number of items
Nunatsiaq News						
Positive	29	7	–	–	–	–
Negative	25	6	–	–	–	–
Neutral	46	11	–	–	–	–
Total	100	24	–	–	–	–
Press Independent						
Positive	60	34	27	17	43	25.5
Negative	0	0	23	15	12	7.5
Neutral	40	23	50	32	45	27.5
Total	100	57	100	64	100	60.5
Globe and Mail						
Positive	38	3	8	1	23	2
Negative	0	0	50	6	25	3
Netural	62	5	42	5	52	5
Total	100	8	100	12	100	10

The patterns in the tone of news stories are consistent with those observed in the tone of headlines, photographs, and cutlines (Table 6.10). Such a pattern again supports the general observation that the northern media tended to favour neutral and positive news items, a pattern which is consistent with that of community weeklies in the South. A researcher reported, "Seen from southern, Westernized journalistic perspective, the writing style of *The Press Independent* seems juvenile. But that is an ignorant observation. The inverted-pyramid style [in which the most significant information comes first and the supporting evidence follows] is present throughout much of the copy, but once in a while writing that seems to meander, take its time, and flow gratuitously, creeps up" (Chase 1991-2).

Classifying news stories as positive, negative, or neutral obviously required independent evaluation by each researcher. For purposes of clarification and, perhaps more importantly, to explore some of the inherent values and judgments exercised by each of the researchers, Table 6.11 shows some of the researchers' descriptions of news stories in each classification.

As Table 6.11 shows, the descriptive language used by the researchers was highly variable, inherently subjective, and personal. There are areas of agreement and areas of divergence. The word choices and judgments suggest the researchers' individual biases and limitations. All researchers, even those working with more purely quantitative data, have such biases and limitations, which affect their evaluations and judgment. The purpose here is to render the biases more transparent.

In the table, the word "turbulent" suggests a story not only "negative" in tone but somehow out of control. Although the words have different nuances, the various researchers use "accurate," "factual," and "balanced" as generally equivalent descriptors but categorize them differently, as either "positive" or "neutral." To me, "meandering" seems more negative than

Table 6.11

Examples of story tone described by researchers, 1991-2

	Press Independent	*Nunatsiaq News*	*Globe and Mail*
Positive	balanced	happy	nostalgic
	good news	factual	supportive
	human interest	instructive	sympathetic
Negative	vague	biased	tragic
	turbulent	didactic	dramatic
		sarcastic	angry
Neutral	accurate	factual	balanced
	meandering	dry	pragmatic
		critical	

neutral, suggesting not just the story's tone but also the researcher's difficulty in following the narrative – more a judgment of reporting and writing style than of tone. The researcher has chosen the broad and imprecise word "dramatic" to describe a "negative" tone. The researcher covering *Nunatsiaq News* uses "didactic" to describe a "negative" tone and "instructive" to describe a "positive" one, although the words are, in effect, two shades of the same colour.

Years ago, I worked for a brief (and frustrating) time with researchers who insisted on assigning quantitative values to words such as those found in Table 6.11. They translated highly subjective language into pseudo-objective, numerically rendered documents, which then were used to forecast developments. Rather than advocate that kind of approach, I think the information in Table 6.11 provides an opportunity to clarify both the thoughtfulness and the limitations of the researchers' work.

The most significant feature of the data in Table 6.12 is the scope of topics covered by northern media, compared to the relatively narrow spectrum observed in the southern media. In fact, the *Globe and Mail*'s coverage was even narrower than these data suggest. The data show only the percentage of items published on each issue, not the total editorial space devoted to

Table 6.12

Percentage of northern coverage represented by each northern topic, 1991-2

Topic	Nunatsiaq News	Press Independent	Globe and Mail
Aboriginal politics	29	15	5
Mine disaster	–	15	40
Education	6	14	–
Land claims	15	7	–
Federal/territorial politics	12	9	5
Union/labour	7	9	10
Business	9	8	–
Environment	2	6	5
Traditional lifestyles	8	5	–
Health care	5	5	–
Local personalities	–	4	5
Justice	–	2	10
Substance abuse	3	2	–
Crime	–	1	–
Art	3	–	5
Social programs	2	–	–
Child abuse	–	–	5
Northern "philosophy"	–	–	5
Human rights	–	–	5

Note: Due to rounding, columns do not always total 100 percent.

them. In terms of total newspaper column-inches devoted to a single topic (for example, the Giant mine explosion), the *Globe and Mail*'s coverage was significantly narrower than that of the other two papers. Furthermore, the relatively large percentages listed for the *Globe and Mail* are the result of the very small number of items published on the North.

The northern media concentrated on issues of Aboriginal politics, land claims, education, and federal/territorial politics. Noted one researcher, "Both the *Nunatsiaq News* and the *Press Independent* concentrated on political and business issues, to do with the north. Most of their articles related the topics to aboriginal people. There was very little writing about spiritual or cultural matters, however" (Prystay 1992-3). Other researchers noted differences in the writing style of the northern newspapers: "Another major difference between the northern and the southern newspapers is the lack of direct quotations and attributions in northern papers" (Clairmont 1992). This may be attributable to a lack of journalism training and/or to cultural differences and differences between small-scale "community" journalism and that of a major metropolitan daily newspaper.

The southern media focused on the Giant mine disaster, labour issues related to it, and reform of the justice system. In its coverage of justice reform, the *Globe and Mail* in 1991 did indeed focus directly on a northern Aboriginal issue at the same time as its northern counterparts. It also touched directly on Aboriginal issues in its story on child abuse in residential schools and the human rights concerns related to the relocation of Inuit people and communities.

Table 6.13

Topics in the *Press Independent*, 1991-2

Topic	% 1991	% 1992
Aboriginal politics	26	6
Mine disaster	0	26
Education	19	10
Land claims	11	4
Federal/territorial politics	9	8
Union/labour	0	16
Business	2	12
Environment	4	8
Traditional lifestyles	9	3
Health care	4	5
Local personalities	9	0
Justice	4	0
Substance abuse	0	3
Crime	2	0

Note: Due to rounding, columns do not total 100 percent.

Yellowknife's *Press Independent* also focused on deaths in that city's Giant gold mine. This reflects the immediate newsworthiness of the story, as well as the paper's repositioning as a publication for all of the Yellowknife community. The *Press Independent* showed other changes in its coverage between 1991 and 1992, as illustrated in Table 6.13.

In its attempt to serve the Aboriginal as well as the non-Native communities in Yellowknife, the *Press Independent*'s coverage of Aboriginal politics, land claims, education, local personalities, and traditional lifestyles decreased to less than half the quantity of coverage in previous years, in most categories. At the same time, the paper increased its emphasis on business, labour, and, to a lesser degree, the environment. Overall, the effect of attempting to serve a wider community seems to have resulted in narrower editorial content that was similar in some respects to that of southern media.

The great imbalance in coverage of northern Aboriginal issues in Canadian media affects the public perception of those issues. In the South, extensive media coverage is restricted to singular events of extraordinary tragedy – be it the Giant mine explosion, suicide in Davis Inlet, or drowning caribou herds in a swollen river in northern Quebec.

This preference for, or tendency toward, "disaster coverage" – a product of conventional training and thinking in southern journalism schools and media – creates a perception of the North as hostile, dangerous, remote, and foreign. It can be argued that this approach to journalism is always problematic and distorts the news no matter what region it represents. In an underrepresented, marginalized region such as the North, it exacerbates existing problems and raises serious questions of ethics and propriety. Such coverage exaggerates the worst tendencies of journalistic practice and perpetuates colonial thinking about northern issues, lands, and peoples. Rendered invisible are the long-term issues vital to the future of northern people, specifically self-government and land claims. This imbalance ends up affecting the ability of readers in all regions of Canada to understand the fundamental questions most important to the North and, often, to the rest of Canada as well.

As "Canada's national newspaper," the *Globe and Mail* has set itself a challenging task to cover even the disparate southern regions with a semblance of parity. The North, with its sparse population, large territory, and multiple languages, seems relegated to perpetual obscurity in its pages. Moreover, even in the existing, limited southern coverage of northern issues, as this study has shown, the focus of that coverage is tailored for southern audiences, and follows an agenda of southern priorities not shared by Aboriginal people. It appears that Canada's "third solitude" will remain solitary, and excluded, in the southern media.

The northern media surveyed here performed their function in a manner similar to that of many community newspapers, except that they served not just one community, but a regional cluster of isolated communities. They focused on local politics, leaders, and events that, by definition, were northern issues. Yet it is surprising how much editorial space those papers devoted to southern issues – about 60 percent of the *Press Independent* and about one-third of the *Nunatsiaq News*. It seems that northern newspapers, perhaps by virtue of their southern news-gathering methods and management structure, tend to import a "southern agenda" for selection of news content.

This does not mean, however, that northern papers are failing their Aboriginal audiences completely. Southern culture has had a tremendous impact on life in the North, especially through satellite transmission of television programming. The mixture of northern and southern issues in those papers seems to reflect that dynamic.

It is interesting to note that the indigenous contribution to newspaper content was greater in Yellowknife than in Iqaluit, perhaps reflecting that city's role as seat of the territorial government. Media ownership may also play a role – the *Press Independent* was owned by one of the publicly funded Aboriginal communications societies and the *Nunatsiaq News* by a private company. However, despite its Aboriginal ownership, the *Press Independent* attempted to increase readership and revenue through expansion into the entire Yellowknife community. It appears that northern newspapers have inherited the "market-driven" strategies of their southern progenitors, regardless of whether such strategies actually work.

The news media hold great potential for Aboriginal people as they move toward a new era of self-government in the North. One facet of the media's role will be to act as liaison among all Canadians with news of important northern issues. In this sense, the media can assist the various ethnic groups in Canada to better understand each other. Ideally, this "cross-cultural" learning process moves information and cultural values north as well as south. However, as this study shows, cultural exchange by the media is a one-way street. Northern people are learning a great deal about the South and, to varying degrees, are assimilating many of its values. The cultural pipeline south, however, ends somewhere above the sixtieth parallel.

7
Old Patterns, Future Directions

We have seen that the northern communications picture is full of contradictions, that northerners are both privileged and disadvantaged in terms of media coverage and media access. We have also seen that, although all of the northern provinces and territories experience similar problems in negotiating time, travel, climate, topography, and budgets, there are significant differences in the ways in which the various peoples and regions address those problems.

The best way to see where northern communications are headed is to rewind and then fast-forward. Thus, this concluding chapter reviews some of the old patterns in northern communications and then examines some of the challenges of the new technologies. When we review past patterns, we see that much has changed. Yet many of yesterday's themes persist – in neo-colonial portrayals and in policies and programs that begin as attempts to change colonialist patterns. Slowly, northern communications are pushing past this reactive state, and proactive programs are taking over. Today's generation of media producers remembers less the representations of old films than the emergence of indigenous broadcasting and the exhilaration of knowing what technology can do when it is consciously used to promote cultural survival.

In the changing political picture, especially the emergence of Nunavut Territory, northerners are becoming national and global newsmakers in their own right, instead of colonized peoples primarily represented to the Outside world by others. The Inuit Circumpolar Conference (ICC) – the international organization of Inuit – has had considerable influence on the various circumpolar governments. While the governments still marginalize Inuit, the reality is that Inuit pushed governments to pursue cooperative interests and develop or expand Arctic policies. The 1998 ICC General Assembly held in Nuuk, Greenland, marked yet another milestone in the organization's history. The delegates committed themselves to strengthening programs and policies in areas crucial to the future of Arctic journalism, communications, culture, and education.

Carl Christian Olsen, who headed the Greenland delegation, has been involved in Greenlandic and international indigenous cultural policy, education, and politics for many years. He helped to found Ilisimatusarfik – the University of Greenland, where he is a professor – and is currently researching international language policy and laying the foundation for a Greenland Language Secretariat under the Greenland Home Rule Government. In August 1998, he sent me an e-mail outlining the latest developments in ICC: "We will establish [an] ICC Commission on Language and Communications and [an] Inuit Press Agency [an international, Inuit-run news service] ... We will also investigate indigenous participation [in the development of] the proposed [international] University of the Arctic under the Arctic Council."

Challenging the Colonial Mentality

The more vocal northerners become, the stronger will be the challenge to conventional colonial thinking. The coming decades may well see an increase in the visibility (and audibility) of northerners. Let us consider how far things have come since 1943, when an optimistic headline in the *Financial Post* of 3 April heralded the joyous consequences of the Second World War: "War Unlocks Our Last Frontier–Canada's Northern Opportunity" (Grant 1988, 121). At the same time, the movie *Look to the North,* narrated by the warm, authoritative voice of Lorne Greene, "minimized the dominant American presence, highlighted the 'joint co-operation' aspect, and particularly stressed the opportunities provided for the postwar development" of the North (ibid., 149).

More than twenty years later, in April 1969, the *New York Times* sent a reporter to join an eighteen-stop, two-week public relations junket in the eastern Arctic. In Igloolik the reporter heard Inuit at a "town meeting" express concern "that they are losing their own culture." Like many others before and since, the reporter depicted the Inuit as "caught between two cultures" – the Inuit's "own leisurely one of hunting, socializing and living by the season and the white man's structured style of schools, jobs and living by the clock" (Walz 1969, 8-9). Only a person completely out of touch with what it takes to hunt in the Arctic would call the hunter's life "leisurely." Perhaps the reporter thought Inuit hunters worked for recreation, rather than for their families' food.

In 1970 another article for the *New York Times* followed established noble-savage tradition in praising the "natural" attributes of Inuit, and heralding "progress": "Dishonesty is almost foreign to the Eskimo's nature ... Since the Canadian Government made the Eskimo a ward of the state much of the primitive way of life has vanished. The overnight hunt is a thing of the past and the tent has been replaced by box-like structures with oil stove heat." This would be news to Inuit who still use their summer camps, and hunt and fish in winter. Inuit women are entirely absent from the story.

It would be comforting to discover that such opinions belong entirely to the past. Sadly, this is not the case. In 1997 Marc G. Stevenson, who has worked for northern government and served as a consultant to Aboriginal organizations, produced a study that claimed to address "cultural persistence" and "Central Inuit social organization" in general, but virtually ignored Inuit women. This purportedly comprehensive study relies entirely on interviews with men and mentions women only in passing – implying that the whole of Inuit social organization and culture can be understood through male eyes and men's lives (Stevenson 1997).

Such sexism is not the only shortcoming in Stevenson's work. He also perpetuates colonial views of the inability of Inuit to understand the difference between their own spiritual traditions and Christian doctrine. He writes: "Most Inuit, and even some lay preachers, failed to grasp throughly [sic] many of the basic concepts of Christianity. For example, Angmarlik at Kekerten in 1902 preached a religious doctrine that fused many elements of the old religious order with the new ideology" (Stevenson 1997, 127). Stevenson contends that Inuit fused tradition and Christian ideology because they "failed to grasp" Christian concepts, rather than, as the distinguished Pangnirtung elder Etuangat, Jose Kusugak, and other Inuit have told me, from a conscious and deliberate effort to ensure cultural continuity. Such patronizing views persist, despite all the years of changes and challenges.

When I first went North in the early 1980s, I expected to find journalism vastly improved from the early coverage I had followed in the libraries and archives of Ottawa and Toronto. I was soon jolted into a more accurate sense of the realities. Some of this awareness is reflected in the entries to my journals:

> In one community, I meet a journalist from a prominent publication. He clutches a Ken Kesey novel and speaks with the self-assurance of one who has, in three days, become an expert. The jokes about this are so rampant it's hard to believe he hasn't heard them. He tells me he will write about the beauty of his hike and "the lifestyle changes of the Inuit people." He rejects the offer of names [of people in the community to interview]: "I don't need to talk to anyone else, I'm leaving tomorrow. I had two Inuit guides on the hike, I've already talked to two of the Native people." Two men for a portrait of "the Inuit lifestyle" – never mind women, children, other men, other generations. Having hiked outside the community, he has returned to wall

himself into a building and watch movies. "I've met two Natives," he says again.

It is not just Aboriginal northerners who are in need of more accurate representation, although they have long been the primary subjects of journalistic misrepresentation of the North. All northerners are misrepresented at one time or another, in one way or another. The North continues to be exoticized, romanticized, and distanced (not just geographically) from the rest of the world. Northerners in general continue to be portrayed as a special breed of people (the very persistence of the word "breed" suggests something apart from humanity). And, as we observed earlier on, there are layers of misrepresentation – of northerners, Aboriginal northerners, northern and Aboriginal women.

But, as we have seen, Native people are not passive recipients of media misrepresentation. They have pioneered important media initiatives and brought their own voices to an ever widening public. Increasingly, they have taken over the representation of themselves – in print, in radio, and on television. Northern first peoples have not just been victims in the centuries-long process of colonizing communications; they have been energetic agents of decolonization and constructive change. Roth reminds us that, among other revolutionary developments in northern communications, the Northern Broadcasting Policy "was the result of a concerted pressure group strategy by Northern First Nations communities and their supporters. Until the early eighties, a variety of experimental domestic satellite-access projects demonstrated First Peoples' skills in organization, management, design and administration of training programs, and maintenance of complex broadcasting undertakings" (Roth 1996, 73).

Setbacks and frustrations continue to accompany each forward move. It is impossible to avoid the conclusion that northern news media should be strengthened and their services expanded. Despite considerable ingenuity in retaining media and programs, the 1990 cutbacks resulted in severely curtailed – or lost – services to people who often thought that they were already receiving inadequate services before the cutbacks.

The Aboriginal and non-Aboriginal northerners I have interviewed or encountered over the years have spoken passionately and frequently of the need for increased Aboriginal participation in the processes of communication and government. As was discussed in earlier chapters, there is widespread support for more and improved Aboriginal language resources in the North. Among the indigenous political and community leaders who were interviewed, there is consensus that more materials and programs should be available in all living languages. But not everyone agrees on the nature or extent of the programs. A Yukon Aboriginal politician and a community leader with expertise in Aboriginal languages both considered that Yukon would be ill-advised to adopt the Northwest Territories language policy of making all Aboriginal languages official along with English and French: "I think the direction we'll go in, in Yukon, is more like the Chinese Canadian community. We will keep our languages for community support and our families. But seven different languages in this tiny territory. We can't afford to keep them official" (Carol Geddes, personal communication, 1990). Glen Chartier stressed the need for a carefully balanced language policy, developed in concert with Aboriginal people: "some of the [political] parties are making special effort ... to involve aboriginal people. But we also see a danger in that ... we don't want as aboriginal people to be co-opted. First of all, we don't want to be assimilated. We do want to work at a degree of integration which is suitable to us and to Canadian society" (Morin, Chartier, and Campone 1990, 171).

The challenge of resisting assimilation without flatly rejecting transformation has been crucial for indigenous peoples. Gail Guthrie Valaskakis clarifies the intricate relationship between tradition and transformation, colonizer and colonized: "In the writing of outsiders, native American traditional practice is often misunderstood as feathers and fantasy or, worse, as oppressive reification of the distant past. But Indian traditionalism is not these; nor is it lost in transformation or revived as a privileged expression of resistance. It is an instrumental code to action knitted into the fabric of everyday life" (Valaskakis 1988, 268). Past and present are inseparable. Valaskakis's eloquent description of her Lac du Flambeau, Wisconsin, Chippewa childhood reflects the experiences of Inuit and other colonized peoples:

> We were very young when we began to live the ambivalence of our reality. My marble-playing, bicycle-riding, king-of-the-royal-mountain days were etched with the presence of unexplained identity and power. I knew as I sat in the cramped desks of the Indian school that wigwams could shake with the rhythm of a Midewiwin ceremonial drum, fireballs could spring from the whispers of a windless night, and Bert Skye could (without warning) transform himself into a dog. I knew that my great-grandmother moved past the Catholic altar in her house with her hair dish in her hand to place greying combings of her hair in the first fire of the day, securing them from evil spirits ... We [Indians and non-Indians] were equally and irrevocably harnessed to each other ... I was both an Indian and an outsider (Valaskakis 1988, 268).

Aboriginal Filmmaker Loretta Todd says Canadians must put aside the persistent colonial mentality and recognize the integrity of indigenous cultures: "It is time for Canadian society to view us not as dying cultures, but dynamic cultures. Despite policies of assimilation, we have survived" (Todd 1991).

New Technologies, Old Values

These days, the biggest noise in communications is being made by the creators and marketers of new technologies, or more sophisticated versions of old technologies. In 1994 *Nunatsiaq News* published a twelve-page "Special Report on Telecommunications." Although not clearly identified as an advertising supplement, the so-called report, which featured "advertorial" stories by *Nunatsiaq News* staff, was in reality an advertisement for NorthwesTel. Two years later, in 1996, NorthwesTel introduced its new satellite phone service "for the Great Canadian Workplace." The full-page black and white advertisement in *Nunatsiaq News* featured a photo-collage of a small portable phone superimposed on a photograph of an idyllic, misted mountain landscape, with a pair of worn leather hiking boots in one corner. The ad, which was obviously intended to be published in a variety of publications and locations, used imagery inappropriate to the region served by *Nunatsiaq News* and to the realities of many of the people who would find this technology useful. At the centre of the page, the mountain landscape features a foreground consisting of a large stand of tall evergreens. On another part of the page, a pine cone sits suspended between segments of white space and text: "Making a call from your desk downtown is one thing. But what if your desk is a tree stump in the back of beyond? No problem. Our new satellite mobile phone service extends to virtually every square inch of the continent" (NorthwesTel 1996a, 11). The advertiser's interpretation of "every square inch of the continent" as a vacationer's paradise is closer to historical colonial-romanticism than to the future of this Inuit-dominated region or of most other regions where satellite phones are most relevant and useful. The leap from "downtown" to "a tree stump in the back of beyond" suggests a backpacking holiday in the wilderness, not a life of survival on the (sometimes treeless) land. I doubt that this is a coincidence, nor do I think it entirely unintentional. It is likely that more backpackers than residents of Nunavut – or any other remote region – will be able to afford this new technology, at least in its early years.

I have no wish to minimize the importance of the new satellite phones. If, as promised, they are superior to the old bush radio, they may well enhance the safety of people who live and work out on the land. Perhaps someone at Advertising Central will catch up to the realities of Nunavut and other remote regions across the globe, and learn to pitch their product to the people who really live here.

Both the advertisement and the earlier advertorial in *Nunatsiaq News* raise a number of issues concerning the product, the target audience, the representation of remote regions and of the people who live and work there, and links between government and business, and business and news.

The product is important to people in remote locations everywhere. The satellite distribution system is already well established in the North, thanks in large part to the federal government's funding of satellites and broadcasting (especially TVNC). Satellite telephone service is not a luxury or a convenience; it can be a lifesaver for people living and working on the land. Pangnirtung elder and midwife Annie Okalik once told me of the time she delivered a baby long distance. The parents were camped far from home, and she relayed instructions and continuing encouragement to the father by radio. Such occurrences are not uncommon, but from a business viewpoint the North is a thinly populated advertising universe. As in the case of northern news media, here is a situation that calls for government subsidy so that the people who most need the technology have access to it. That, I think, is an example of appropriate linking of government and business.

Less appropriate is a media-advertiser link that has become all too familiar, north and south – the "advertorial" – a pseudo-news story sometimes not immediately recognizable as advertising, whose primary purpose is to sell a product. There are alternative ways to handle this if a newspaper does not want to reject it out of hand (an unlikely option, given the lure of advertising revenue, especially for a small newspaper). The supplement can be clearly labelled in large type, making it immediately identifiable as advertising. The paper can also refuse to print bylines with the stories, even if its reporters write them. Otherwise, the familiar names imply that this is just another section of the newspaper.

My other concern is with the representation of people in "the back of beyond." Advertisers are slowly realizing that diversity isn't just about ethics: it increases the potential market for sales. The regions most likely to need satellite phones are filled with people, many of them Aboriginal, a few of them from Outside. Both the written and the visual language of the ad suggest a tension between the romance of *visiting* and the reality of *working* and living in remote locations. True, the ad was designed for a broad readership, but even when the company specifically targeted Nunavut audiences, there was a similar dissonance between reality and fiction.

In 1996 NorthwesTel staged "NorCOM '96, Bringing the World to You" (NorthwesTel 1996b, 13), an exposition in Iqaluit that hyped the Internet, video conferencing, ATM (asynchronous transfer mode), satellites, and other technological developments and included a satellite-transmitted trip to the Calgary Zoo. Virtual "travelling" to places unlike home (such as the Calgary Zoo) may well have delighted Nunavut audiences, but if the exposition was meant to communicate, and ultimately to sell, the usefulness of new technologies, such choices seem odd, and culturally and geographically irrelevant.

The information superhighway and other technological breakthroughs and developments will continue to extend the possibilities for northern communications, and for north-south and circumpolar connections. However, we must remember that the technology will not make the connections between people and media outlets, journalism and literacy, language and power. It will not be a panacea for accuracy in representation – there are no guarantees as to the accuracy of the information that is carried in print, on line, in the air.

In 1997 the Nunavut Implementation Commission (NIC) came up with an idea for putting new technologies to work for the people of Nunavut. Their proposal will use communications technology to support the decentralized government most Inuit want. Their plan is to develop "community teleservice centres." Each community would have its own centre, which would provide access for all residents to free or low-cost use of electronic communication equipment, including computers and modems, fax machines, scanners, and videoconference equipment. Paid staff would maintain the equipment and train people in its use. The centres would be large enough to accommodate community-wide videoconferences (Bell 1997, E7).

NIC researcher Randy Ames said most electronic communications have flowed into Nunavut from the South. The new service would utilize a broadband telecommunications system to send information from North to South. "For example ... an elder in Pond Inlet could be paid to give a lecture in Inuktitut to a university class in the South" (Bell 1997, E7). In addition to equipment, each centre would have a meeting room for community gatherings and videoconferences, a separate room for training, and kitchen and child-care facilities (*Nunatsiaq News* 1997, E7).

One of the assumptions of old-order colonial thinking is that "peripheral" people learn from "core" people, and not the other way around. The time is long overdue to break that ethnocentric paradigm. The exceptional development of northern communications suggests a way out – and a way to develop more progressive paradigms. We have seen that despite its marginalization, and for a variety of reasons, northern communications in Canada are among the most highly developed in the world. With Nunavut's progressive use of new technologies, the "core" in that territory is likely to be less centrally located – both ideologically and spatially – than elsewhere in the country. Projects such as the proposed teleservice centres will enable Nunavut residents to interact and govern themselves without relegating some people and communities to the margins. In this way, Nunavut may provide a useful model for decentralizing power and administration in other governments and regions.

It is unfortunate that most of today's public discussion of new information technologies is focused on technological change, as if such change occurred in a human-free vacuum, and as if the information emerged on its own and was not generated, created, or selected by people with various experiences, biases, and agendas. That is a dangerous pretence, not only for the North but for the communication universe as a whole. There is a desperate need for attention to the impact of new technologies on questions of ethics and human rights, and on *people*. No matter how sophisticated the technology, nothing can replace the careful work of responsible journalists. No technology in and of itself can provide universal access to all people, without prejudice to where they live or how much they earn. These are the real challenges for the northern communicators of the future.

In the final analysis, these concerns are not unique to northern communications. The North contains humanity's entire communications future in microcosm. Our well-being, and perhaps our survival, will depend on our ability to abandon the obsession with how to send the information out, and to pay careful attention to what messages are sent, and by whom.

Appendix A:
Native News Network of Canada
Statement of Principles

Journalists can change or influence the thinking of those who are mere bystanders or news followers ... How can the public judge, if they never have a chance to read? First of all, you need to hire Native writers. Let them write the stories they feel are important and let readers decide if this is what they've been looking for all these years.

Bud White Eye,
founder of NNNC, "Journalism and First Nations,"
in *Deadlines and Diversity: Journalism Ethics in a Changing World,*
ed. V. Alia, B. Brennan, and B. Hoffmaster
(Halifax: Fernwood, 1996)

The human being has been given the gift to make choices, and ... guidelines, or what we call original instructions. This does not represent an advantage for the human being but rather a responsibility.

Oren Lyons,
"Spirituality, Equality and Natural Law,"
in *Pathways to Self-Determination: Canadian Indians and the Canadian State,*
ed. L. Little Bear, M. Boldt, and J.A. Long
(Toronto: University of Toronto Press, 1986)

Native News Network of Canada (NNNC) is dedicated to the gathering and distributing of print and broadcast news, features, reviews, and opinion by, about and for First Peoples. Its purpose is to inform all people and enable them to make judgments on the issues of the day, and to this end, to give expression to the interests of people who are under-represented in "mainstream" news media.

The ethical practice of journalism is paramount. An ethical journalism is a journalism of courage and conscience. It must reflect the diversity of the society, in terms of both hiring of journalists and representing people in news media. To carry out its purpose, NNNC has adopted the following principles:

1   Journalism should be fair, accurate, honest, conscientious and responsible.

2   Journalists and media outlets should be free from government or other outside interference; journalists must be free to discuss, question, or challenge private or public actions, positions or statements.

3   Journalism should

encourage creativity in writing and broadcasting, and foster the different, authentic voices of Aboriginal people;

promote the public's right to know;

critically examine the conduct of those in the public and private sectors;

expose any abuse of the public trust, evidence of wrongdoing or misuse of power;

advocate reform or innovation whenever need, in the public interest;

avoid unfair bias, distortion, or sensationalism in written and broadcast text and in printed or broadcast images;

clearly distinguish editorials and opinion from reporting;

present information in context;

present information without irrelevant reference to gender, culture, colour, "race," sexual preference, religious belief, marital status, physical or mental disability;

treat racial, ethnic or other derogatory terms as obscenities, used in quoted material only when essential to a story;

avoid photography or art work which fosters racial, ethnic, gender or other stereotypes;

respect individuals' dignity and right to privacy; avoid unnecessary intrusion into private grief;

except in extreme cases in which information vital to the public interest cannot be obtained in any other way, obtain information in a straightforward manner, without misrepresenting the journalist's identity;

except in rare cases in which information vital to the public interest can not be obtained in any other way, tape-record, videotape, or photograph an interview only with the interviewee's knowledge and permission;

avoid identifying the names or addresses of individuals whose safety might be jeopardized;

preserve NNNC's independence from the vested interests of any particular individual, organization, institution or community;

encourage thoughtful criticism of the news media as well as the society at large.

4   We recognize that journalists are citizens. An NNNC journalist should

be free to be active in the community, perform work for religious, cultural, social or civic organizations and pursue other activities of commitment or conscience, provided these activities do not distort the quality of his or her coverage;

disclose any involvement in outside organizations, political or other activities, to the NNNC editors and the public;

avoid covering stories in which he or she has a conflict of interest (for example, most stories concerning close relatives or friends);

disclose to sources if he or she is doing freelance work for a media outlet other than NNNC (for example, if an interview will be used for a story submitted to another news organization);

avoid plagiarizing, by carefully quoting from or attributing information to other sources, and by assuring that his or her name is only used to identify the journalist's own work;

honour pledges of confidentiality, which should be made with great care, and only when necessary to serve the public's need for information;

make respect the watchword of journalistic practice – respect for subjects and sources, for other journalists, for the public we serve, and especially for the First Nations which are the backbone and the raison d'être of NNNC.

Dan Smoke-Asayenes
President, Native News Network of Canada
Treasurer, Native Journalists' Association

Valerie Alia, Ph.D.
Advisory Board Member, Native News Network of Canada
Distinguished Professor of Canadian Culture,
Western Washington University

April 1997

Appendix B:
A Brief to the Royal Commission
on Aboriginal Peoples

Communication is at the core of First Nations concerns. In a democratic society, news media ensure that information is communicated to the public. Many of the myths and misperceptions which persist among non-Aboriginal people are perpetuated by non-communication, poor communication, or one-sided communication.

Current efforts to remedy inaccuracies in "mainstream" news coverage of Aboriginal issues are an important beginning. But they are not enough. Non-Aboriginal journalists are slowly becoming better educated to the issues and peoples they report. "Mainstream" news media are broadcasting and publishing reports and columns by (usually part-time or freelance) Aboriginal journalists.

Aboriginal people remain underrepresented in these media, both in accurate coverage and in employment. Where they are hired, they are often subject to the last-hired, first-fired syndrome, leaving employment statistics at the status quo. The Aboriginal-run news media are unfunded or underfunded, and must often rely on volunteer labour to continue. The crucial and highly successful Aboriginal communications societies which government helped to establish are threatened with extinction.

Non-Aboriginal news media are not hiring many First Nations journalists, and even if they were, this would solve only a small part of the problem. First Nations journalists must be employable and employed, and they must have the option of this employability in Aboriginal and non-Aboriginal news media.

The depth and diversity of Aboriginal perspectives must be communicated, through both First Nations and "mainstream" news media, to as broad a public as possible.

The past several years have seen a number of developments in Aboriginal communications – some of them sharply contradictory. At the same time that Television Northern Canada (TVNC) received funding and captured the northern airwaves, Aboriginal Communications Societies and journalism training programs experienced distressing, sometimes devastating, funding cutbacks. The result has been the demise of programs for training Aboriginal journalists – including opportunities for early years or first-year experience after graduating (apprenticeship year), the curtailment of news services by and for First Nations peoples, the cutting of jobs for qualified First Nations journalists, the extension of already overburdened facilities and personnel, sometimes to the breaking-point.

Communications training programs have produced leaders – in politics, business and social services as well as journalism. Graduates of these programs have gone on to lead national organizations and found newspapers and radio stations. There is a need for increased training. Yet the training programs are disappearing.

Communication and Journalism, a brief to the Royal Commission on Aboriginal Peoples, Toronto, Ontario. 21 October 1992, by the Native News Network of Canada, Bud White Eye, President, and Dr. Valerie Alia, Member, Advisory Board[10]

Among the cutback casualties were the University of Western Ontario's Program in Journalism for Native People and the program sponsored by Arctic College in the Northwest Territories. These programs bypassed obstacle-creating credentials to open doors for prospective journalists – the result was excellence on many fronts.

First Nations newspapers, magazines, radio and television provide an effective training ground for journalists, as well as an opportunity to sell their work. If we are to increase the participation of First Nations journalists in the communication of their communities' priorities and perspectives, we must continue to foster these crucial training programs. This means promoting programs which facilitate entrance of Aboriginal students into university, as well as those which exist outside the college or university system.

In a depressed economy, equal opportunity legislation and private company programs are of little use to Aboriginal journalists who have not earned conventional credentials – regardless of the extent of their skills or expertise.

It is more urgent than ever that Aboriginal perspectives reach a wider public. We therefore offer the following recommendations, for consideration by the Royal Commission on Aboriginal Peoples:

Recommendations from the Native News Network of Canada (NNNC)

1 That there be immediate and substantial efforts to revitalize the Aboriginal Communication Societies, and fund transition programs aimed at facilitating their financial independence.
2 That a program be established, of incentives to journalism schools to encourage and educate Aboriginal journalists, to include transition programs, scholarship funds, and adjustments to entrance requirements as needed.
3 That a counselling program be established, earmarked for the development of programs and projects in Aboriginal communications.
4 That a funding program be established, as a bridge between First Nations students, teachers, administrators and news media.
5 That the central importance of effective communications be acknowledged in according recognition to the sovereign rights of First Nations peoples in Canada.
6 That programs be created and supported with long-term funding, for the purpose of promoting understanding and collaboration between Aboriginal and non-Aboriginal journalists.

Appendix C: Catalogue of Northern Community Radio

CBC Radio and Television are available in most communities; fax transmission cannot be used in communities that have only radio-phone service. Information includes languages spoken in each community and population, based on the 1996 Canadian Census and the December 1995 Yukon Census.

Table C1

Nunavut community radio			
Community	Population	Languages	Media
Arctic Bay	639	Inuktitut, English	Community radio and TV, equipment from IBC
Arviat	1,559	Inuktitut, English	Community radio
Baker Lake	1,385	Inuktitut, English	Community radio
Bathurst Inlet	80	Inuinnaqtun, English	HF radio
Broughton Island	488	Inuktitut, English	Community radio, Community Airport Radio Station (CARS): weather and communications
Cambridge Bay	1,351	Inuinnaqtun, English	Community radio, LPAM Inuit Radio Society (not currently operating)
Cape Dorset	1,118	Inuktitut, English	Community radio, CARS
Chesterfield Inlet	337	Inuktitut, English	Community radio, CARS
Clyde River	708	Inuktitut, English	Community radio, CARS
Coral Harbour	669	Inuktitut, English	Community radio
Gjoa Haven	879	Inuktitut, English	CARS
Grise Fiord	148	Inuktitut, English	Community radio
Hall Beach	543	Inuktitut, English	Community radio
Igloolik	1,174	Inuktitut, English	CARS
Iqaluit (Frobisher Bay)	4,220	Inuktitut, English, French	Eastern Arctic radio and TV centre, IBC-TV production centre, satellite uplink
Kimmirut (Lake Harbour)	397	Inuktitut, English	Community radio, CARS
Kugluktuk (Coppermine)	956	Inuinnaqtun	Community radio
Nanisivik	317	Inuktitut, English, French	Community radio, CARS
Pangnirtung	1,243	Inuktitut, English	Community radio, CARS
Pelly Bay	496	Inuktitut, English	Community radio, CARS
Pond Inlet	1,154	Inuktitut, English	Community radio and TV, CARS
Rankin Inlet	2,058	Inuktitut, English	Community radio, IBC-TV production centre
Resolute	198	Inuktitut, English	No radio (CBC only)
Sanikiluaq	631	Inuktitut, English	Community radio, CARS
Whale Cove (Tikirarjuaq)	225	Inuktitut, English	Community FM radio, CARS

Table C2

Northwest Territories community radio

Community	Population	Languages	Media
Aklavik	727	English, Inuvialuktun	Low-power FM station, community TV, Anik satellite – CBC/TVNC
Colville Lake	90	North Slavey, English	HF radio, Colville Lake Band (Dene)
Deline (name changed from Fort Franklin, 1993)	616	North Slavey, English	No radio
Detah	190	Dogrib, Chipewyan, English	CJCD Radio (microwave)
Enterprise	86	English	NorthwesTel VHF radio-phone
Fort Good Hope	644	North Slavey, English	Community radio, CARS, NorthwesTel radio-phone
Fort Liard	512	South Slavey, English	Community radio – Fort Liard Dene Band, CARS
Fort McPherson	878	Gwich'in, English	CARS, Community radio – Tetlit Gwich'in Band
Fort Providence	748	English, South Slavey, French	VHF radio-phone
Fort Resolution	536	English, Chipewyan	VHF radio-phone, CARS
Fort Simpson	1,257	English, South Slavey	VHF radio-phone
Fort Smith	2,441	English, Chipewyan, Cree	VHF radio-phone
Hay River	3,611	English, South Slavey, Chipewyan	VHF radio-phone
Hay River Reserve	253	South Slavey, Chipewyan, English	CBC radio and TV from Hay River
Holman	423	Inuinnaqtun, English	CARS
Inuvik	3,296	English, Inuvialuktun, Gwich'in, North Slavey	VHF radio-phone, CKEV-FM
Jean Marie River	53	South Slavey, English	NorthwesTel mobile radio-phone
Kakisa	29	South Slavey, English	NorthwesTel mobile radio-phone from terminal outside community
Lutselk'e (Snowdrift)	304	Chipewyan, English	No community radio, CBC only
Nahanni Butte	75	South Slavey, English	NorthwesTel mobile radio-phone
Norman Wells	798	English, North Slavey, Dogrib, English	VHF radio-phone Community radio – Lac La Martre Dene Band
Paulatuk	277	Inuvialuktun, English	CARS
Rae-Edzo	1,662	Dogrib, English, French	Community radio, Beacho Kho Radio Society
Rae Lakes	256	Dogrib, English	Mobile radio-phone
Repulse Bay	559	Inuktitut, English	Community radio, CARS
Sachs Harbour	135	Inuvialuktun, English	Community radio, CARS
Snare Lake	135	Dogrib, English	Radio-phone, no CBC, no other service
Taloyoak (Spence Bay)	648	Inuktitut, English	Community radio, CARS

©

§   *Table C2*

Community	Population	Languages	Media
Trout Lake	68	South Slavey, English	NorthwesTel mobile radio-phone
Tsigehtchic (Arctic Red River)	162	Gwich'in	NorthwesTel VHF radio-phone
Tuktoyaktuk	943	Inuvialuktun, English	Community radio
Tulita (Fort Norman)	450	North Slavey, English	VHF radio-phone, Community radio
Wha Ti (Lac La Martre)	413	Dogrib, English	Community radio, Lac La Martre Dene Band
Wrigley	167	South Slavey, English	VHF radio-phone
Yellowknife	17,275	English, French, Dogrib, North Slavey, South Slavey, Chipewyan, Cree, other languages	VHF radio-phone; CFYK-AM, news/information, CBC affiliate, English and other languages; CJCD-AM, music, news, public service, and sports, private ownership, re-broadcast in Hay River; CKLB-FM, country and western, Native Communications Society ownership, re-broadcast in Aklavik, Deline, Detah, Ft. Good Hope, Ft. Liard, Ft. McPherson, Ft. Providence, Ft. Resolution, Ft. Simpson, Ft. Smith, Hay River (CKNM), Inuvik, Iqaluit, Jean Marie River, Kakisa, Lutsel'ki, Nahanni Butte, Norman Wells, Rae Lakes, Rae-Edzo, Snare Lake, Trout Lake, Tsigehtchic, Tulita, Wha Ti, Wrigley

Table C3

Yukon Territory community radio			
Community	Population	Languages	Media
Whitehorse	23,000	English, French, Northern Tutchone, Southern Tutchone, Gwich'in, Tlingit, other languages	Pirate and bush radio (various locations); CFWH-AM, varied programming, CBC affiliate, English, occasional broadcasts in other languages; CHON-FM, country and western with news, public service, sports, NNBY ownership, English, South and North Tutchone, Gwich'in; CKRW-AM, adult contemporary (music, news, public service, sports, women's programming, Klondike Broadcasting Company ownership, English)*

* Re-broadcast in Beauval (CIPI), Buffalo Narrows (CIBN), Canoe Narrows (CLCC), Carcross (CKRW), Cole Bay (CFBB), Dawson City (CFYT), Dillon (CKBR), Faro (CKRW), Green Lake (CHGL), Haines Junction (CKRW), Ile La Crosse (CILX), Jans Bay (CJBR), Pine House (CSBL), Mayo (CKRW), Meadow Lake (CFDM), Patnuak (CFPK), Turner Lake (CJTL), Watson Lake (CKRW). Whitehorse also has a private cable television station, Northern Television Systems, with bilingual English-French programming and 5,000 subscribers. Also: CFWE-FM, "Alberta's Aboriginal Voice" broadcast by Aboriginal Multi-Media Society of Alberta from Edmonton, covers some northern regions of provinces and Yukon.

Appendix D:
Catalogue of Northern Newspapers and Magazines

Entries for publications produced in southern Canada or elsewhere are included because they have northern readership, distribution, and impact, or are of national or international significance. The amount of information for each publication varies according to its importance and the available information. The list includes publications no longer in print, which are available through libraries, archives, or on-line services.

Northwest Territories

Above and Beyond: Yellowknife. Quarterly magazine (glossy, colour). First Air in-flight magazine; tourist-oriented stories on arctic society, politics, culture, news analysis. Distribution: 50,000 (Canada, United States, England, Italy, Germany, and other countries). Established 1988.

L'Aquilon: Yellowknife. Weekly French-language newspaper (formerly monthly).

Deh Cho Drum: Fort Simpson. Weekly. Northern News Service Limited. Serves Fort Simpson, Fort Liard, Fort Providence, Jean Marie River, Wrigley, Trout Lake, Nahanni Butte.

Dene Cultural Institute Quarterly: Hay River. Dene Cultural Institute.

Dene Nation Newsletter: Yellowknife. Dene Nation.

The Hub: Hay River. Weekly newspaper. Hub Publications, Inc.

Inuvik Drum: Inuvik. Weekly newspaper. Northern News Services. Beaufort-Mackenzie Delta region; covers Inuvik, Aklavik, Fort McPherson, Tsigehtchic (Arctic Red River), Paulatuk, Tuktoyaktuk, Sachs Harbour, Holman Island. Circulation: 1,900. Estimated readership: 3,800.

Mackenzie Times: Fort Simpson. Territorial newspaper serving the areas from Lake Athabasca to Arctic Delta – Greater Mackenzie delta region; distributed in Yukon; Dene, Métis, non-Native news.

Midnight Sun: Igloolik. 1960s-70s.

Native Press: Yellowknife. (See also *Press Independent*). Founded as bi-weekly newspaper, replaced by *Press Independent;* revived as a quarterly in 1996.

Native Women's News: Yellowknife. Native Women's Association in the NWT.

News/North: Yellowknife. Weekly newspaper. Founded as *News of the North;* Northern News Services. Some Native news (increasing use of Native reporters and inclusion of Native news, after *Press Independent* ceased publication); mostly western Arctic. Highest circulation in NWT: 12,000. Regional News Bureaus: Deh Cho Region, Fort Simpson; Mackenzie Delta Region, Inuvik; Kivalliq Region, Rankin Inlet; Baffin Region, Iqaluit. Established in 1945.

The Norther: Fort Smith. Mackenzie Arts and Graphics.

Northern Women Talk: Yellowknife. NWT Advisory Council on the Status of Women.

Press Independent: Yellowknife. Weekly newspaper. Founded as *Native Press* bi-weekly newspaper; Native Communications Society of the NWT; Dene and Métis news with some Inuvialuit, Inuit, and non-Native northern issues; changed to weekly after 1990 budget cuts. Circulation: 5,000+. Ceased publication in 1993, after years of struggling to stay afloat.

Slave River Journal: Fort Smith. Weekly newspaper. Serves Fort Smith, Lutselk'e, and Fort Resolution in the NWT and Fort Fitzgerald and Fort Chipewyan in northern Alberta.

Tapwe: Hay River. Boreal Press Ltd.

Tukisiviksat: Yellowknife. Department of Information, Government of the NWT.

Tusaayaksat: Inuvik. Newspaper published every two weeks. Founded 1985, Inuvialuit Communications Society (formerly published by the Committee on Original Peoples' Entitlement). English and Seglit dialect; distributed to all six Inuvialuit communities, including each of 800-odd households. Funding lost in 1990; publication was increased to twice monthly to meet government tender eligibility standards (Thorbes 1990). (ICS founded as Inuit Okangit Inumgun in 1976; reorganized in 1984 as the Inuvialuit Communications Society.)

ULU News: Yellowknife. Arctic Winter Games Corporation.

Up Here: Yellowknife. Magazine; six issues a year. Glossy, colour; non-controversial, tourist-oriented stories on culture, history, business, science; profiles; Aboriginal and non-Aboriginal subjects.

The Yellowknifer: Yellowknife. Twice-weekly newspaper. Northern News Services, non-Aboriginal, but has large number of Aboriginal readers; focus on community news with some broader NWT/northern coverage. Circulation: 6,200, Yellowknife and NWT. Founded 1972.

Nunavut

Ajurnangimmat Magazine: Arviat (formerly Eskimo Point). Inuit Cultural Institute. Replaced *Ajurnarmat.*

Arctic Circle: Iqaluit. (See entry under National Publications.)

Inuit Okaoheet: Cambridge Bay. Kitikmeot Inuit Association.

Inummarit: Igloolik. Inummarit Cultural Association.

Kivalliq News: Rankin Inlet. Weekly newspaper. Newest publication of Northern News Services. Circulation: 1,400. Bilingual, Inuktitut and English. Serving the Kivalliq (Central Arctic) region. Communities served: Arviat, Baker Lake, Chesterfield Inlet, Coral Harbour, Repulse Bay, Rankin Inlet, Whale Cove.

Newsweek of Pond Inlet: Newspaper, Pond Inlet. 1970s.

Nuna: Cambridge Bay. Oblate Fathers of the Canadian Arctic.

Nunatsiaq News: Iqaluit. Weekly newspaper. Formerly *Inukshuk;* focus on Nunavut with broader northern coverage; distributed to more than 40 Arctic communities. Inuit and non-Inuit news and journalists, correspondents in several communities, bilingual English/Inuktitut; claims to be only self-supporting Canadian paper published in a Native language (but *Makivik News* is self-supporting and trilingual). Published by Nortext. Circulation: 3,000. Also publishes *Nunavik Edition* (for northern Quebec) and a supplement/sister publication in Iqaluit, *Capital News.*

Rankin Times: Rankin Inlet. (Ceased publication.)

Suvaguq: Pond Inlet.

Ugaqta: Arviat (formerly Eskimo Point). Inuit Cultural Institute.

Yukon Territory

L'Aurore Boréale: La voix française de la dernière frontière. Whitehorse. Yukon-wide. Founded 1982, ceased publication for a time in 1992, following budget cuts. Yukon's only French-language newspaper, published by L'Association Franco-Yukonnaise.

Dännzhà': Whitehorse. Monthly magazine. Yukon-wide; four-colour cover, black/white inside; Ye Sa To Communications Society; Aboriginal staff, subjects; theme issues (e.g., family violence); electoral information. Suspended after funding cuts, has intermittently resumed publication.

Dawson News Letter: Dawson City. Quarterly.

Klondike Sun: Dawson City. Twice monthly newspaper. Volunteer staff; printed by *Yukon News.*

Northern Journal: Whitehorse. Monthly newsprint magazine. Arts, nostalgia, history, comment; non-Aboriginal.

The Northern Review: Whitehorse. Yukon College. Founded in 1988. The only scholarly journal published North of 60 in Canada.

The Optimist: A Voice for Yukon Women: Whitehorse. Quarterly magazine. Founded in 1974, formerly a monthly newsprint newspaper/magazine; Yukon Status of Women Council. Wide coverage of Yukon communities; writing by women from all Yukon cultures and communities, tends to have a Whitehorse focus; readers in British Columbia, elsewhere. Circulation: about 800, including US.

Pelly Button: Pelly Crossing. Newsletter.

The Raven: Faro. Weekly newspaper. Volunteer staff; covers area politicians and local/regional news.

Raven's Eye: BC and Yukon's Aboriginal Newspaper: Edmonton. Monthly. Published by AMMSA. Founded 1997. Circulation: 7,600.

Shakat: Summer supplement to *Dännzhà'* and the former *Yukon Indian News.*

Skagway News: Skagway, Alaska. Weekly newspaper. Distributed and read in Yukon because of transportation/communication link (connected by highway, bus route, and the White Pass and Yukon Railway).

Skookum Jim News: Whitehorse. Ceased publication.

Whitehorse Star: Whitehorse. Daily, except Sunday. One of the two major Yukon newspapers; Whitehorse focus but covers all other Yukon news; extensive election coverage within Whitehorse area.

Yukon Indian News: Whitehorse. Ye Sa To Communications Society (1974-91); founded as a newspaper; evolved into the magazine *Dännzhà'.*

Yukon News: Whitehorse. Published twice weekly. Second of the two major Yukon newspapers; based in Whitehorse but has commitment to Yukon-wide coverage; some reporting from smaller communities; extensive election coverage; Yukon-wide distribution. Founded 1962. Circulation: 5,000.

Western Native News: See Alberta listings; see also *Kahtou* (British Columbia).

Alberta

Aboriginal Times: Calgary. Monthly. Founded 1996. National distribution: 8,000.

Achimovin Newsletter: Peace River. Sagitava Friendship Society.

Alberta Native News: Edmonton. Monthly newspaper. Nationwide readership, coverage; distributed to Native bands and Métis settlements in Alberta, Yukon, and NWT. On masthead: "No Government Grants."

Alberta Sweetgrass: Edmonton. Monthly. "Alberta's Aboriginal Newspaper." Published by AMMSA. Founded 1993. Circulation: 7,100.

Arrows to Freedom: Drumheller. Quarterly. Drumheller Native Brotherhood.

Camsell Arrow: Edmonton. Periodical by and about North American Indians, published by the Charles Camsell Indian Hospital. Available on microfilm.

Enoch Echo: Winterburn. Enoch Band.

First Nations Free Press: Working Together: Sherwood Park. Monthly.

Internacs: Lac La Biche. National Aboriginal Communications Society.

Kainai News: Standoff. Weekly newspaper. Founded 1968 in Hobbema, now published at Standoff; severe cuts to funding in 1990.

Mannawanis Messenger: St Paul. Mannawanis Native Friendship Centre Society.

Napi News: Pincher Creek. Napi Friendship Association.

Native Journal: Edmonton. Monthly newspaper. H. Gaudet, publisher. Distributed free across Canada and parts of the United States, and also by subscription. Features a section on mining and exploration and a directory of mining advertisers, suggesting that part of the purpose is to promote mining and exploration on Aboriginal lands. The masthead indicates that the paper is not a "charitable organization" but does not clarify the sponsorship of the organization.

Native Network News: Edmonton. Monthly.

Native People: Edmonton. Newspaper. Alberta Native Communication Society; founded in 1968.

Native Woman: Edmonton. Monthly.
Peace Hills Country Newspaper: Hobbema. Monthly.
Slave Lake Native Friendship Centre Newsletter: Slave Lake.
Western Native News: Edmonton. Monthly. Masthead includes note: "*Western Native News* is published monthly without government assistance for distribution to Native Bands in British Columbia and Yukon." *Kahtou* (see British Columbia) is also published in collaboration with the *Western Native News* news group.
Windspeaker: Edmonton. Weekly newspaper. Temporarily suspended regular publication following 1990 funding cuts. The only newspaper west of Ontario to survive the federal cuts, by changing from a regional to a national newspaper, and developing AMMSA and its Web site. Now calls itself "Canada's National Aboriginal News Source." Published by the Aboriginal Multi-Media Society of Alberta (AMMSA). Founded 1983. About 75 percent of *Windspeaker's* circulation is paid subscriptions; this, with various marketing activities, totally replaced government funding lost in 1990. National circulation: 18,000; estimated readership: 100,000. Special sections published several times a year, including the Classroom Edition and the Guide to Indian Country.

British Columbia
Awa'K'Wis Newspaper: Monthly. Port Hardy. According to the summer 1998 Aboriginal Media Services Web site, it has ceased publishing until further notice.
Coqualeetza News: Sardis. Coqualeetza Cultural Centre.
Dakelh dustl'us: Prince George. Carrier Sekani Tribal Council.
The First Citizen: Vancouver. Community newsletter; published 1969-71.
Ha-Shilth-Sa: Port Alberni. Ten issues a year. Nuu-chah-nulth Tribal Council.
Indian Time: Vancouver. Pan-American Indian League; published 1950-9.
Indian Voice: Vancouver. Founded in 1969 by British Columbia Indian Homemakers' Association.
Kahtou: Sechelt. Monthly newspaper. Abandoned all public funding in favour of private ownership and extended its coverage from Vancouver to provincewide. See also *Western Native News* (Alberta). Distributed free to 8,000 Native families, band offices, and friendship centres.
Moccasin Telegraph: Quesnel. Quesnel Tillicum Society, Native Friendship Centre.
Native Voice: Vancouver. Published in 1946 by the Native Brotherhood of British Columbia.
Nawican Friendship Centre Newsletter: Dawson Creek.
Nesika: The Voice of B.C. Indians: Vancouver. Union of B.C. Indian Chiefs.
Nitep News: Vancouver. University of British Columbia Native Indian Teacher Education Program.
Raven's Eye: See heading under Yukon Territory.
RedWire Magazine: Vancouver. Magazine written by and for urban Aboriginal youth.
Secwepemc News: Kamloops. Monthly. Chief Louis Centre.
The Thunderbird: British Columbia/national. Privately owned and operated; published and edited by Andrew Paull, founder of the North American Indian Brotherhood, 1949-55.
The Totem Speaks: British Columbia/national. Privately owned and operated; published and edited by Andrew Paull, 1953.
Unity: Union of B.C. Indian Chiefs.
Western Native News: British Columbia/Yukon. See Alberta.

Manitoba
Achimowin: Thompson. Weekly. Formerly *Achimouin Weekly.*
Annoosh: Norway House. Norway House Band.
Eskimo: Churchill. Twice a year. Oblate Fathers of the Hudson Bay Vicariate.
First Perspective: Winnipeg. Monthly. National distribution: 10,000. Founded 1991.
Grassroots: Winnipeg. Monthly. Distribution: 6,000. Founded 1996.
Indian Life Magazine: Winnipeg. Magazine; six issues a year. Covers Intertribal Christian Communications in Canada and the United States.
The Interlake Ensign: Ashern. Interlake Reserves Tribal Council Inc.

Mesanaygun: Ceased publishing until further notice, August 1997.
Natotawin: Listen to Me: The Pas. The Pas Indian Band.
Networks (Language Development in Native Education): Winnipeg. Eight issues a year. Teaching English as a second language.
The New Nation: Thompson. Ceased publication.
New News: Churchill. Continued by *Keewatin Echo.*
The Scout: Brandon. Indian-Métis Friendship Centre.
Taiga Times: Churchill.
Weetamah: Manitoba's Aboriginal Newspaper: Winnipeg. Every two weeks. Mikisiw Publishing. Distributed throughout Manitoba, Northwestern Ontario, Saskatchewan, and Alberta. Circulation: 10,000, includes all First Nations and Métis communities, Tribal councils, Aboriginal and non-Aboriginal businesses and organizations. Financed solely through advertising revenues. National and provincial news, opinion, arts and entertainment, business and career opportunities.

New Brunswick, Nova Scotia, and Prince Edward Island

Agenutemagen: Six issues a year. Indians of New Brunswick and Prince Edward Island; publishes news, calendar of events, information, and features.
Mal-l-mic News: Fredericton. Publishes irregularly. New Brunswick Association of Métis and Non-Status Indians.
Micmac-Maliseet Education: Fredericton. Publication of the Micmac-Maliseet Institute.
Micmac-Maliseet Nations News: Truro, NS. Monthly. Published by the Micmac/Maliseet Nations, serving Nova Scotia, New Brunswick, Eastern Quebec, Prince Edward Island, and Newfoundland. Founded 1990. Distribution: 3,000.
Micmac News: Nova Scotia. Originally founded in 1932 and revived in the mid-1960s and then in 1970 it was revived and published by the Union of Nova Scotia Indians; publication suspended after 1990 funding cuts; 1988-9 circulation: 6,000; after cancellation of the NCP, circulation dropped to 2,000. Played a key and courageous role in bringing forward information resulting in freeing of Donald Marshall (a Micmac wrongly convicted of murder).
Na-goot-koog News: Maliseet, New Brunswick. "Eastern Canada's only Native people's weekly."

Newfoundland and Labrador

Caribou: Flat Bay, Newfoundland. Newfoundland Federation of Indians.
Kinatuinamot Ilengajuk: Nain, Labrador. Quarterly.
Labrador Craft Producers Association Newsletter: Happy Valley-Moose Bay, Labrador.
Labrador Friendship Centre Newsletter: Happy Valley, Labrador.
Them Days: Happy Valley, Labrador. Quarterly. Labrador Heritage Society and Older Timers League.

Ontario

Aboriginal Voices: See entry under National and International Publications, below.)
AIAI Newsletter: Wallaceburg. Walpole Island Research Centre. Association of Iroquois and Allied Indians.
Anishinabek News: North Bay. Monthly newspaper. No federal or provincial government funding; Union of Ontario Indians; head office, Nipissing First Nation. Founded 1991. Distribution: 5,000.
A-ni-skay-ah-che-mo-win: Timmins. Grand Council Treaty 9.
Coraid News: Orillia. Native Peoples of Ontario.
Council Fire: Kenora. Grand Council Treaty 3.
Council Fires: Blind River. Monthly. North Shore Tribal Council.
Focus North: Thunder Bay. Lakehead Centre for Northern Studies.
Jibkenyan: Wallaceburg. Twenty-five issues a year. Walpole Island Band Office.
Kenomadiwim News: Port Arthur. Thunder Bay Friendship Centre.
Ministikok: Moose Factory. Ceased publication.

NativeBeat: Forest. Three Sisters Multi-Media. Ceased publication mid-1990s.

Native Canadian: Toronto. Founded as *Boozhoo,* Newsmagazine of the Native Canadian Centre of Toronto; Toronto and Ontario focus; some national coverage.

Northern Woman Journal: Thunder Bay. Quarterly. Northern Women's Centre.

N'Swakamok Native Friendship Centre Newsletter: Sudbury.

OMAA: Sault Ste Marie. Newsmagazine; six issues a year. Ontario Métis and Aboriginal Peoples Association; news and analysis, Ontario/northern Ontario focus.

Ontario Indian: Toronto. Union of Ontario Indians, 1978.

Ontario Native Women's Association Newsletter: Thunder Bay.

Native Times: Toronto. Canadian Indian Centre of Toronto, 1968-81.

Tellum ... As It Is: London. Published at University of Western Ontario by Program in Journalism for Native People (PJNP); ceased publication in 1990 when university ended program.

United Native Friendship Centre Newsletter: Fort Frances.

Wawatay News: Sioux Lookout. Monthly newspaper. Serves northern Ontario Aboriginal people; Wawatay Communications Society; founded 1974; English, Ojibway-Cree; severe funding cuts in 1990.

Quebec

Arqutitsait: Kativik Regional Government.

Atikamekiw Sipi: La Tuque. Quarterly.

Atuaqnik, le journal du Québec arctique: Fort Chimo (now Kuujjuaq).

Chiiwetin: Chibougamau. Cree Indian Centre of Chibougamau Inc.

Cree Ajemoon: Chibougamau. Quarterly newspaper. Cree Indian Centre of Chibougamau; founded in 1973.

First Nations Education Council: Wendake. First Nations Education Council.

Makivik News: Kuujjuaq, Nunavik (Inuit northern Quebec). Magazine. Published by Makivik Information Department, Makivik Corporation for Nunavik residents; published in Inuktitut (syllabics), English, and French (each edition is fully trilingual); thriving, due to financing of the Makivik Corporation through the James Bay and Northern Quebec Agreement.

Micmac Journal: Restigouche. Restigouche Institute of Cultural Education.

Micmac Maliseet Nations News: Distributed to Micmac Maliseet Nations people in eastern Quebec and other provinces (see entry under New Brunswick.)

The Nation: Montreal. Six issues a year. Only print medium serving the James Bay Cree in northern Quebec and Ontario – 21 communities, 30,000 people. News, culture, opinion, sports, environment, development projects, Cree traditional pursuits, in English and Cree. Founded 1993. Distribution: 5,000.

Povungnituk Newsletter from the Vallees: Povungnituk (Anita and Frank Vallee).

Tepatshimuwin-Teoashemoun (Le Message/The Message): Village Huron. Conseil Attikamek-Montagnais (Innu).

Waskahegen: Better Housing for Native People: Mistassini. Waskegen Corporation.

Saskatchewan

Canadian Native Law Reporter: Saskatoon. Quarterly. Native Law Centre, University of Saskatchewan. Formerly the *Canadian Native Law Bulletin.*

Indian Outlook: Federation of Saskatchewan Indians, 1960-3.

Indigenous Times: Saskatoon.

Journal of Indigenous Studies/La Revue des Études indigène: Regina. Twice a year. Gabriel Dumont Institute of Native Studies and Applied Research.

Native Brotherhood Newscall: Prince Albert. Native Brotherhood of Indians and Métis Society, Saskatchewan Penitentiary.

New Breed Magazine: Regina. Monthly. Indian and Métis news, features, and analysis; national coverage, regional and Saskatchewan focus; administered by Saskatchewan Native Communications Corporation; following 1990 funding cuts, set up plans to generate revenue through fundraising, advertising, and subscriptions.

News for Saskatchewan Indian Women: Regina. Department of Indian Affairs and Northern Development.

Northian Newsletter: Saskatoon. Society for Indian and Northern Education.

Saskatchewan Indian: Monthly. Federation of Saskatchewan Indians; founded in 1970. Abcom Publishers.

Saskatchewan Sage: Saskatchewan's Aboriginal Newspaper: Edmonton, Alberta. Monthly. Published by AMMSA. Founded 1996. Circulation: 7,100.

Tansi: Regina. Saskatchewan Association of Friendship Centres and the Native Court Worker Services of Saskatchewan.

National and International Publications

Aboriginal Voices: Toronto. Monthly magazine (colour, glossy). Founded in 1996 by publisher, Gary Farmer; first editor, Miles Morrisseau (founder and former editor of *Nativebeat* newspaper at Kettle Point, Ontario). Focuses on arts and culture; some coverage of other issues; nation-wide; US and other international coverage.

Aboriginal Women: Hull, Quebec. Indian and Northern Affairs Canada (INAC) publication.

Akwesasne Notes: Rooseveltown, NY, Mohawk Nation. Monthly newsprint magazine. Founded 1974. One of the main sources of information from the American Indian Movement (AIM) of the 1970s; focus on US and Canadian news, analysis and features; also covers some international news (e.g., articles on Australian Aboriginal people and the UN indigenous peoples' movement; earlier version founded 1969.

Arctic Circle: Iqaluit/Ottawa. Magazine (glossy, colour). Varied from monthly to bi-monthly to less often. Published by Nortext; Aboriginal and non-Aboriginal writers; politics, news analysis, society, culture, environment, and science; circumpolar/international focus; included CARC Members' Update insert with environmental news; covered entire North "above 60"; journalists and topics encompassed wide range of issues, some controversial; in-depth social, environmental, and political analysis by and about Aboriginal and non-Aboriginal northerners. Best of the northern magazines, it ceased publication in 1994. Subscribers urged to continue reading *Nunatsiaq News*, newspaper published by Nortext, which had also published *Arctic Circle.*

Assembly of First Nations Bulletin: Ottawa. Monthly. AFN Secretariat.

The Beaver: Winnipeg. Magazine of the Hudson's Bay Company. Six issues a year. Historical focus, primarily from a non-Aboriginal perspective, although greater diversity of material and viewpoints in recent years.

Canadian Journal of Native Studies: Brandon, MB. Twice a year. Academic journal, publication of the Society for the Advancement of Native Studies, Brandon University; official publication of the Canadian Indian/Native Studies Association; articles and book reviews; Canada, US, and international subjects.

Canadian Native News Services: Ottawa. Monthly news service.

Dreamspeaker: Hull, Quebec. Indian and Northern Affairs Canada.

Études/Inuit/Studies: Quebec City. Twice a year. Academic journal; published at Université Laval, by the Inuit and Circumpolar Study Group and Inuksiutiit Katimajiit Association; national, circumpolar, and international subjects; articles and book reviews.

Inuit: Ottawa. Magazine of the Inuit Circumpolar Conference.

Inuit Art Quarterly: Ottawa. Quarterly magazine (glossy, some colour). In recent years, increasing involvement of Inuit writers and artists; feature articles, profiles, reviews; only periodical devoted to Canadian Inuit art.

Inuit Today: Ottawa; moved to Iqaluit (then Frobisher Bay) in 1983. Monthly/every other month. National distribution, primarily to Inuit communities. Magazine of the Inuit Tapirisat of Canada, in the 1980s – an outgrowth of ITC's first newsletter, *Tapirisat Newsletter* (founded in 1971 at the head office in Edmonton, which was moved to Ottawa in 1972). Newsletter evolved into *Inuit Monthly* in 1972, *ITC News*, and *Inuit Today.*

Inuktitut: Ottawa. Monthly magazine. Published by the Department of Indian Affairs and Northern Development; English and Inuktitut (syllabics), fully bilingual; some of its editors (e.g., Peter Ernerk) were Inuit; features on arts, social issues, culture, language, profiles.

Kakivak: Ottawa. Newsletter of the ITC in the late 1980s, which I helped to design and edit in 1986-7. Inaugural issue 13 June 1986. Bilingual Inukitut-English.

Native Business Summit Review: Toronto. Native Business Summit Foundation of Canada.

Native Canadian Relations Theme Area Newsletter: North York, ON. York University Faculty of Environmental Studies.

The Native Nurse: Ottawa. Newsletter of the Indian and Inuit Nurses of Canada.

Native Peoples Magazine: US, non-Native publication focusing on arts and cultural issues of Native peoples of the Americas.

Native Perspective: Ottawa. National Association of Friendship Centres, 1975-8.

Native Studies Review: Saskatoon. Twice a year. University of Saskatchewan Native Studies Department.

Native Theatre School News: Toronto. Association for Native Development in the Performing and Visual Arts.

Native Women's Association of Canada Newsletter: Toronto.

NIIPA Portrayals: Hamilton, ON. Native Indian/Inuit Photographers Association.

Northern Perspectives: Ottawa. Six issues a year. Newsletter of the nonprofit Canadian Arctic Resources Committee (CARC). Since 1986. Non-Aboriginal publication usually written by scholars in a fairly accessible interdisciplinary style. Environmentalist/conservationist perspectives focus on environmental and social issues, mostly concerning Inuit but including other northern first peoples and international Aboriginal issues (e.g., a 1995 issue on Aboriginal rights and land claims in New Zealand); twenty-year index available.

Northern Sciences Network Newsletter: Edmonton. Twice a year. UNESCO MAB-NSN (Man and the Biosphere-Northern Sciences Network) Secretariat, The Danish Polar Center, Copenhagen.

Northline/Point Nord: Ottawa. Association of Northern Studies.

Nouvelles Indiennes: Ottawa. Indian and Inuit Affairs Program, 1954-82.

Samefolket: Östersund, Sweden. Journal of Sámi affairs; calls itself the "oldest indigenous and native controlled publication in the world." It was first published as *Lapparnas egen tidning,* starting in 1904 and, as *Samefolket,* has been published continuously since 1918.

Suvaguuq: Ottawa. Quarterly. National newsletter on Inuit social and cultural issues. Pauktuutit Inuit Women's Association of Canada. Direct delivery to households in Nunavik; insert in northern newspapers in Nunavut and elsewhere.

Tawow: Ottawa. Department of Indian Affairs, 1970-80.

Transition: Hull, Quebec. Indian and Northern Affairs Canada.

Treaty News: Hull, Quebec. Indian and Northern Affairs Canada.

Appendix E:
Catalogue of Northern Internet Resources

Valerie Alia and Brenda G. Nores

For a handful of sites listed below, a particular search engine has been suggested. For these few, secondary access via a search engine appears to be required.

Aboriginal Directors Video Collection 1997
  http://www.nfb.ca/aboriginal97/
  A wonderful resource, with outstanding videos by some of Canada's finest filmmakers, unfortunately virtually unavailable outside Canada. The National Film Board of Canada (NFB) put this information out on its internationally available site with promotional material and prices, without informing the public that many people would be unable to order the videos in the collection.

Aboriginal Multi-Media Society of Alberta (AMMSA)
  http://www.ammsa.com
  See also http://www.ammsa.com/ams/amscanadapubs.html
  Includes a quick guide to Canada's thirteen Aboriginal communications societies, with logos, addresses, and phone numbers for each society.

Aboriginal Film & Video Arts Alliance
  http://www.culturenet.ucalgary.ca/afvaa/afvaa.html

Aboriginal Voices
  www.uli.cal/clients/abc/cmall/abvoices
  http://www.cacmall.com/abvoices/index.html
  National/international arts and cultural magazine designed by Saw-Whet Communications Inc.

Above and Beyond
  http://www.above-n-beyond.com/
  Magazine

AIROS
  http://airos.org/
  The American Indian Radio on Satellite network, based in Lincoln, NE. Radio distribution and video and public television programs through its VMV service. Can be reached by e-mail through its assistant manager, John Gregg (Iñupiat/Hopi): jgregg@unlinfo.unl.edu

Alberta Native Friendship Centres Association
  E-mail: anfca@nativecentres.org

Alberta Sweetgrass
  http://www.ammsa.com/sweetgrass/
  E-mail: edsweet@ammsa.com
  Newspaper published by AMMSA, based in Edmonton. Founded 1994. Monthly.

American Native Press Archives
http://anpaserver.ualr.edu
Founded in 1983. Based in the Department of English and Ottenheimer Library, University of Arkansas at Little Rock. One of the world's largest repositories of Native thought. Now includes not only newspapers and periodicals but material related to Native press history and Native writers and publishers. It's worth looking at this site just for the teasers – in July 1998, the home page included a photocopy of the front page of the *Cherokee Phoenix* from 21 February 1828.

L'Aquilon
http://users.internorth.com/~aquilon/
Magazine for NWT francophones, Yellowknife.

Arctic Art Gallery
http://www.arcticartgallery.com/links/index.htm
Links to art-related Nunavut and NWT Web sites.

Arctic Circle
http://www.lib.uconn.edu/ArcticCircle/

Arctic Institute of North America (AINA)
http://www.ucalgary.ca/aina/
E-mail: tkeys@ucdasvml.admin.ucalgary.ca
Maintains extensive database/search resource, ASTIS; publishes *Arctic* journal. Based in Calgary. Institute created by an Act of Parliament in 1945 to advance the study of Canada's North.

Arctic Studies Center
http://nmnhwww.si.edu/arctic
Main office: National Museum of Natural History, Smithsonian Institution, Washington, DC.
E-mail: arctics@nmnh.si.edu
Alaska office: Anchorage Museum of History of Art, Anchorage, Alaska.
E-mail: aronc@muskox.alaska.edu

ARDICOM Digital Communications Ltd.
http://www.inuvialuit.com/ardicom/
Consortium formed by Arctic Cooperatives Ltd., Northern Aboriginal Services Company, and NorthwesTel, equipped by Northern Telecom to create a two-way, high-speed digital communications network. Founded in 1998. Ardicom Digital Communications Ltd. links all 58 communities in the NWT and Nunavut, to provide services through the Arctic Co-op's cable network and in some communities NorthwesTel's telephone network to support information services such as videoconferencing, telemedicine, distance education, and the Internet.

Association Touristique du Nunavik, Kuujjuaq
http://www.nunavik-tourism.com/French_nun/f-main.html

British Columbia Association of Indian Friendship Centres
E-mail: admin@bcafc.com
Links to friendship centres across Canada. Includes employment services, list of centres and related sites, other information. Centre locations: Alberta, British Columbia, Saskatchewan, Manitoba, Ontario, Quebec, Maritimes/Atlantic, Northwest Territories/Yukon, American Indian Centres.

Canadian Arctic Resources Committee
http://www.carc.org/
Publishes newsletter; non-Aboriginal environmentally focused organization. May need Metacrawler or Infoseek to access.

Canadian Broadcasting Corporation (CBC)
http://www.cbc.ca/
Head office in Toronto; audio and videotapes and other resource and programming materials; level of Aboriginal broadcasting is much lower than it used to be, nationally and regionally, except in CBC's northern service regions (NWT, Nunavut, Nunavik, Yukon, Labrador).

CBC North (CBC Northern Service)
http://www.tvnc.ca/members/doc.html
Among the services available is a Real Audio service, from which one can download CBC broadcasts from Iqaluit, Whitehorse, Yellowknife, and Inuvik.

CBC North Igalaaq
http://www.cbcnorth.cbc.ca/ig_eng.htm
Northern on-line magazine in Inuktitut syllabics and English.

Canadian Journal of Native Studies
http://www.lights.com/sifc/natstud.htm
Journal, Canadian Indian/Native Studies Association, based at Brandon University, Brandon, MB.

Center for North Atlantic Studies, University of Århus, Denmark
http://www.aau.dk/uk/hum/cnatlant/index.html
University of Århus, Denmark. Houses the Library of the North Atlantic, The Polar Web, Polar Libraries and Archives. Publishes the journal *North Atlantic Studies*, North Atlantic Monographs, and *Nordatlantisk Voerk*.

Center for World Indigenous Studies Home Page
http://www.halcyon.com/FWDP/cwisinfo.html

Deh Cho Drum
http://www.nnsl.com/dehcho/index.html
Newspaper for Deh Cho (Big River) region of NWT, based in Fort Simpson (see Northern News Services below).

Dreamspeaker Magazine
www.inac.gc.ca/pubs/dreams/index.html
Indian and Northern Affairs Canada. Since 1995.

First Nations House of Learning
http://www.longhouse.ubc.ca/
Vancouver. University of British Columbia Aboriginal education degree program.

The First Perspective On-Line
www.mbnet.mb.ca/firstper/
Canada-wide on-line version of newspaper.

Greg Lincoln's Web site
members.aol.com/glincoln45/frame.html
Run by a member of the Yup'ik village of Toksook Bay in western Alaska, the Web site offers visitors an introduction to traditional Yup'ik drum dancing and singing, including stereophonic sound and a "Village Mall" with handmade crafts for sale.

Igloolik Isuma Productions and Tarriaksuk Video Centre
http://www.isuma.ca
E-mail: isuma@isuma.ca
Dediated to encouraging and supporting indigenous, community-based Inuit media productions. Founded in 1988 by former employees of IBC as an alternative source of Inuit-produced Inuktitut language television.

Index of Native American Poetry online
http://www.nativeweb.org/resources/arts_humanities/literature/poetry_online/

Indian and Northern Affairs Canada
http://www.inac.gc.ca/table.html

Indian Country Today
www.indiancountry.com
On-line version of an excellent newspaper covering issues nationwide in the United States, Canada, and other countries.

Infoculture: CBC's Online Arts & Culture Magazine
http://www.infoculture.cbc.ca/infoculture.html

Inuit Art Foundation
http://www.inuitart.org/
Publishes *Inuit Art Quarterly.*

Inuit Art Quarterly
http://www.cmpa.ca/va15.html
Journal, based in Nepean, ON.

Inuit Broadcasting Corporation (IBC)
http://www.tvnc.ca/members/ibc.html (AltaVista, Infoseek, Metacrawler)

Inuit Circumpolar Conference (ICC)
http://www.inusiaat.com
The international umbrella organization for Inuit.

Inuit Desktop Publishing/Word Processing Software
http://www.gy.com/www/ww1/in_p.htm
Gamma UniType International for Windows 95 and NT *Inuit Software Digest* ComStar Company 2043

Inuit Relationship to the Environment
siksik.learnnet.nt.ca/Inuuqatigiit/RelationshipEnvironmenttoc.html
Resources for teaching K-12.

Inuit Software Digest
http://www.gy.com/www/in.htm

Inuit Tapirisat of Canada (ITC)
http://www.magi.com/~itc/itc.html
The Canadian national umbrella organization for Inuit, ITC has a long history of involvement in pioneering print and broadcast media projects.

Inukshuk Productions
http://home.istar.ca/~inukshuk/
Inuit music.

Inuvialuit Communications Society
http://www.tvnc.ca/members/ics.html
Communications society for the western Inuit.

Inuvialuit Development Group
http://www.inuvialuit.com/irc/inuvcorp.html

Inuvik Drum
http://www.nnsl.com/ops/pub/publish.html
Newspaper for Beaufort-Mackenzie Delta region of NWT, based in Inuvik (see Northern News Services below).

Inuvik TV Ltd.
http://www.inuviktv.com/tvrates.html

Isaacs/Innuit Gallery-Internet
http://www.novator.com/UC-Catalog/Isaacs-Internet.html

Kahtou
http://www.uniserve.com/lifeenergy/wnews/wnews.htm
http://www.uniserve.com/shaman/home/htm
ben@uniserve.com
Newspaper, based in Sechelt, BC. Web page created 1995.

Kiluutaq School, Umiujaq, Nunavik
http://www3.sympatico.ca/kiluutaq.school

Kivalliq News
http://www.nnsl.com/ops/pub/kpromo.html
Newspaper, based in Rankin Inlet, serving Kivalliq (Central Arctic) (see Northern News
Services below).

Klondike Sun
http://www.yukonweb.wis.net/community/dawson/klondike_sun/ (Yahoo! Metacrawler)
Bi-monthly newspaper based in Dawson City, Yukon.

Labrador Inuit Association (LIA)
http://bunko.lib.uconn.edu/HyperNews/get/arcticforum/66.html

Labrador Métis Association
http://www.iosphere.net/~holwell/nlrsh/metis.html

Links River, North of Sixty: Online Life in Canada's Northwest Territories
http://www.denendeh.com/linksriver/pages/stats.htm
NWT community statistics and profiles.

Makivik News
http://www.makivik.org/
Makivik Corporation, Nunavik (northern Quebec Inuit). Viewing Makivik's pages requires
a browser capable of displaying frames. Published in English, French, and Inuktitut.

McMichael Canadian Art Collection
http://www.mcmichael.com/
Kleinberg, ON. Devoted exclusively to Canadian art. Major collections of First Nations
and Inuit art. One of the first galleries to take Aboriginal art out of the natural history
museum context and bring it into the art gallery mainstream.

The Métis Nation of Ontario
http://www.metisnation.org/
Information on training initiatives, scholarships and bursaries, history and culture.

Métis Nations of Alberta: Executive
http://www.metis.org/pages/executive_bourque.html
Edmonton.

Micmac-Maliseet Nations News
E-mail: nstn2436@fox.nstn.ca
Newspaper, based in Truro, NS.

Missinipi Broadcasting Corporation (MBC)
http://www.link.ca/~mbcnet/

The Nation
http://www.cmpa.ca/si26.html
E-mail: beesum@odyssee.net
Magazine, based in Montreal, serving James Bay Cree in northern Quebec and Ontario.

National Aboriginal Communications Society (NACS)
http://www.ammsa.com/ams/amscanadapubs.html

National Association of Friendship Centres
http://www.nativecentres.org/nafcplus.htm
E-mail: nafcgen@nafc-aboriginal.com

National Museum of the American Indian
www.si.edu/cgi-bin/nav.cgi
Smithsonian Institution. Exhibitions, films, archives, research, and recordings can be accessed online.

Native American Communication Resources on the Internet
http://hanksville.phast.umass.edu/misc/NAmedia.html
Includes a broad listing of indigenous print and broadcast media from Canada, the United States, Latin America, and other regions. Lists documentary photography exhibits. Also hosts an on-line newsletter, *Community News for the Matanuska-Susitna Valley, Alaska.*

Native American Journalists Association (NAJA) on the World Wide Web
http://www.medill.nwu.edu/naja/html/startpage.html
The major North American association of indigenous journalists (includes Canadian and northern journalists); information clearing house. On-line service offers job information, NAJA history, Native publications on-line, discussion groups, and "NAJA hot news." NAJA headquarters are in Minneapolis, but the site is housed at the Medill School of Journalism at Northwestern University.

Native American Technology and Art
www.lib.uconn.edu/NativeTech/poetry/index.html
Collection of poems and stories.

Native Communications Society of the NWT (NCS)
http://www.tvnc.ca/members/ncs.html

Native Cyber Trade
www.atiin.com
Business oriented. Pages on arts/crafts, nations, indigenous gaming, resources (links).

Native Journalists' Association of Canada (NJA)
http://bioc09.uthsca.edu/natnet/archive/nl/9408/0021.html

Native Media – Film and Video Organizations, Journals and Newspapers, Radio and Television
http://info.pitt.edu/~mitten/media.html
Site maintained by Lisa Mitten, based at Hillman Library, University of Pittsburgh. Includes Aboriginal Directors Video Collection (NFB); Kifaru Productions, producers of the Native American Relations Video Series; Na Maka O Ka'Aina, Native Hawaiian video production company; Native American Press Archives; Native American Public Telecommunications; Native Voices Public Television; Vision Maker Video; several newspapers, print media networks, radio, and television outlets from the United States and Canada.

Native Media Resource Center
http://www.wco.com/~berryhp/
E-mail: pbnmrc@wco.com
Produced by Peggy Berryhill, maintained by Susan Ruschmyer.
A woman-owned Native organization that produces educational materials about indigenous communities "in order to promote racial harmony and cross-cultural understanding." Projects include audio, print, and electronic media.

Native Pages from StFXU
http://juliet.stfx.ca/~rmackinn/native.htm
Micmac resources; Aboriginal Resource Centre, book collection, other resources. Based at Saint Francis Xavier University, Antigonish, NS.

Native Peoples Magazine
http://www.nativepeoples.com/
Non-Native US publication with mostly Native American writers, excellent photography and art.

NativeWeb
http://www.nativeweb.org/
A collective project whose purpose is "to provide a cyber-community for Earth's indigenous peoples." Wide range of information and resource materials (legal issues, jobs, geographic information, events listings, news sources, organizations).

Net Warriors – Indigenous Peoples Global Caucus
http://hookele.com/netwarriors/96/index.html
http://hookele.com/netwarriors/97/index-netwarriors.html

News/North
http://www.nnsl.com/frames/nnservices/newsnorthpromo.html
On-line service of the newspaper. Headquarters in Yellowknife; regional news bureaus. Also publishes *Yellowknifer, Deh Cho Drum, Inuvik Drum,* and *Kivalliq News.*

Northern Native Broadcasting Terrace (NNBT)
http://www.tvnc.ca/members/nnbt.html
Headquarters in Terrace, BC.

Northern Native Broadcasting Yukon (NNBY)
http://www.yukonweb.com/business/nnby/
Canada's largest Aboriginal broadcaster. CHON-FM radio and NEDAA-TV; *Your Eye on the Yukon* (NNBY Television); Keyah Productions – industrial, educational, and training videos.

Northern News Services
http://www.nnsl.com/ops/pub/publish.html
E-mail: nnsl@nnsl.com
"100 percent Northern Owned & Operated; Politically Independent." Founded 1972. Head office in Yellowknife, NWT. Bureaus: Deh Cho (Fort Simpson); Mackenzie Delta (Inuvik); Keewatin (Rankin Inlet). Non-Aboriginal ownership; journalism by and for Aboriginal people is slowly increasing.

Northern Perspectives
http://www.carc.org/pubs/np.htm
Published by the Canadian Arctic Resources Committee (CARC). See also other CARC Publications, Ottawa.

Northern Review
http://www.ayamdigut.yukoncollege.yk.ca/review
Based at Yukon College in Whitehorse.

Northlink
http://www.tvnc.ca/northlinkn.html
TVNC Northlink Newsletter. Web site is a clearinghouse for many Aboriginal communications outlets.

Nunatsiaq News
http://www.nunatsiaq.com/
Home Page: http://www.nunanet.com/~nunat/index.hml
Nunavut weekly newspaper, Inuktitut syllabics and English. Also Nunavik edition and *Capital News* (Iqaluit). Inuktitut text available at Web site by downloading the Nunacom font.

Nunavik.Net
http://www.nunavik.net/srvcom.htm
A freenet provider offering Internet connections to people, via public access sites in community centres and other locations in the Nunavik communities of Kuujjuaraapik, Inukjuak, Akulivik, Kangiksuaq, Kangiqsualujjuaq, Quaqtaq.

Nunavut.com
http://www.nunavut.com
Nortext (publisher of *Nunatsiaq News*). Inuktitut and English. Cross-platform Inuktitut font can be downloaded, free, on a Mac or PC, on any Internet browser, and with any computer software and printer. Founded 1998. Plan is to include news stories, searchable databases, Internet tools, and links to other Nunavut-related information sources.

Nunavut Implementation Commission
http://www.nunanet.com/~nic
The organization charged with creating the Nunavut government.

Okalakatiget Society (OS)
http://www.tvnc.ca/members/os.html
Communication society for the Inuit of Labrador; based in Nain.

Ontario Métis Aboriginal Association (OMAA)
http://www.omaa.org/tour.html
Aboriginal Links – major resource centre for political, legal, environmental, social, and cultural information for indigenous peoples throughout Canada; several sites for Nunavut, NWT, Yukon, and the northern regions of the provinces. Treaties, maps of reserves in territories and provinces, organizations (e.g., Assembly of First Nations, Federation of Saskatchewan Indian Nations, Crees of Northern Quebec, Nunavut Planning Commission).

Pauktuutit Inuit Women's Association
http://www.arctic.ca/~jonalik/iwa.htm
Created at the 1997 Pauktuutit (Inuit Women's Association) annual general meeting in Puvirnituq, Nunavik, to include women from across the Arctic who were not able to attend the AGM, as a preliminary to creating a permanent site to act as the official Internet voice of Inuit women in Canada.

Raven's Eye
http://www.ammsa.com/raven/
E-mail: edraven@ammsa.com
Newspaper published by AMMSA.

Resources
http://www.vanderbilt.edu/snap/resources/resources.html
For learning and teaching about Native America. Resources for classroom use. Includes a list of several sites.

Saskatchewan Sage
http://www.ammsa.com/sage/
E-mail: edsage@ammsa.com
Newspaper published by AMMSA.

Savis Dene First Nation (Tadoule Lake) Band No. 303
http://www.winnipeg.freenet.mb.ca/mfntc/sayisi.html (Yahoo! Metacrawler)
North-central Manitoba.

Slave River Journal Interactive
http://www.auroranet.nt.ca/srjl
On-line version of newspaper, based in Fort Smith, NWT.

Spirit of Aboriginal Enterprise
http://www.fnc.ca/
Business-oriented.

Taqramiut Nipingat Inc. (TNI)
http://www.tvnc.ca/members/tni.html

Television New Zealand (TVNZ), c/o Nga Matatiki Rorohiko: Maori Electronic Resources
Television/Radio
http://www.auckland.acnz/lbr/maotv htm
http://www.exeutive.govtnz/m.../maori news tv htm

Television Northern Canada (TVNC) Web site
http://www.tvnc.ca/
Canada's public Aboriginal television network. Web site opened in 1996. Includes on-line version of *Northlink*, TVNC's monthly newsletter, founded November 1995.

Treaty Areas
http://ellesmere.ccm.emr.ca/wwwnais/select/indian/english/html/indian.html

Wawatay Native Communication Society (WNCS)
http://www.tvnc.ca/members/wawatay.html
Northern Ontario. Publishes *Wawatay News*.

Weetamah
http://www.abinfohwy.ca/Weetamah/weetpage.htm
On-line version of Aboriginal newspaper, Manitoba, northwestern Ontario, Saskatch-ewan, Alberta.

Windspeaker
http://www.ammsa.com/windspeaker/
E-mail: edwind@ammsa.com
Newspaper, Aboriginal Multi-Media Society of Alberta (AMMSA)

Yellowknifer
http://www.nnsl.com/frames/nnservices/yellowkniferpromo.html
Newspaper based in Yellowknife.

Yukon College
http://www.tvnc.ca/members/yukon.html

Yukon Indian Women Association
http://www.yukonweb.com/government/womensdir/groups.html

Yukon News
http://www.yukonweb.com/community/yukon_news/
Access through Lycos, Yahoo! or Metacrawler.
E-mail: stever@Yukon-News.com
Newspaper.

Sámi Web Sites
Ajjte Website
http://jokkmokk.se/ajtte/index.htm
Ajjte is the Sámi museum in Jokkmokk, Sweden. Text in Swedish.

Aanta Forsgren's Web Site
http://www.itv.se/boreale/samieng.htm
A mix of information and business pages, with political content from Sámi youth organizations.

Finnish Ministry of Foreign Affairs, Website for the Sámi of Finland
http://www.vn.fi/vn/um/finfo/english/saameng.html

Samefolket
http://www.samefolket.se/index htm
On-line version of the world's oldest indigenous-controlled publication. Monthly maga-zine based in Sweden. Features an excellent mix of materials, including scholarly articles, coverage of events (e.g., the May 1998 issue included coverage of a talk by Mikhail Gorbachev at the University of Trømso, Norway, concerning the indigenous people of

Siberia). In recent years, the content has been expanded beyond coverage of Sámi issues to coverage of indigenous issues worldwide. There are links to publications and news services in Canada, the United States, Australia, New Zealand, Russia, and other countries.

Sámi-net discussion area
http://www.student.oulu.fi/~tryhanen/saminet/english.html

Sámi Parliament in Sweden Web Site
http://www.sametinget.se/english/index.html
Text in English and Swedish.

Sámi Radio
http://www.ylefi/samiradio/contents.htm
Based in Finland, with ties throughout Sammiland (Sapmi). Web site has Internet-accessible audiotaped programs, including an interview with Johan M. Nuorgam, the first Sámi-speaking radio journalist.

Web site for the Taiga Network
http://www.sll.fi/TRN/TaigaNews/News17/Hoerjedalen.html
Includes a page describing a Sámi land case in the province of Harjedalen (non-Sámi controlled).

UNESCO Web site addressing the status of the Sámi languages
http://amacrine.berkeley.edu/finnugr/uralic-table.html

University of Linkoping
http://www.lysator.liu.se/nordic/scnfaq23.html

Westnet Inc.
http://www.smorgasbord.se/sweden/culture/lifestyle/sami.html
Includes a Sámi Web page (non-Sámi controlled).

Appendix F:
Catalogue of Broadcast Sites for
Television Northern Canada
(TVNC)

British Columbia
Alexandria, Alexis Creek, Alkali Lake, Atlin, Bella Bella, Bella Coola, Blueberry River, Broman Lake, Burns Lake/Babine, Canim Lake, Cheslatta, Dease Lake, Dog Creek, Doig River, East Moberly, Fort Babine, Fort Ware, Gitsegukla, Gitwangak, Gitwinksihlkw (name changed from Canyon City, 1989), Good Hope Lake, Greenville, Halfway River, Hartley Bay, Hazelton, Iskut, Kincolith, Kispiox, Kitamaat Village, Kitkatla, Kitwancool, Klemtu, Lower Post, Masset, Mcleod Lake, Metlakatla, Morrice Town, Nautley, Necoslie, Nemaia Valley, New Aiyansh, Port Simpson, Red Bluff, Skidegate, Soda Creek, Stony Creek, Sugar Kane, Tache, Takla Landing, Telegraph Creek, Terrace, Toosey, Topley, Tsay Keh Dene, Ukatcho, West Moberly

Labrador (Newfoundland)
Goose Bay, Hopedale, Makkovik, Nain, Postville, Rigolet

Northwestern NWT
Holman Island (Uluqsaqtuuq), Inuvik, Paulatuk, Sachs Harbour (Ikaahuk), Tuktoyaktuk

Northern Quebec (Nunavik)
Akuilivik, Aupaluk, Inukjuak, Ivujivik, Kangiqsualujjuaq, Kangiqsujuaq, Kangirsuk, Kuujuaraapik, Povungnituk, Quaqtaq, Salluit, Tasiujaq, Umiujaq

Nunavut
Arctic Bay, Arviat (name changed from Eskimo Point, 1989), Baker Lake, Broughton Island, Cambridge Bay, Cape Dorset (Kinngait), Chesterfield Inlet, Clyde River, Coral Beach, Coral Harbour, Gjoa Haven, Grise Fiord (Aujuittuq), Hall Beach (Sanirajak), Igloolik, Iqaluit, Kimmirut (changed from Lake Harbour, 1996), Kugluktuk (changed from Coppermine, 1996), Nanisivik, Pangnirtung, Pelly Bay (Arviliqjuat), Pond Inlet (Mittimatalik), Rankin Inlet (Kangiqtinq), Repulse Bay (Naujat), Resolute (Qausuittuq), Sanikiluaq (formerly Belcher Islands), Taloyoak (changed from Spence Bay, 1992), Umingmaktok (Bay Chimo), Whale Inlet

Western Northwest Territories
Aklavik, Deline (name changed from Fort Franklin, 1993), Detah, Fort Good Hope, Fort Liard, Fort McPherson, Fort Providence, Fort Resolution, Fort Simpson, Fort Smith, Hay River (K'atlode), Jean Marie River (Tthedzehk/edli Koe), Kakisa (K'aagee Tu), Lutselk'e (name changed from Snowdrift, 1992), Nahanni Butte (Nah?aa Dehe), Norman Wells, Rae-Edzo (Behcho Ko/?edzo), Rae Lakes (Gameti), Snare Lake (Wekweti), Trout Lake (Sambaa K'ee), Tsigehtchic (changed from Arctic Red River, 1994), Tulita (name changed from Fort Norman, 1996), Wha Ti (name changed from Lac La Martre, 1996), Wrigley (Tthedzeh Koe), Yellowknife

Yukon
Beaver Creek, Burwash Landing, Carcross, Carmacks, Dawson City, Destruction Bay, Faro, Haines Junction, Lake Leberge, Mayo, Old Crow, Pelly Crossing, Ross River, Teslin, Upper Liard, Watson Lake, Whitehorse

Notes

1 Despite the many advances and the "slow increase in the level of federal government support for indigenous broadcasting in Australia," Meadows says "it still pales by comparison with Canada" (Meadows 1995). Indigenous media are the fastest-growing media in Australia; this includes print, radio, film, video, television, and work in progress to develop multimedia and on-line services (NIMAA 1998). As in Canada, radio is the most advanced. In 1998 more than one thousand hours of indigenous radio went out weekly over indigenous and non-indigenous community stations, the Australian Broadcasting Corporation (ABC), and the Special Broadcasting Service (SBS); there were ninety-four licensed radio stations, eighty of them in remote communities. Australia's equivalent to NNBAP and NACS is the Broadcasting for Remote Aboriginal Communities Scheme (BRACS), developed in 1987 to deliver satellite radio and television to 28,000 people. BRACS serves about fifty indigenous media associations broadcasting on non-indigenous community radio, in the language of each community's choice. In 1996 Australia established the National Indigenous Radio Service (NIRS), a satellite service somewhat akin to TVNC. ABC also produces two national indigenous programs. In 1993 – ten years after it was conceived – the National Indigenous Media Association of Australia (NIMAA) was officially recognized and incorporated. "NIMAA represents the collective of Indigenous media bodies Australia-wide" and aims to increase "availability of culturally appropriate and effective media service for Aboriginal and Torres Strait Islander peoples" (NIMAA 1998).
2 Although it is admirable to consider media in Australia, Canada, France, Ireland, New Zealand, Norway, Finland, Sweden, Wales, Scotland, and the United States (represented by Arizona, South Dakota, Montana, and Wisconsin), the reason for selecting this particular collection of countries is never quite explained, and the inaccuracies and omissions render Browne's study a disservice to the very media he seeks to examine and promote.
3 In Alaska, Yukon, Nunavut, the Northwest Territories, and some other northern regions, the word "Outside" (always capitalized) refers to anywhere south of one's home ground (usually south "of 60"). I have extended this usage to refer to Outsiders – people from anywhere else. The term refers to anyone whose primary home is not in the North, and does not include immigrants from Outside, who have made the North their home.
4 Two years after the film was finished, Nanook died in a famine that took many Inuit lives.
5 The translation in the text is from its author. I found it difficult to comprehend and made further inquiries. According to Pete Steffens (personal communication, 1998), *prostory* has several meanings, each of which falls into one of two categories: "vernacular" or "the people's language," and "vast, open spaces." It seems that Taksami had the latter definition in mind. However, it also seems likely that the journal's founders were looking at the broader context, and perhaps both meanings since it is dedicated to the languages and cultures of Russian northern peoples, and to the Russian North itself.
6 I do not find all the factors that Petrone cites equally credible. The "deluge of immigration" (1990, 95), for example, is not a plausible explanation in my estimation.
7 *Dännzhà'* is the spelling used for the cover of the magazine published by the Ye Sa To Communications Society. The word, which means "the Native sun" in the southern

Tutchone language, is also transliterated as *Dan Sha,* and has been used in this form in other Ye Sa To publications, including the *Dan Sha News.*

8   A former ITC land-claims field worker, Joanasie Salamonie starred in the feature film *The White Dawn,* which filmmaker Phillip Kaufman based on James Houston's novel, and in *Nanook Taxi,* Ed Folger's film about a Cape Dorset hunter who comes to Frobisher Bay to work as a taxi driver. A beloved humorist and raconteur, Salamonie continued to make frequent appearances on IBC and to help run alcohol and drug treatment programs until his death in March 1998 (Amagoalik 1998, 9; Dialla 1998, 7; *Nunatsiaq News* 13 March 1998, 3).

9   When the award was announced at Copps Coliseum in Hamilton, Ontario, Jerry Alfred was not there to receive it. Like most northern nominees, he was unable to travel that far and had to watch the ceremonies on television.

10 There is a need to set the record straight. There has apparently been some confusion as to the authorship of this document, as evidenced by the citation errors in the volumes and reports of the Royal Commission on Aboriginal Peoples (RCAP). I wrote the brief in consultation with NNNC President Bud White Eye and the NNNC board members. It was based largely on a paper I had presented in 1990 in a panel on northern Aboriginal communications at the Inuit Studies Association conference in Fairbanks, Alaska (Alia 1990). The paper was published in the conference proceedings as "Northern News: Canada's Communication Cutbacks," in a 1992 special issue of *Études/Inuit/Studies* (Alia 1992b, 37-45). Bud White Eye and NNNC vice-president Dan Smoke-Asayenes made the formal oral presentation on behalf of NNNC to the commission at its Toronto hearing, 21 October 1992. Unfortunately, a (non-Aboriginal) NNNC member had removed my name from an earlier transcript of the brief. It was reinstated and submitted to the RCAP, but may have been released with the misattribution to some of the commission's members or researchers.

References

People Interviewed or Consulted, 1990-6
This is only a partial list. Most of those interviewed or consulted were guaranteed anonymity. This list includes only the people who chose to speak on the record, or whose anonymity could be protected in the text. Where an occupation or title is listed, it refers to the position held by the individual at the time of the interview. Place names refer to where the interviewees were from. Dates refer to the years in which the interviews took place; some people were interviewed several times. The interviewers were Valerie Alia, Lorna Roth, and the researchers and assistants listed in the Acknowledgments.

In addition to conducting formal interviews, the author consulted several people at workshops and conferences. Two important consultations took place at a discussion of the nature of literacy, cultural literacy, literacy education, and cross-cultural understanding of literacy at the November 1990 Canadian Museums Association conference "Literacy and the Museum: Making the Connections," in Ottawa; and a discussion of media ethics, cross-cultural news coverage, and other issues, at the conference "Ten Years After 'Jimmy's World': The Search for a Green Light Ethic," 2-5 October 1990, sponsored by the Poynter Institute for Media Studies in St Petersburg, Florida.

Adamson, Shirley. Director of Communications, Council for Yukon Indians, Whitehorse. 1990

Alfred, Jerry. Head, land claims; editor, *Pelly Button* newsletter. Selkirk First Nation (Northern Tutchone), Pelly Crossing, YT. 1991.

Anawak, Jack. MP (Liberal), Nunatsiaq Riding, Ottawa. Interviewed by Lorna Roth, 1990.

Anderson, Toby. Director of Land Claims, Labrador Inuit Association, Nain, Labrador. 1990.

Anderson, William. Senior Radio Producer, Okalakatiget Communications Society, Nain, Labrador. 1990.

Andreschuck, Marilyn. Executive Director, Riverton and District Friendship Centre, Riverton, MB. 1991.

Angeconeb, Garnet. Director, Independent First Nations Alliance, Sioux Lookout, ON. 1990.

Badger, Mark. Head, broadcast journalism, University of Alaska, Fairbanks (works with Alaska Native journalists and communities). August 1990.

Bell, Doug. Publisher, *Yukon News*; former Yukon deputy commissioner and lieutenant governor, Whitehorse. 1990-1.

Bell, Jim. Editor, *Nunatsiaq News*. Iqaluit, NT. 1990-6

Berglund Nielsen, Jorn. Journalist and journalism professor, Commercial College of Greenland, Nuuk. 1992.

Bill, Doris. Editor, *Dännzhà'*, Whitehorse. 1991.

Blondin, Ethel. MP (Liberal), Western Arctic, NT. 1990-1.

Boyles, Jim. Station manager, CBC, Whitehorse. 1991.

Brydges, Douglas. Editor, *Geraldton Times-Star,* Geraldton, ON. 1992.

Burns, Milt. Economic development co-ordinator. Federation of Saskatchewan Indian Nations. 1992.

Butler, Jim. Editor, *Whitehorse Star.* 1990-6.

Byblow, Maurice. MLA (NDP) Faro, YT; Minister of government services, communication and transportation. 1990.

Cachagee, Doreen. Chief, Chapleau Cree First Nation, Chapleau, ON. 1990.

Callahasingh, Perle. MP, Lesser Slave Lake, AB. 1990.

Cardinal, Mike. MLA, Peace River, AB. 1990.

Chartier, Clem. Advisor, Métis Society of Saskatchewan, Saskatoon. 1990.

Chrisjohn, Alan. Former director, Program in Journalism for Native People, University of Western Ontario, London, ON. 1990-4.

Cottingham, Bruce E.Consultant, Indian governments, community organizations, small business, Silverton, BC. 1990-1.

Courchene, Joyce. Executive director, Indigenous Women's Collective of Manitoba, Winnipeg. 1990.

Crump, John. Communications advisor, Premier's Office; land claims; Government of the Yukon. 1990-1.

Cunningham, Duncan. Assistant to the president, Baffin Regional Inuit Association, Iqaluit, NT. 1990.

Cunningham, Gord. Project officer, First Peoples' Fund, Toronto. 1993.

de Uriarte, Mercedes. Professor of journalism, University of Texas at Austin, formerly with the *Los Angeles Times*; with Maggie Balough, editor *Austin American-Statesman,* developing a cross-cultural training program for newspaper staff, to improve news coverage of, and participation by, members of minority communities (at Poynter Institute for Media Studies, St Petersburg, FL). 1991.

Diamond, Billy. Chief, Waskaganish Band, Waskaganish, QC. 1990.

Dubinsky, Lon. Consultant, museums and literacy, Montreal and Ottawa. 1991-6.

Edmondson, Jim. Policy analyst, Executive Council office, Yukon government, Whitehorse (has also worked for GNWT). 1990-3.

Ernerk, Peter. MLA, Aivilik (Rankin Inlet, Coral Harbour, Repulse Bay, Chesterfield Inlet), Rankin Inlet, NT. 1990-6.

Fallding, Helen. Broadcast journalist, NNBY, Whitehorse. 1990-6.

Flowers, Bill. General manager, Torngat Fish Producers Co-operative; candidate 1979 provincial election, Happy Valley, Labrador. 1990.

Foster, Kathy. Communications, Taku River Tlingit, Atlin, BC. 1990.

Fowler, Dick. Attorney general, Alberta; MLA (Métis). 1990.

Fox, Ray. Broadcast journalist, CBC, Native Perspectives Program; Board of directors, TVNC, representing NACS; head, NACS, Lac La Biche, AB. 1990-1.

Fry, Frank. Producer, NEDAA-TV, NNBY. 1990-2.

Gaudet, Lynn. Lawyer and legal education consultant, Whitehorse. 1990-1.

Gaudy, Joe. Native liaison officer, Department of National Defence, Goose Bay; PC candidate, experience in five political campaigns, Happy Valley, Labrador. 1990.

Geddes, Carol. Filmmaker, writer, Aboriginal communications and development consultant, Whitehorse (Teslin First Nation; Tlingit). 1990-6.

Gladue, Helen. President, Advisory Council of Treaty Women, Winterburn, AB. 1990.

Goose, Louis. Inuvialuit Communications Society, Inuvik, NT. 1990.

Harper, Ella. Broadcaster (weekly news feed to CHON-FM), receptionist, Selkirk First Nation (Northern Tutchone), Pelly Crossing, YT. 1990.

Hayden, Joyce. MLA (NDP) Whitehorse South Centre, Whitehorse. 1990.

Henry, George. Vice-president of First Nations, Yukon College, Whitehorse; one of the founders of NNBY and TVNC. 1990-1.

Holzer, Haley. Assistant, Province of British Columbia, Ministry of Regional Development, Atlin, BC. 1990.

Houston, Rhonda. Executive director, Ka-Wawiyak Friendship Centre, Powerview, MB. 1990.

Hunt, Alan. Instructor, administrative and management studies, Yukon College, Whitehorse. 1990.

Isaac, Alexie. Television broadcaster (Yup'ik), Alaska. 1990.

Isaac, Darrin. Land claims, Selkirk First Nation (Northern Tutchone), Pelly Crossing, YT. 1990.

Jacquot, Lou. Faculty advisor, Yukon Native Teacher Education Program, Yukon College, Whitehorse. 1990-1.

Jenkins, Fred. Government agent, Province of British Columbia, Ministry of Regional Development, Atlin, BC. 1990.

Joe, Danny. MLA (NDP) Tatchun (Northern Tutchone), YT. 1990.

Joe, Margaret. MLA Whitehorse North Centre (NDP), Whitehorse. 1990-1.

Joe, Pat. MLA candidate (PC), Whitehorse, YT. 1990.

Johnston, Sam. Speaker of the Assembly and MLA, Campbell (Teslin First Nation/Tlingit), YT. 1990-1.

Kane, Ken. Chair, Northern Native Broadcasting Yukon; chair, TVNC, Whitehorse. 1990-3.

Kassi, Norma. MLA, Old Crow, YT (Gwich'in). 1990.

Keenan, David. Chief, Teslin First Nation (Tlingit), Yukon. 1990-1.

Kilabuk, Ipeelee. MLA (Independent) Baffin Central, Pangnirtung, NT. 1990.

Kilmer, John. Volunteer fire fighter, repair businessperson, Atlin, BC. 1990.

Kluthe, Dilys. Coordinator, Continuing Education, Yukon College, Whitehorse. 1990-1.

Krupnik, Igor. Anthropologist (northernist), Moscow. 1990-6.

Kuptana, Rosemarie. Director-at-large, TVNC; Inuit Women's Association; former head of IBC Ottawa; president, ITC. 1990-3.

Kusugak, Peter. Department of Indian and Northern Affairs; NDP Executive Council for Nunatsiaq Riding; candidate for MP, 1988 federal election; Hamlet Council (1976), Iqaluit, NT. 1990.

Law, William. Network features producer, Radio Arts, CBC, Edmonton, AB (now a freelance journalist in England). 1990-6.

Lawrence, Richard. Instructor, English and journalism, Yukon College; instructor, WordPower literacy centre, Whitehorse, Carmacks, Pelly Crossing, Ross River, YT. 1990.

Littlejohn, Katherine. Research officer, Gabriel Dumont Institute of Native Studies and Applied Research, Saskatoon (at Canadian Museums Association "Literacy and the Museum" conference). 1990.

McCaffray, Charles. President, Yukon College, Whitehorse. 1990.

McCullough, Mark. Faculty advisor, Yukon Native Teacher Education Program, Yukon College. 1990.

McLaughlin, Audrey. MP (NDP) for Yukon; Leader, New Democratic Party; Member, Privy Council, Whitehorse. 1990-1.

Magiskan, William, Jr. Chief, Aroland First Nation, Nahona, ON. 1990.

Mark, Efsie. Receptionist, Cree Indian Centre, Chibougamou, QC. 1990.

Mary, Cindy. Whitehorse-Atlin mail bus (van), Atlin, BC. 1990.

Mary, Wayne. Whitehorse-Atlin mail bus driver and volunteer fire fighter, Atlin, BC. 1990.

Moore, Nellie. Broadcaster, Fairbanks, AK. 1990.

Moreno, Phil. Human relations training for Native people (experimental programs using communications skills); artist; (Tlingit); Alaska and BC; Sitka, AK. 1990.

Morin, Gerald. Secretary. Métis Society of Saskatchewan. 1990.

Newkirk, Reggie. Executive director, Yukon Human Rights Commission, Whitehorse. 1990.

Njootli, Stan. Land claims, Vuntut Gwitch'in Band, Old Crow, YT. 1990.

Oberlyn, Ros. Broadcaster; CBC Northern Service, *Focus North*, Whitehorse. 1990-1.

Okpik, Abraham. Elder, Iqaluit, NT. (Interviewed by V. Alia in 1985, 1986, 1989; interviewed in 1990 by Lorna Roth).

Pearson, Bryan R. MP candidate (PC), 1988 federal election; former mayor, Frobisher Bay (Iqaluit); campaign manager, federal elections, Iqaluit, NT. 1990.

Penikett, Tony. Premier, Yukon; minister of health and human resources; MLA (NDP), Whitehorse West. 1990-1.

Rabbitskin, Roderick. Senior announcer, Cree Communications Society, James Bay, QC. 1990.

Robbins, Ronald. Director, Communications Branch, Government of the Yukon; TVNC board of directors, representing government of Yukon, Whitehorse. 1990-1.

Saganash, Romeo. Vice-chair, Grand Council of the Crees, Nemaska, QC. 1990.

Sangi, Vladimir. Founder, Association of Small Peoples of the Soviet North; poet; member of Nivgh northern Aboriginal community; currently in Moscow. 1990.

Schechter, Elaine. Anthropologist; journalist; specialist on Greenland home rule; was wire service reporter in Greenland. New York. 1990-1.

Sebastian, Gordon. Lawyer, Native law office; MLA candidate (Independent), Hazelton, BC. 1990.

Seethram, Seeth. Vice-president academic, Yukon College, Whitehorse (later president, Yukon College). 1990-1.

Selleck, Lee. Editor, *Press Independent* (and the former *Native Press*), Yellowknife. 1990-2.

Smith, Bobbi. Director, Yukon Women's Directorate, Whitehorse. 1990-1.

Smoke-Asaneyes, Dan. National treasurer, Native Journalists' Association; co-host, *Smoke Signals* radio program; president NNNC; London, ON. 1990-6.

Sparvier, Florence. Director, Kluane Tribal Council, Burwash Landing, Yukon. 1990.

Studer, Carol. Café/store owner; regional weather information service, Atlin, BC. 1990.

Tredger, Jim. Principal, Selkirk First Nation school, Pelly Crossing, YT. 1990.

Ward, Elda. Policy analyst, Women's Directorate, Government of the Yukon, Whitehorse. 1990-1.

White Eye, Bud. President, NNNC (later policy analyst, Association of Iroqois and Allied Indians). 1990-6.

Williams, Maureen. Editor, *Wawatay News*, Sioux Lookout, ON. 1990.

Wilson, Fred. Reporter/announcer, CFNR, Northern Native Broadcasting Terrace, BC. 1990.

Works Cited

Abramovitch, Ingrid. 1990. "Arctic Quebec: Drug Problem 'Epidemic,' Female Inuit Mayor Says." *London Free Press.*

Achirgina, Tatiana. 1994. "Development of Self-Government by Small Nations of Chukotka Area (Including Eskimo-Yupik Nation)." Unpublished paper, Ninth Inuit Studies Conference, Iqaluit.

Adams, Duncan. 1997. "Twenty Years Later: ICC Celebrates a Landmark." *Nunatsiaq News*, 4 July, 17.

Adams, Howard. 1975. *Prison of Grass: Canada from a Native Point of View.* Toronto: General Publishing.

Adamson, Shirley. 1990. Radio interview by Ken Kane. Whitehorse: CHON-FM.

Adler, Leonore Loeb, ed. 1977. *Issues in Cross Cultural Research.* New York: New York Academy of Sciences.

Alia, Valerie. 1987. "Another Look at Nanook." *Up Here*, September/October, 63-4.

–. 1989a. "Closing the Circle." *Up Here*, September/October, 18-20.

–. 1989b. "Re-identifying the Inuit: Name Policies in the Canadian North." *Onomastica Canadiana* 71, no. 1:1-12.

–. 1990. "Northern News: Canada's Communication Cutbacks." Paper presented at Seventh Inuit Studies Conference. Fairbanks, Alaska. August.

–. 1991a. "Aboriginal Peoples and Campaign Coverage in the North." In *Aboriginal Peoples and Electoral Reform in Canada.* Edited by R. Milen, 105-46. Vol. 9 of *Research Studies of the Royal Commission on Electoral Reform and Party Financing.* Toronto and Oxford: Dundurn Press.

–. 1991b. "Aboriginal Perestroika." *Arctic Circle* 2, no. 3:23-31.

–. 1991c. *Communicating Equality.* Whitehorse: Government of the Yukon.

–. 1991d. "Northern Art and Craft." In *Canada North of 60.* Edited by Jürgen Boden, 99-137. Toronto: McClelland and Stewart.

–. 1991e. "Northern Media Survey." Unpublished paper, University of Western Ontario Graduate School of Journalism, London, ON.

–. 1991f. "The Powwow Is More Than Just a Carnival of Color." *London Free Press*, 16 July, A7.

–. 1992a. "Aboriginal Perestroika," *Surviving Together: A Journal on Relations with the Former Soviet Union* 10, no. 1: 11-13.

–. 1992b. "Northern News: Canada's Communication Cutbacks." In *Regard sur l'avenir/ Looking to the Future*. Edited by M. Dufour and F. Thérien, 37-45. Ste Foy, QC: Association Inuksiutiit Katimajiit. Special issue of *Études/Inuit/Studies*.

–. 1994. *Names, Numbers and Northern Policy: Inuit, Project Surname and the Politics of Identity*. Halifax: Fernwood.

–. 1995. "Nunavut: Where Names Never Die." *Ideas*. CBC Radio documentary and transcript. 13 and 20 February.

Alia, Valerie, Brian Brennan, and Barry Hoffmaster, eds. 1996. *Deadlines and Diversity: Journalism Ethics in a Changing World*. Halifax: Fernwood.

Amagoalik, John. 1977. "Will the Inuit Disappear from the Face of This Earth?" *Inuit Today* 6, no. 4: 52-4.

–. 1993. "They Came, They Polluted, They Left." *Nunatsiaq News*, 23 July, 9.

–. 1994. "The Written Word." *Nunatsiaq News*, 11 March, 9, 11.

–. 1996a. Talk on Nunavut given at University of Western Ontario, London. 16 January.

–. 1996b. "My Little Corner of Canada." *Nunatsiaq News*, 19 January, 9.

–. 1998. "Joanasie." *Nunatsiaq News*, 13 March, 9.

Ames, Randy. 1989. *Nunavut: Political Choices and Manifest Destiny*. Ottawa: CARC.

Arctic Institute of North America. 1995. *Annual Report 1995*. Calgary: AINA.

Armstrong, Sally. 1990. "Audrey McLaughlin: 'I Know Who I Am, and I Know Where I'm Going.'" *Homemaker's*, January/February, 10-24.

Arsenault, Adrienne. 1990. "Summary of Research Findings." Unpublished paper, University of Western Ontario Graduate School of Journalism, London, ON.

Asch, Michael, ed. 1984. *Home and Native Land: Aboriginal Rights and the Canadian Constitution*. Toronto: Methuen.

Atherton, Tony. 1991. "Canada's Third National Network?" *Ottawa Citizen*, 23 June, D1.

Atkinson, Jim. 1989. Third Kaska Nation Assembly. Broadcast of proceedings, NEDAA-TV, NNBY, 11 November, Whitehorse.

Bear, Leroy Little, Menno Boldt, and J. Anthony Long, eds. 1984. *Pathways to Self-Determination: Canadian Indians and the Canadian State*. Toronto: University of Toronto Press.

Bell, David. 1975. *Power, Influence, and Authority: An Essay in Political Linguistics*. New York: Oxford University Press.

Bell, Jackie, and Mike Mattson. 1996. "Inuit Broadcasting Corporation at the NMC." *New Currents* 3 (4 October): n.p.

Bell, Jim. 1995. "TVNC Leaps into Daily Newscast." *Nunatsiaq News*, 24 April, 1, 2.

–. 1996a. "Footprints 2: Road to Nunavut Paved with Electrons." *Nunatsiaq News*, 22 November, 16, 17.

–. 1996b. "IBC Gets Nasty Surprise in Latest Budget." *Nunatsiaq News*, 22 March, 14.

–. 1996c. "Yellowknife Broadcast Boss Wants Inuit Money." *Nunatsiaq News*, 5 July, 12.

–. 1997. "New Communication Tools for Nunavut." *Working in Nunavut*. Special supplement to *Nunatsiaq News*, E7, 23.

–. 1999. "Editorial: Canada's Telecommunications Slum." *Nunatsiaq News*, 28 January, 9.

Berger, Thomas R. 1977. *Northern Frontier, Northern Homeland: The Report of the Mackenzie Valley Pipeline Inquiry*. Vols. 1 and 2. Toronto: James Lorimer.

–. 1985. *Village Journey: The Report of the Alaska Native Review Commission*. New York: Hill and Wang.

Berry, John W., Rudolf Kalin, and Donald M. Taylor. 1976. *Multiculturalism and Ethnic Attitudes in Canada*. Ottawa: Minister of State for Multiculturalism.

Black, Martha. 1986. *Martha Black (My Ninety Years)*. Edmonds, WA: Alaska Northwest.

Blomquist, David. 1981. *Elections and the Mass Media*. Washington, DC: American Political Science Association.

Boldt, Menno, and J. Anthony Long, eds. 1985. *The Quest for Justice: Aboriginal Peoples and Aboriginal Rights*. Toronto: University of Toronto Press.

Bonacich, Edna. 1980. "Class Approaches to Ethnicity and Race." *The Insurgent Sociologist, Special Issue: Race and Class in 20th Century Capitalist Development,* 10, no. 2.

Bowman, Lee. 1997. "Human Ancestors May Have Neared Arctic Circle." *Globe and Mail,* 28 February, A18.

Brice, Susan. 1990. *Report of the Advisory Council on Community-Based Programs for Women.* Victoria: Minister of Government Management Services and Minister Responsible for Women's Programs, 18 June.

Brisebois, Debbie. 1983. "The Inuit Broadcasting Corporation." *Anthropologica* 25, no. 1: 107.

Bristow, Gary, Robert Kuptana, and Richard Condon. 1992. Unpublished letter to the editor of the *Daily Telegraph,* 27 September.

British Columbia. 1980. "Manpower Services in Northern British Columbia with Special Reference to the Transition from Traditional to Wage Economy." Paper presented to Third Annual Interprovincial Conference of Ministers with Responsibility for Northern Development. Thompson, MB. 9-11 September.

–. 1990a. *Multicultural Policy of the Province of British Columbia.* Victoria: Ministry of Provincial Secretary.

–. 1990b. *Regional Communications Grants.* Victoria: Communications Policy and Programs Branch, Ministry of Regional Development.

Brown, George, and Ron Maguire. 1979. *Indian Treaties in Historical Perspective.* Ottawa: Indian and Northern Affairs Canada, Research Branch.

Browne, Donald R. 1990. "Aboriginal Radio in Australia: From Dreamtime to Prime Time?" *Journal of Communication* 40, no. 1:111-20.

–. 1996. *Electronic Media and Indigenous Peoples: A Voice of Our Own?* Ames: Iowa State University Press.

Brownlow, Kevin. 1979. *The War, the West, and the Wilderness.* New York: Alfred Knopf.

Buckley, Andrea. 1991. "Grounded Planes Put Profits in Tailspin." *Yukon News,* 11 January, 3.

–. 1992. "French Paper Cancelled After Budget Cuts." *Yukon News,* 19 June, 1-2.

Burgess, Marilyn, and Gail Guthrie Valaskakis. 1995. *Indian Princesses and Cowgirls: Stereotypes from the Frontier.* Montreal: OBORO.

Burns, Nick. 1992. *Super Shamou* comic book. Translated by Micah Lightstone. Iqaluit/Ottawa: Inuit Broadcasting Corporation.

Butler, Jim. 1990. "Lament for a Region." *content,* January-February, 16-7.

Cairns (no first name given). 1990. Brief 691, Yellowknife, 24 May. In Pierre Lortie, *Public Hearing Transcripts,* T-0349. Ottawa: Royal Commission on Electoral Reform and Party Financing.

Canada. 1972. *Canada's North, 1970-1980.* Ottawa: Department of Indian and Northern Affairs.

–. 1978. *Native Claims: Policy, Processes and Perspectives.* DINA Publication 95-5095-00-88-A1. Ottawa.

–. 1986. *Report of the Task Force on Broadcasting Policy* (Caplan-Sauvageau Report). Ottawa: Ministry of Supply and Services.

Canadian Broadcasting Corporation. 1982. Yukon Territorial Election Coverage. Various tapes. CBC Northern Service, Whitehorse.

–. 1985. Yukon Territorial Election Coverage. Radio, various dates. CBC Northern Service, Whitehorse.

–. 1990. *CBC Northern Service.* Ottawa: CBC.

–. 1993. *Journalistic Standards and Practices.* Toronto: CBC.

Canadian Multiculturalism Council. 1988. *Reflections from the Electronic Mirror: Report on the National Forum of Multiculturalism in Broadcasting/Les médias électroniques, Miroir de la société? Rapport du forum national sur le multiculturalisme et la radiodiffusion,* 13, 14 May. Toronto: Canadian Multiculturalism Council.

Canadian Museums Association. 1990. *Literacy and the Museum: Making the Connections.* Ottawa: CMA.

Canadian Press. 1992. "Nation's First Northern TV Network Launched Today." *Winnipeg Free Press,* 21 January, 29.

Canadian Radio-television and Telecommunications Commission (CRTC). 1980. *The 1980s, A Decade of Diversity: Broadcasting, Satellites, and Pay-TV. Report of the Committee on Extension of Service to Northern and Remote Communities.* Hull: Canadian Government Publishing Centre, Supply and Services Canada.

–. 1983. *The Northern Broadcasting Policy.* Federal Government News Release. 10 March.

–. 1985. *A Broadcasting Policy Reflecting Canada's Linguistic and Cultural Diversity.* Ottawa: CRTC Public Notice 1985-139, 4 July.

–. 1986a. *Broadcasting Act: Cable Television Regulations, 1986.* Ottawa: CRTC. *Canada Gazette* Part II, 120(17), 3334-53, plus amendments, 1 August.

–. 1986b. *Regulations Respecting Radio Broadcasting.* Ottawa. CRTC.

–. 1998. *Decision CRTC 98-171. Canadian Satellite Communications Inc. Across Canada – 199712008.* Ottawa: CRTC, 23 June.

Carriere, Paul, and Dann Downes. 1992. "After the Axe: A Content Analysis of News Coverage of Two Native Newspapers." Paper presented at the Canadian Communication Association annual meeting, Charlottetown, PEI.

Cernetig, Miro. 1992. "The Big Melt." *Globe and Mail,* 10 October, A1, D1, D5.

Charlie, Patricia. 1990. "Summary of Research Findings." Unpublished research paper, Whitehorse.

Chase, Steven. 1991-2. "Aboriginal Communications in the Canadian North: Contextualized Content Analysis." Unpublished paper, University of Western Ontario Graduate School of Journalism, London, ON.

Chrisjohn, Allan. 1986. "Native Journalism and Academia." In "National Aboriginal Communications Society, Retrospective: Twenty Years of Aboriginal Communications in Canada." Unpublished monograph.

CKRW Radio. 1985. Yukon Territorial Election Coverage, various dates. Whitehorse.

–. 1982. Yukon Territorial Election Coverage, various dates. Whitehorse.

Clairmont, Susan. 1992. "Aboriginal Communications in the Canadian North: Contextualized Content Analysis." Unpublished paper, University of Western Ontario Graduate School of Journalism, London, ON.

Clarridge, Christine. 1998. "Makah Days – and a Media Craze." *Seattle Times,* 29 August, A1, A8.

Coates, Ken S., and William R. Morrison. 1988. *Land of the Midnight Sun: A History of the Yukon.* Edmonton: Hurtig.

Coolican, Murray. 1985. *Living Treaties, Lasting Agreements: Report of the Task Force to Review Comprehensive Claims Policy* (Coolican Report). Ottawa: Department of Indian Affairs and Northern Development.

Coon Come, Matthew. 1990. Brief 287, 13 March. In Pierre Lortie, *Public Hearing Transcripts.* Ottawa: Royal Commission on Electoral Reform and Party Financing.

Craven (no first name given). 1990. Brief 340, 26 March, Victoria. In Pierre Lortie, *Public Hearing Transcripts,* T-0083. Ottawa: Royal Commission on Electoral Reform and Party Financing.

Crowe, Keith. 1979. "A Summary of Northern Native Claims in Canada: The Process and Progress of Negotiations." *Études/Inuit/Studies* 3:131-9.

–. 1991. *A History of the Original Peoples of Northern Canada.* Rev. ed. Montreal: McGill-Queen's University Press.

Curley, Austin, and Associates. 1993. *Evaluation Report: Northern Native Broadcast Access Program.* Hull, QC: Department of Canadian Heritage.

Curry, Don. 1995. *Fact or Fantasy? Diversity and Employment Equity Handbook for Journalism Schools.* North Bay, ON: Canadian Centre for Social Justice.

Dahl, Roy K. 1990a. "Money Trouble to Close Two Papers." *Native Press,* 17 August.

–. 1990b. "NACS Closes Doors in Ottawa." *Native Press,* 17 August.

Daniels, Ernie. 1990. Brief 573, 19 April, Winnipeg. In Pierre Lortie, *Public Hearing Transcripts,* T-0169. Ottawa: Royal Commission on Electoral Reform and Party Financing.

David, Jennifer. 1998, "Seeing Ourselves, Being Ourselves: Broadcasting Aboriginal Television in Canada." *Cultural Survival Quarterly* (Summer): 36-9.

Davis, Robert, and Mark Zannis. 1973. *The Genocide Machine in Canada: The Pacification of the North.* Montreal: Black Rose.

de Poncins, Gontran, in collaboration with Lewis Galantière. 1941. *Kabloona.* New York: Reynal and Hitchcock.

de Uriarte, Mercedes, and Maggie Balough. 1990. "The Ethics of Diversity: Multicultural Challenges in Our Newsrooms and in Our Coverage." Paper presented at conference "Ten Years After 'Jimmy's World': The Search for a Green Light Ethic." St Petersburg, Florida, 4 October.

Dialla, Andrew. 1998. "Goodbye to Joanasie Salamonie." *Nunatsiaq News,* 13 March, 7.

Dietz, Mary Lorenz, Robert Prus, and William Shaffir, eds. 1994. *Doing Everyday Life: Ethnography as Human Lived Experience.* Toronto: Copp Clark Longman.

Ericson, Richard, Patricia Baranek, and Janet B.L. Chan. 1991. *Representing Order: Crime, Law, and Justice in the News Media.* Toronto: University of Toronto Press.

Ernerk, Peter. 1971a. Editorial. *Tukisiviksat* 1, no. 1.

–. 1971b. Editorial. *Tukisiviksat* 1, no. 4.

–. 1987. "The Inuit as Hunters and Managers." *The Beaver* 67, no. 1:62.

Étienne, Mona, and Eleanor Leacock, eds. 1980. *Women and Colonization: Anthropological Perspectives.* New York: Praeger.

Fairman, Shane. 1990. Oral testimony. 14 May, Whitehorse. In Pierre Lortie, *Public Hearing Transcripts.* Ottawa: Royal Commission on Electoral Reform and Party Financing.

Farmer, Gary. 1998. "Letter from the Editor: Time in a Computer Chip." *Aboriginal Voices,* July-August, 6.

Fetherling, Douglas. 1990. *The Rise of the Canadian Newspaper.* Toronto: Oxford University Press.

Fiddler-Berteig, Ona. 1990. "Update: Saskatchewan Native Communications Corporation." *New Breed,* 24 April.

Fienup-Riordan, Ann. 1995. *Freeze Frame: Alaska Eskimos in the Movies.* Seattle: University of Washington Press.

Fine, Doug. 1998. "Eskimos Warm to the Digital Age." *Washington Post,* 9 August, 1.

First Nations Film and Video World Alliance. 1993. "Organizational Plan by Working Group." Unpublished manuscript.

Flaherty, Robert, J., in collaboration with Frances Hubbard Flaherty. 1924. *My Eskimo Friends: "Nanook of the North."* Garden City, NY: Doubleday, Page and Company.

Fleras, Augie. 1988. "Renegotiating Aboriginal-Government Relations in Canada: A View from Herbert Blumer." Paper presented to the Interactionist Research conference, University of Windsor.

Fleras, Augie, and Jean Leonard Elliot. 1992. *The 'Nations Within': Aboriginal-State Relations in Canada, the United States and New Zealand.* Toronto: Oxford University Press.

Forsgren, Aanta. 1998. "Use of Internet Communication among the Sámi People." *Cultural Survival Quarterly* (Winter): 34-6.

Franks, C.E.S. 1989. "Native Canadians: The Question of Their Participation in Northern Public Services." *Population Research and Policy Review* 8 (January): 79-95.

Frideres, James S. 1983. *Native People in Canada: Contemporary Conflicts.* Scarborough, ON: Prentice-Hall.

Fumoleau, René. 1973. *As Long as this Land Shall Last: A History of Treaty 8 and Treaty 11, 1870-1939.* Toronto: McClelland and Stewart.

Gault, John. 1984. "The Strangers among Us" *Toronto Life,* July.

George, Jane. 1998. "KSB Uses Television Puppets to Reach Children." *Nunatsiaq News,* 9 October, 33.

Girard, Bruce. 1992. *A Passion for Radio: Radio Waves and Community.* Montreal: Black Rose.

Gitksan Wet'suwet'en Education Society. 1992. "Gitksan Wet'suwet'en School of Journalism." Hazelton, BC: Gitksan Wet'suwet'en Education Society.

Giuliani, Maura. 1983. "The Inuit Broadcasting Corporation," *North/Nord,* 16-9.

Globe and Mail. Updated periodically. *Style Book.* Toronto: Globe and Mail.

Gould, Gary P. 1990. Brief RCE-721-A, M-1375. In Pierre Lortie, *Public Hearing Transcripts.* Ottawa: Royal Commission on Electoral Reform and Party Financing.

Graburn, Nelson H.H. 1982. "Television and the Canadian Inuit." *Études/Inuit/Studies* 6, no. 1:7-17.

Grace, Sherrill E. 1996. "Exploration as Construction: Robert Flaherty and *Nanook of the North.*" *Essays on Canadian Writing,* no. 59 (Fall): 123-46.

Grant, Shelagh D. 1988. *Sovereignty or Security? Government Policy in the Canadian North, 1936-1950.* Vancouver: UBC Press.

Griffith, Richard. 1953. *The World of Robert Flaherty.* New York: Duell, Sloan, and Pearce.

Groves, Robert, Christopher McCormick, et al. Brief RCE-782/A, 12 June. In Pierre Lortie, *Public Hearing Transcripts.* Ottawa: Royal Commission on Electoral Reform and Party Financing.

Hall, Stuart. 1980. "Race, Articulation and Societies Structured in Dominance." In *Sociological Theories: Race and Colonialism,* 305-45. Paris: UNESCO.

Hamelin, Louis-Edmond. 1972. "L'Ecoumene du Nord Canadien." In *The North/Le Nord.* Edited by W.C. Wonders, 25-40. Toronto: University of Toronto Press.

–. 1978. *Canadian Nordicity.* Montreal: Harvest House.

Hardie, Garth. 1990. "Summary of Research Findings." Unpublished paper, University of Western Ontario Graduate School of Journalism, London, ON.

Harper, Kenn. 1986. *Give Me My Father's Body: The Life of Minik, the New York Eskimo.* Frobisher Bay: Blacklead Books.

Hechter, Michael. 1986. "Rational Choice Theory and the Study of Race and Ethnic Relations." In *Theory of Race and Ethnic Relations.* Edited by John Rex and David Mason. Cambridge: Cambridge University Press.

Herbert, Wally. 1989. *The Noose of Laurels.* New York: Atheneum.

Hernandez, Debra Gersh. 1995. "J-School Faculties Get F in diversity," *Editor & Publisher,* 9 September, 7, 13.

Holman, John. 1990. "Radio Stations struggling." *Native Press,* 17 August.

Hutchison, David. 1990. "Broadcasting Policy in Canada and the United Kingdom: Politics, Technology and Ideology." *Canadian Journal of Communications* 15, no. 2:76-95.

Immaroitok, Bernadette K., and Peter Jull. 1984. "Inuktitut: Surviving in the Arctic's New Age!" *Sweetgrass* 1, no. 1:15-6.

Inuit Broadcasting Corporation. 1985. *Position Paper on Northern Broadcasting.* Iqaluit: IBC.

Inuit Circumpolar Conference. 1989. "Draft Principles and Elements on Communciation and Information." *Draft Principles for a Comprehensive Arctic Policy.* Lachine, QC: ICC.

Inukshuk, Rhoda. 1996. "A Message from the President." *Kakivak* 1, no. 1:1.

Ipellie, Alootook. 1983a. "*Inuit Today* Magazine." *North/Nord* (Spring):20-3.

–. 1983b. "My Story." *North/Nord* (Spring):54-8.

Isaacs, Harold R. 1989. *Idols of the Tribe: Group Identity and Political Change.* Cambridge: Harvard University Press.

Jackson, Michael. 1984. "The Articulation of Native Rights in Canadian Law." *University of British Columbia Law Review* 18:255-87.

Jacobs, Alex Karoniaktatie. 1986. "The Politics of Primitivism: Concerns and Attitudes in Indian Art." *Akwekon* 2, no. 3.

Jacquot, Lou. 1992. "Teacher Predicts College Success." *Yukon News,* 6 March, 5.

Janeway, Elizabeth. 1980. *Powers of the Weak.* New York: Alfred A. Knopf.

Jobson, Keith, and Richard King, eds. 1983. *Aboriginal Title, Rights and the Canadian Constitution.* Victoria: University of Victoria Press.

Jocks, Conway. 1996. "Talk of the Town: Talk Radio." In *Deadlines and Diversity: Journalism Ethics in a Changing World.* Edited by Valerie Alia et al., 173-85. Halifax: Fernwood Books.

Kane, Ken, et al. 1990. *Television Northern Canada (TVNC).* Whitehorse: Northern Native Broadcasting Yukon.

Killick, Adam. 1996. "Surfing the Net in Whitehorse." *Globe and Mail,* 18 January, A20.

King, Mike. 1989. "Death of Inuit Leader Casts a Shadow over Northern Election Today." *Montreal Gazette,* 10 April, A5.

Kinnear, (no first name given). 1990. Brief 812, July 23, Iqaluit. In Pierre Lortie, *Public Hearing Transcripts*. Ottawa: Royal Commission on Electoral Reform and Party Financing. 1-0476

Klingle, Paul, et al. 1985. *The Costs of Choice: Report from the Task Force on Access to Television in Underserved Communities*. Ottawa: Minister of Supply and Services Canada (CRTC Information Services), Catalogue no. BC 92-32/1985.

Korbin, Kelley. 1990. "Summary of Research Findings." Unpublished paper, University of Western Ontario Graduate School of Journalism, London, ON.

Langford, Cooper. 1990. "Native Station Rules." *Native Press*, 28 September.

Law, William, and Gurston Dacks. 1990. "True to the North." *Ideas*. CBC Radio, 2, 9 April.

Lawrence, Guy. [1965] 1990. *40 Years on the Yukon Telegraph*. Quesnel, BC: Caryall Books.

Leacock, Eleanor Burke, and Richard Lee, eds. 1982. *Politics and History in Band Societies*. Cambridge: Cambridge University Press.

Leyda, Jay. 1977. *Voices of Film Experience*. New York: Macmillan.

Linttell, Perry. 1988. "The History of CBC Northern Service Broadcast Recordings." *Canadian Journal of Native Studies* 8, no. 2:291-3.

Lopatka, Sharon, Daphne Ross, and Rosella Stoesz. 1990. *Northwest Territories Data Book 1990/91*. Yellowknife: Outcrop.

Lortie, Pierre. 1990. *Public Hearing Transcripts*. Ottawa: Royal Commission on Electoral Reform and Party Financing.

Lougheed and Associates. 1986. *Report on the Native Communications Program and the Northern Native Broadcast Access Program*. Ottawa: Secretary of State Canada.

MacArthur, Mary. 1990. "Journalism Dean Sees No Hope at all for Native Program." *London Free Press*, June, B3.

McBride, Gordon. 1994. "Spelling Mistake Embarrassing." *Nunatsiaq News*, 16 December, 7.

McClellan, Catharine, with Lucie Birckel, Robert Bringhurst, James A. Fall, Carol McCarthy, and Janice R. Sheppard. 1987. *Part of the Land, Part of the Water: A History of the Yukon Indians*. Vancouver: Douglas and McIntyre.

MacGregor, Roy. 1989. *Chief: The Fearless Vision of Billy Diamond*. Markham, ON: Penguin.

McLaren, Leslie. 1993. *Aboriginal Communications in the Canadian North*. London, ON: University of Western Ontario Graduate School of Journalism, April.

McNeil, Bill, and Morris Wolfe. 1982. *Signing On: The Birth of Radio in Canada*. Toronto and New York: Doubleday.

Macpherson, Rod. 1990. "Suit Planned against GNWT." *News/North*, 15 October, A1.

Malinowski, Bronislaw. 1922. *The Argonauts of the Western Pacific*. New York: E.P. Dutton.

Manwell, Roger, ed. 1950. *Robert Flaherty Talking in Cinema 1950*. London: Pelican.

Maori Radio Network. 1996. *Maori Radio Network Now in Stereo*. News release, 12 August.

Maser, Peter. 1988. "Turner Wants Arctic Treaty." *Calgary Herald*, 8 February, A3.

Massot, Charles. 1994. *Kabloonak* (feature film). France/Canada co-production.

Masten (no first name given). 1990. Brief B-449, 19 March, Fredericton. In Pierre Lortie, *Public Hearing Transcripts*, T-0041. Ottawa: Royal Commission on Electoral Reform and Party Financing.

Meadows, Michael. 1993. "The Way People Want to Talk: Media Representation and Indigenous Media Responses in Australia and Canada." Unpublished Ph.D. thesis, Griffith University, Brisbane.

–. 1995. "Ideas from the Bush: Indigenous Television in Australia and Canada." *Canadian Journal of Communications* 20, no. 2: n.p.

–. 1996. "Reclaiming the Public Sphere: Indigenous Journalism in Australia and Canada." *Australian Studies in Journalism* 5:61-81.

Meadows, Michael, and Anthony Brown. 1995. *Northern Voices, Northern Choices – Television Northern Canada: A Background Report*. Brisbane: Queensland University of Technology, Centre for Media and Policy Practice.

Meyer, Leona. 1990. Brief 565, 29 April, Thompson, MB. In Pierre Lortie, *Public Hearing Transcripts*, T-0100. Ottawa: Royal Commission on Electoral Reform and Party Financing.

Michael, Patrick L. 1987. *The Yukon Legislative Assembly: Parliamentary Tradition in a Small Legislature*. Whitehorse: Government of the Yukon.

Milen, Robert A. ed. 1991. *Aboriginal Peoples and Electoral Reform in Canada*. Vol. 9 of *Research Studies of the Royal Commision on Electoral Reform and Party Financing*. Toronto and Oxford: Dundurn Press.

Miller, Jarrod. 1998. "A Network to Call Our Own." *Aboriginal Voices*, July-August, 26-9.

Miller, J.R. 1996. *Shingwauk's Vision: A History of Native Residential Schools*. Toronto: University of Toronto Press.

Minore, J.B., and M.E. Hill. 1990. "Native Language Broadcasting: An Experiment in Empowerment." *Canadian Journal of Native Studies* 10, no. 1:97-119.

Minority Rights Group. 1994. *Polar Peoples: Self-Determination and Development*. London: Minority Rights Publications.

Mitcham, Allison. 1989. *Atlin: The Last Utopia*. Hantsport, NS: Lancelot.

Montreal Gazette. 1989. "Ottawa Won't Accept Band Council Election." 15 May, A4.

–. 1990a. "Army Will Replace Police on Barricades." 18 August, A1.

–. 1990b. "The Mohawk Crisis." 31 August, A4-A7, photograph.

Morgan, Lael. 1998. "Indigenous Journalists: Two Provocative Provinces, Worlds Apart." *Cultural Survival Quarterly* (Summer): 32-5.

Morin, Max, Glen Chartier, and Ron Campone. 1990. Brief 501, 17 April, Saskatoon. In Pierre Lortie, *Public Hearing Transcripts*, T-0143. Ottawa: Royal Commission on Electoral Reform and Party Financing.

Morrisseau, Miles. 1991. "Alanis Obomsawin: Documenting the Native Reality." *Nativebeat*, August, 3-4.

–. 1994. "Alanis Obomsawin." *Nativebeat*, March, 1.

–. 1997. "Caught Up in the Web." *Aboriginal Voices* 4, January-March, 53.

–. 1998. "Sometimes Big Brother Is Your Brother." *Aboriginal Voices* 5, July-August, 9.

Morse, Bradford W. 1984. *Aboriginal Peoples and the Law: Indian, Métis and Inuit Rights in Canada*. Ottawa: Carleton University Press.

Mostyn, Richard. 1990. "Skagway Road Blockade Is Looming; Band Wants Clan System." *Yukon News*, 12 December, 1, 2.

National Aboriginal Communications Society. 1986. "Retrospective: Twenty Years of Aboriginal Communications in Canada." Unpublished monograph.

Native Media Resource Center. 1998. *Native Stations List*. Sebastopol, CA: NMRC.

New Zealand. 1998. Office of the Minister of Maori Affairs and Office of the Minister of Communications. 1998. *Maori Radio Going Well*. Press release, 19 May.

NIMAA. 1998. *NIMAA: "The Voice of Our People."* Fortitude Valley, Queensland, Australia: National Indigenous Media Association of Australia.

NorthwesTel. 1994. "Special Report on Telecommunications." *Nunatsiaq News*, 25 March.

–. 1996a. "Introducing Phone Service for the Great Canadian Workplace." *Nunatsiaq News*, 19 January, 11.

–. 1996b. "NorCOM'96: Bringing the World to You." *Nunatsiaq News*, 19 January, 13.

Northwest Territories. 1971. *Report of the Territorial Council*. Yellowknife: GNWT.

Nunatsiaq News. 1994. "CFRT-MF 107.3." *Nunatsiaq News*, 11 March, 30.

–. 1997. "What's in a Teleservice Centre?" *Nunatsiaq News*, E7.

–. 1998. "A Well-loved Resident Passes Away." *Nunatsiaq News*, 13 March, 3.

Nuttall, Mark. 1994. "Greenland: The Emergence of an Inuit Homeland." In *Polar Peoples*, 1-28. London: Minority Rights Group.

Obomsawin, Alanis. 1992. *Kanehsatake: 270 Years of Resistance* (documentary film).

Outcrop Ltd. 1987. *Northwest Territories Data Book*. Yellowknife: Outcrop.

Paine, Robert. 1977. "The Nursery Game: Colonizers and Colonized in the Canadian Arctic." *Études/Inuit/Studies* 1, no. 1:5-32.

Penner, Keith. 1983. *Indian Self-Government in Canada: Report of the Special Committee* (Penner Report). Ottawa: Supply and Services.

Petersen, Robert. 1984. "The Pan-Eskimo Movement." In *Arctic*. Edited by David Damas, 724-8. Washington, DC: Smithsonian Institution.

Petrone, Penny. 1988. *Northern Voices: Inuit Writing in English*. Toronto: University of Toronto Press.

–. 1990. *Native Literature in Canada: From the Oral Tradition to the Present.* Toronto: Oxford University Press.

Picard, André. 1989. "Soviet Inuit Granted Permission to Attend International gathering." *Globe and Mail,* 11 April, A5.

Platiel, Rudy. 1992. "North Channels Its Resources." *Globe and Mail,* 18 January, A5.

Powless, Kate. 1990a. "PJNP: Brief History." *Tellum,* June, 6.

–.1990b. "PJNP: Dying a slow death." Editorial. *Tellum,* June, 6.

Pross, Paul A., ed. 1975. *Pressure Group Behaviour in Canadian Politics.* Toronto: McGraw-Hill Ryerson.

Prystay, Chris. 1992-3. "Print Coverage of Northern/Aboriginal Issues in the *Nunatsiaq News.*" Unpublished paper, University of Western Ontario Graduate School of Journalism, London, ON.

Purich, Donald. 1986. *Our Land: Native Rights in Canada.* Toronto: James Lorimer.

Qitsualik, Rachel. 1988. "Cyber-Inuit." *Nunatsiaq News,* 25 September, 10.

Reitz, Jeffrey G. 1980. *The Survival of Ethnic Groups.* Toronto: McGraw-Hill Ryerson.

Remie, Cornelius H.W. 1983. "Culture Change and Religious Continuity among the Arviligdjuarmiut of Pelly Bay, N.W.T., 1935-1963." *Études/Inuit/Studies* 7, no. 2:53-77.

Rhode, Eric. 1976. *A History of Cinema.* New York: Da Capo Press.

Riggins, Stephen Harold. 1992. "The Media Imperative: Ethnic Minority Survival in the Age of Mass Communication." In *Ethnic Minority Media: An International Perspective.* Edited by Stephen Harold Riggins, 1-22. Newbury Park, CA: Sage Publications.

Robertson, Gordon. 1987. "Innovation North of Sixty: The Iqaluit Agreement." *Policy Options* 8, no. 4: 9-12 May.

Robinson, Bart T. 1990. "Our Home, and Native Land." *Equinox,* September-October, 4.

Robinson, Eric, and Henry Bird Quinney. 1985. *The Infested Blanket.* Winnipeg: Queenston House.

Robinson, Laura. 1993. "Baffin, in Nunavut 1999: In the Words of the People." *Up Here,* August-September, 14-7.

–. 1998. "A Lyrical Inuit Story." *Aboriginal Voices,* July-August, 52.

Robinson, Viola M. 1990. Brief 769, 5 June, Sydney, NS. In Pierre Lortie, *Public Hearing Transcripts,* T-0407. Ottawa: Royal Commission on Electoral Reform and Party Financing.

Roman, Andrew J. 1990. "The Telecommunications Policy Void in Canada." *Canadian Journal of Communication* 15, no. 2:96-110.

Ross, Val. 1996. "The Mainstreaming of Inuit Art." *Globe and Mail,* 13 January, C1, C10.

Rostaing, Jean-Pierre. 1985. "Native Regional Autonomy: The Initial Experience of the Kativik Regional Government." *Études/Inuit/Studies* 8, no. 2: 3-40.

Roth, Lorna. 1991. *CBC Northern Service and Electoral Reform.* Ottawa: Royal Commission on Electoral Reform and Party Financing.

–. 1995. "(De)Romancing the North." *Border/Lines* 36:36-43.

–. 1996. "The Politics and Ethics of Inclusion: Cultural and Racial Diversity in Canadian Broadcast Journalism." In *Deadlines and Diversity: Journalism Ethics in a Changing World.* Edited by Valerie Alia, Brian Brennan, and Barry Hoffmaster, 72-91. Halifax: Fernwood.

Roth, Lorna, and Gail Guthrie Valaskakis. 1989. "Aboriginal Broadcasting in Canada: A Case Study in Democratization." In *Communication for and against Democracy.* Edited by Marc Raboy and Peter A. Bruck. Montreal: Black Rose.

Rotha, Paul. 1983. *Robert J. Flaherty: A Biography.* Philadelphia: University of Pennsylvania Press.

Royal Commission on Aboriginal Peoples. 1997. Vol. 3, *Gathering Strength.* Hull: Supply and Services Canada.

Royal Commission on Electoral Reform and Party Financing. 1990. *Summary of Issues of Hearings from the Royal Commission on Electoral Reform.* Ottawa: Royal Commission on Electoral Reform and Party Financing.

Russell, Frances. 1990. Untitled column. *Winnipeg Free Press,* 17 February, 12.

Sainte-Marie, Buffy. 1998. "Honoring or Exploitation?" *Aboriginal Voices,* July-August, 7.

Salter, Liora. 1980. "Two Directions on a One-Way Street: Old and New Approaches in Media Analysis in Two Decades," *Studies in Communications* 1: 85-117.

Saskatchewan Indian Federated College. 1993. "Journalism Institute Set for the Summer." *SIFC Powwow Times* 10: n.p.

Saunders, Patricia. 1991. "TVNC Hits the Air." *News/North,* July 29.

Schiller, Bill. 1987. "How They Made an Indian School a School for Indians." *Toronto Star,* 7 December, A18.

Shaver, Pat. 1998. "Made for TV Movie Spotlights Crees' Struggle." *Aboriginal Voices,* July-August, 52-3.

Shiell, Les. 1990. "Native Renaissance." *Canadian Geographic,* August-September, 59-66.

Simon, Andrea. 1990. "Another Journalism Program Bites the Dust." *Tellum,* June, 6.

Smellie, Janet. 1990. "Inuktitut Becomes one of Eight NWT Official Languages." *Nunatsiaq News,* 12 April.

Smith, Bruce L., and M.I. Cornette. 1998. "Electronic Smoke Signals: Native American Radio in the United States." *Cultural Survival Quarterly* (Summer):28-31.

Smythe, Daniel. 1990. "Summary of Research Findings." Unpublished paper, University of Western Ontario Graduate School of Journalism, London, ON.

Sorensen, Linda, and Ewen Cotterill. 1990. Brief 681, 24 May, Yellowknife. In Pierre Lortie, *Public Hearing Transcripts,* T-0250. Ottawa: Royal Commission on Electoral Reform and Party Financing.

Soublière, Marion. 1998. "Why Won't the Globe and Mail Correct Its Errors?" *Nunatsiaq News,* April 10, 25-6.

Statistics Greenland. 1997. *Greenland 1997: Statistical Yearbook.* Nuuk: Greenland Home Rule Government.

Stenbaek, Marianne. 1988. "The Politics of Cultural Survival: Towards a Model of Indigenous Television." *American Review of Canadian Studies* 18 (Autumn): 331-40.

Stenbaek-Lafon, Marianne. 1982. "Kalaaliit-Nunaata Radioa – To Be Master of One's Own Media Is to Be Master of One's Own Fate," *Études/Inuit/Studies* 6, no. 1:39-48.

Stevenson, Marc G. 1997. *Inuit, Whalers, and Cultural Persistence: Structure in Cumberland Sound and Central Inuit Social Organization.* Toronto: Oxford University Press.

Svensson, Tom G. 1985. "The Sámi and the Nation State: Some Comments on the Ethnopolitics in the Northern Fourth World." *Études/Inuit/Studies* 8, no. 2:158-66.

Taksami, Chuner. 1990. "Opening Speech at the Congress of Small Indigenous Peoples of the Soviet North." *Indigenous Peoples of the Soviet North.* IWGIA Document No. 67. Copenhagen: International Workgroup for Indigenous Affairs.

Taylor, Kate. 1996. "A Dose of Moses' Medicine." *Globe and Mail,* 20 January, C5.

Television Northern Canada. 1987. Proposal to fund the TVNC satellite distribution network (untitled document). Yellowknife: TVNC.

–. 1993a. *CRTC Intervention – Structural Cable Hearings.* Ottawa: 1 March.

–. 1993b. Television Northern Canada, press kit.

Thomas, Lorraine. 1992. "Communicating Across the Arctic." *CAJ Bulletin,* Spring, 14, 20.

Thompson, Francis. 1992. "British Newspaper Article Deserves 'Harsh Rebuttal' – Holman Mayor." *News/North,* 2 November, A3, A30.

Thorbes, Clare. 1990. "Summary of Research Findings." Unpublished paper, University of Western Ontario Graduate School of Journalism, London, ON.

Tobin, Chuck. 1996. "Alfred First Yukoner to Win Juno." *Whitehorse Star,* 11 March, 1, 3.

Todd, Loretta. 1991. *The Learning Path* (documentary film), National Film Board and TVOntario, Tamarack Productions.

Tom, Gertie. 1987. *Ekeyi: Gyo Cho Chu* (My country: Big Salmon River). Whitehorse: Yukon Native Language Centre.

Tuchman, Gaye. 1978. *Making News.* New York: Free Press.

Tusaayaksat. 1996. "1996/97 Community Literacy Projects Fund." 23 February, 19.

Valaskakis, Gail Guthrie. 1982. "Communication and Control in the Canadian North: The Potential of Interactive Satellites." *Études/Inuit/Studies* 6, no. 1:19-28.

–. 1988. "The Chippewa and the Other: Living the Heritage of Lac du Flambeau." *Cultural Studies* 2, no. 3: n.p.

–. 1990. "The Issue Is Control: Northern Native Communications in Canada." In *The Chugach Conference: Communications Issues in the '90s*, 15-20. Anchorage: University of Alaska.

–. 1995. "Sacajawea and Her Sisters: Images and Indians." In *Indian Princesses and Cowgirls: Stereotypes from the Frontier*. Edited by M. Burgess and G. Valaskakis, 11-39. Montreal: OBORO.

Variety. 1923. "Adventures in Far North." Film review, 13 September. Los Angeles.

Walsh, Lyle. 1990. Oral testimony, 20 April. In Pierre Lortie, *Public Hearing Transcripts*, T-0184. Ottawa: Royal Commission on Electoral Reform and Party Financing.

Walz, Jay. 1969. "Canada Promotes Nationalism in the Arctic." *New York Times*, 5 May, 14.

–. 1970. "Civilization, Good and Bad, Invades the Canadian North." *New York Times*, 13 March. Reprinted in *Paterson News*, 8-9 June 1972, 8-9.

Weaver, Sally M. 1981. *Making Canadian Indian Policy: The Hidden Agenda, 1968-1970*. Toronto: University of Toronto Press.

Weiner, Gerry. 1989. Letter. *Windspeaker* 6, no. 52:4.

Weller, Geoffrey R. 1983. "Provincial Ministries of Northern Affairs: A Comparative Analysis." In *Resources and Dynamics of the Boreal Zone*. Edited by R.W. Wein, R.R. Riewe, and I. Methuen, 480-97. Ottawa: Association of Colleges and Universities for Northern Studies.

–. 1988. "Self-government for Canada's Inuit: The Nunavut Proposal." *American Review of Canadian Studies* 18 (Autumn):341-58.

Werezak (no first name given), Joyce Brown, and Peggy Woods. 1990. Brief 505, 17 April, Saskatoon. In Pierre Lortie, *Public Hearing Transcripts*, T-0151. Ottawa: Royal Commission on Electoral Reform and Party Financing.

Whidden, Richard. 1990. Brief 564, 20 April, Thompson, MB. In Pierre Lortie, *Public Hearing Transcripts*, T-0181. Ottawa: Royal Commission on Electoral Reform and Party Financing.

Whipp, Stephen. 1990. Brief 670, 24 May, Yellowknife. In Pierre Lortie, *Public Hearing Transcripts*, T-0346. Ottawa: Royal Commission on Electoral Reform and Party Financing.

White, Geoff. 1990. "Cuts Showed Little Concern for Natives." Editorial. *Calgary Herald*, 2 March, A4.

White, Graham. 1995. "Missed Opportunity." Letter to the editor. *Globe and Mail*, 8 February, A18.

White Eye, Bud. 1996. "Journalism and First Nations." In *Deadlines and Diversity: Journalism Ethics in a Changing World*. Edited by Valerie Alia, Brian Brennan, and Barry Hoffmaster, 92-7. Halifax: Fernwood.

Whitehorse Star. 1990a. *90 Years: Special Edition. The Whitehorse Star. 1900-1990*. Whitehorse: Whitehorse Star, 16 June.

–. 1990b. *The Whitehorse Star Visitor Guide*. Whitehorse: Whitehorse Star, Summer.

–. 1991. "Eskimo News" (Associated Press photograph with cutline), 23 October, 6.

Whyard, Flo. 1997. "Whitehorse-to-Atlin Road Discussed." *Whitehorse Star*, 16 June, 14.

Wilkin, Dwane. 1997. "NWT's Digital Network Late, but Still on Track." *Nunatsiaq News*, 12 September, 10.

Wilson, Clint C., and Felix Gutierrez. 1985. *Minorities and Media: Diversity and the End of Mass Communication*. Beverly Hills, CA: Sage.

Woolgar, Steve, and Dorothy Pawluch. 1985. "Ontological Gerrymandering: The Anatomy of Social Problems and Explanations." *Social Problems* 32:214-27.

Ye Sa To Communications Society. 1988. *Yohunji: A Special Report on Native Communications in the Yukon*. Whitehorse: Ye Sa To Communications Society.

York, Geoffrey. 1990. *The Dispossessed: Life and Death in Native Canada*. London: Vintage.

Yukon. 1998. *Population as of December 1995*. Whitehorse: Yukon Bureau of Statistics.

Zebrinski (no first name given). 1990. Brief 562, 20 April, Thompson, MB. In Pierre Lortie, *Public Hearing Transcripts*, T-0183. Ottawa: Royal Commission on Electoral Reform and Party Financing.

Zellen, Barry. 1998. "'Surf's Up!' NWT's Indigenous Communities Await a Tidal Wave of Electronic Information." *Cultural Survival Quarterly* (Winter): 50-5.

Index

Set in Stone by Artegraphica Design Co.

Printed and bound in Canada by Friesens

Copy editor: Barbara Tessman

Proofreader: Andy Carroll

Indexer: Annette Lorek